BEAR
TRADING

2nd Edition

BEAR
TRADING

2nd Edition

DARYL GUPPY

Wrightbooks

Acknowledgements

All charts created by Ezy Chart© (scale on the left-hand side) or Metastock© (scale on the right-hand side). Data supplied by Just Data, Almax, Key Quotes and William Noall Trading system 2.5.

First edition published in 1998. Second edition published in 2000 and reprinted in 2008.

Wrightbooks,
an imprint of John Wiley & Sons Australia, Ltd
42 McDougall Street, Milton Qld 4064
Office also in Melbourne

© Daryl Guppy 2000   Email: <china@guppytraders.com>   Website: <www.guppytraders.com>
The moral rights of the author have been asserted.

National Library of Australia Cataloguing-in-Publication Data:

Guppy, Daryl J., 1954–
Bear Trading
2nd ed.
Includes index.
ISBN: 1 876627 36 0
1. Investments - Australia. 2. Stocks - Australia.
I. Title.
332.63220994

Cover design by Rob Cowpe

10 9 8 7 6 5 4 3 2

Disclaimer

CONTENTS

C O N T E N T S (Cont'd)

Part IV **GRIN AND BEAR IT**

RUN WITH THE BULLS, HUNT WITH THE BEARS

When you spend three days in an evacuation centre surrounded by floodwater stretching three kilometres on either side and are contemplating an almost total loss of your trading office, I assure you trading, and bear trading in particular, looks easy. In just a few days in January 1998, my world was turned upside down with substantial losses. My stop loss was the one in one hundred year flood level and as my home and office were above this level, I did not bother to insure for flood. I did not count on a one in three hundred year catastrophe so my 'stop loss' was literally washed away.

Recovery required patience, skill, determination and added a piquant flavour to this book.

In just a few days in April 2000 and previously in September 1998, world financial markets took a nose dive dragging the All Ordinaries with it. Many market participants believed they were safe. Their stop loss was set just below the most recent high – if they even bothered to think about it. It was a terrifying ride for novice market participants who believed you make money when the market goes up and lose money when it goes down.

After the initial shock in 1998, many of the novices promptly forgot the experience and in a few years turned to trading Dot Com stocks. This second, updated edition of *Bear Trading* comes just after the nasty Dot Com collapse where an entire segment of the market is enveloped in a bear hug. Every bear is slightly different and this one is no exception. The strategies and tactics covered in the first edition remain valid, although we have added a note of caution to the warrant sector due to low trading volumes. We have added a new chapter, Don't Feed the Bear, in an attempt to unravel the knot of woolly thinking called defensive investing. Going into a huddle is not a good solution when the bear attacks.

Bear attacks do not suddenly materialise. They develop over time and in 1998 and 2000, many experienced equity traders were already trading in a defensive manner. Each collapse delivered money-making opportunities using warrants and other derivatives.

When the first edition of *Bear Trading* was published the hottest market was in warrants. Issued by third-party groups like banks and brokerages, they provided a way for traders to enter a derivative market based on a right to buy or sell underlying shares. Although promoted as a way to hedge portfolios, the market attracted more speculative traders. In a bull market loose cash slops around the system and institutions are quick to develop new products to mop up excess money.

In a bear market everybody is mauled. The first financial products to lose liquidity are those based on loose cash. These include the speculative end of the equity market and speculative derivative instruments. At the turn of the century much of the warrant market is as quiet as a financial graveyard. Trading volume is restricted to a handful of popular stocks. Increasingly, exotic derivatives are being offered to tempt speculative money and to protect the warrant issuer.

Price behaviour has come to resemble the drought and flood characteristics of the traditional penny stock speculative market as discussed in *Share Trading*. In the first edition of *Bear Trading* we highlighted the gap between option theory and warrant trading reality and underlined the primary role of volume in warrant trading success. The decline in the warrant market has further emphasised the importance of these comments. They are as applicable now as they were at the height of warrant trading activity. The same traps apply, but in thin markets the minefield is spread more widely.

In low volume, thinly traded derivative markets the trader can still make a profit but it is much more difficult. It requires much greater practical skills rather than relying on theoretical calculations of fair value.

As are many traders, I am a refugee from the equity markets. Our market skills developed first with investments in blue chips: Coles Myer, Telstra and others. Later, trading skills were honed with volatility in Normandy Mining, Jubilee Gold and the temporary market dips on the way to the top of the bull market. The same bull market spawned new trading derivative instruments in the form of warrants, forced changes in the Australian options market and expanded trading activity on the Sydney Futures Exchange.

Here lies our trading future, because although we can survive in equity bear markets, to really prosper we need to be comfortable with trading from the short side – selling high and buying low. Essentially this means delving into the derivative markets where it is very easy to 'short' the market and profit from a fall in prices. This smacks of immorality, and if so, it is a common indiscretion we commit in life outside of trading the market.

FLOOD INSURANCE

We all 'short' the insurance market when we buy an insurance policy. When my insurance policy is renewed, quite naturally, I will choose one of the two insurance companies providing flood cover. If my house is flooded I expect to collect a lot more than just the cost of the insurance premium. My insurance policy is like a 'put' and no different from buying a 'put' warrant to make money when we believe the market is going to collapse.

For the risk of a small known loss – the insurance premium – I buy a yearly insurance policy. I swap the prospect of a large, possibly catastrophic risk for the prospect of a much smaller risk – the loss of my premium money. The insurance policy expires worthless unless I am hit with another devastating flood. Then my insurance policy is equal to my insured assets. The insurance company's loss is my gain.

This is almost exactly the same as shorting the market. Traders exchange the risk of bear market loss – the value of ordinary equity shares – for a small known loss – the warrant premium or price. If we are wrong, the warrant-issuer gets to keep our premium. If we are right, we get to keep our equity stock.

This comparison does fall apart around the edges if we examine it in detail, mainly because our objective is to increase our assets by trading the premiums. This we explore in Part II. The insurance policy covers an entire range of possible events, from minor loss to complete flooding. Some years we make small claims for minor events. In much the same way, when trading put derivatives we are given the opportunity to exit the position and save part of our premium if the market goes up instead of down.

Insurance is an accepted fact of life and we lose no sleep when we 'short' this market. Why then does it still feel uncomfortable to short the stock market? The bear attacks psychologically. It seems unethical to make a profit while others are losing their shirts. Yet each of those sellers has exactly the opposite view of the market to us. This is no different when we buy shares in a bull market hoping they will go up. Although the market goes up the seller believes the stock is likely to go down, and he breathes a sigh of relief when a mug – you – buys it from him. Every seller and every buyer believe they are winners in at least one sense going up the bull market mountain. It is no different coming down the mountain.

Somehow we don't seem to feel the same guilt in selling our long position just before the peak of a move. We also forget the number of times we hand money back to the market when our short position turns out to be wrong. On balance, the market is just as heartless, uncaring and indifferent as it has always been. Money is made and lost. Our objective is to use techniques to transfer capital to our accounts rather than away from them. And that means hunting with the bears.

When the market goes down it is more difficult to make money using the techniques we grew accustomed to using in the bull market. When the market goes down the best traders make good money by using derivative financial instruments. These complex sounding beasts are really as simple as warrants and options. We explore these below.

ANIMAL FARM

Three animals feed in the market. We all recognise the bull and the bear. Less well known, or less often acknowledged, is the pig. He is the last to leave the party, hanging on for just a little extra profit. We spot him easily, snuffling amongst the ruins of his paper profits.

Without caution, the bull is slaughtered by bear markets, but the unfortunate pig is on the endangered species list. In this book we explore some ways to avoid being slaughtered. Some readers are already on the endangered list. We will show them some strategies for recovery, and almost all of them require a strict diet of reduced-profit expectations. Using a range of trading examples, we show how excellent returns are possible in bear markets, both from trading the long and short sides.

TERMS OF TRADE

To survive we need to understand what works, and just as importantly, what does not work. Some strategies, such as averaging down, are attractive, but closer examination reveals they are not particularly successful. Others, including channel trading, look unattractive but offer steady returns.

We use the Australian resource sector as a proxy for a real bear market. The index declined all through 1997 and 1998 so many of the examples are drawn from this area. Please do not delude yourself. Resources are no different from other market segments, such as banking and insurance. The gold they mine is physical rather than a rich seam of user-pays bank fees, but when the bear bites they react in the same way. We also draw some examples from Asian markets because their currency crisis experience shows a different aspect of the bear.

As in my previous books, most of the trading examples used here are real trades I have personally taken during the resources and Asian bear markets, and on bear-attack dips in the All Ordinaries. You can pick these because the entry and exit points are not at the exact top or bottom of the move. Coming from equity market trading some bear market terms are unfamiliar. We know *long-side trading* refers to buying low and selling high and we use the term in this sense throughout the book. In contrast, *long-term* trades are those where we expect a result in weeks or months.

Throughout this book _short-side trading_ is used in the sense of selling high and buying low. A _short-term_ trade, such as a rally or spike trade, is a trade spanning days or weeks.

We encounter other different and unfamiliar tools and terms throughout the book. They are explained fully as we come across them. This is no teddy bears' picnic. Our objective is to develop a survival pack for bear markets rather than a fully-equipped camping safari. We do not attempt a complete coverage of all the available strategies. Our concern is with survival and once achieved, readers can take the time to follow up the additional reading references scattered through the text.

We start with ordinary shares.

PART I – LONG BEARS

The first part of _Bear Trading_ is centered around equities, or fully paid ordinary shares. These are bread and butter trades for most private traders and can remain so in a bear market. The comfortable living available from trading equities in a bull market hits turbulence when the bear stomps in. Distracted by media hysteria many traders assume all bear markets are the same. Chapter 1, BEAR NECESSITIES takes a closer look at the variety of bear market activity. Defining the nature of a particular market collapse allows us to select the best combination of trading tools.

Equity trading, from the long side, offers a limited range of trading opportunities so BEAR RALLIES defines the first of these. Finding good stocks performing counter trend is easy with computer-assisted searches.

Deciding the best trading tactics is more challenging. These are not true trend trades so short-term tactics are more suitable. The clues come from volume and momentum.

Office towers tumble into rubble in the best disaster movies. In a full bear market the special effects are the same and as Malaysia knows, just as spectacular. The rubble is never totally flat and this offers BEAR SURVIVAL trading opportunities. Many stock prices slip into life support mode, breathing gently, alive but not vigorous. These trading bands, or trading channels, are a steady income for traders content to feed like sparrows – a crumb at a time until the cake disappears – rather than like pigs, always looking for a little extra.

Hope springs eternal, so bullish fundamental traders see bargains as heavyweight stocks fall below book and asset value. The novice buys them with shivers of anticipation at the prospect of a breakout or trend reversal.

In every zoo there is a large sign with the command DON'T FEED THE BEARS. We need one in the market because instead of tossing peanuts to the bear we throw cash at the bear market. The market eats all we can throw and then demands more. When we come under bear attack the first thought is to find a defensive position. Some look for protection behind thick walls. It is usually called a flight to quality and is a key ingredient in a defensive portfolio. Others fight a desperate rearguard action, using dividends to fend off a steady decline in capital value. A few are more aggressive, using forward defence strategies involving counter cyclical stocks in an attempt to outflank the bear. A last group decides to split up believing that diversification is a better option. While each of these strategies can be successful many of those who use them would be better off if they obeyed the sign not to feed the bears. A more objective analysis shows the unexpected risks in these strategies.

Traders DANCING WITH BEARS, Chapter 5, watch their feet carefully. This dancing partner is clumsy and heavy-footed so we use some traditional analysis tools in some new ways to avoid being stomped.

Traders are hampered by instinctive reactions buried deep in human ancestral memory. When it comes to fight or flight too many choose the former, walking right into BEAR TRAPS with an aggressively unsuccessful fighting strategy based on averaging down. This loser can be turned into a winner and Chapter 6 considers how this is done.

PART II – BEYOND THE BEAR

Relying on equity trading alone for survival means fighting with one arm tied behind our back. It is impressive, but not powerfully effective. Two-armed traders turn to derivative financial instruments, such as warrants, options and futures. These are all referred to as *instruments* to distinguish them from ordinary shares.

I am a refugee from the speculative end of the equity market. When I first approached warrant trading I carried baggage from speculative gold stocks. Warrant charts added the same sparkle to profit projections as junior nickel explorers. The joy of specs, apparently, was not dead and Chapter 7, DERIVING SATISFACTION, is an introduction to this pleasant trading mirage. Trading profits do lie here, but not in the shape or style we first expect. This glittering prize is more difficult to grasp.

Hard trading experience throws warrant speculating into perspective. All mirages are a distorted image of something real. PREMIUM TRADERS steps out to find the source of the mirage. Leverage does deliver spectacular returns, but only under certain circumstances. It delivers reliable returns when we master an applied understanding of VOLATILITY AND THE BEAR. The concepts that served us so well in the equity market need modification, and although it means a brush with options trading, the adaptations are not as complex as we feared.

Slowly we slough habits dragged from the equity market. With derivatives trading volume does matter in significantly different ways. We TURN UP THE VOLUME in Chapter 10 to show how it is loudest when trading is most effective. This defines the reality of the mirage, and BEAR VALUE includes new concepts of time and intrinsic worth. We aim for a working knowledge so we are able to transfer the relevant equity trading skills into this new market.

Not an Option

Warrants do provide a way to short the market – to make money when the market goes down – and are similar to options in many ways. It is not our intention to trade options. We want a working knowledge of them so we get a foot in the door before the bear slams it shut.

When I open a book on options trading my head hurts within the first few pages. I am a trader, not a mathematician. I trade crowd reactions at the emotional extremes. Yet I need to know how others think in this very mathematically-constructed market if I am to trade it successfully. In our discussion of derivatives we have tried to remove the pain of options by considering the way the peculiar behaviour of warrants is different from equity market patterns. We look for trading opportunities in these differences, and show how options' theory explains practical trading opportunities.

As your trading skills develop you can return to explore options-style strategies in greater depth and we provide some relevant references.

The reader may well ask why we do not cover the options market, as this is a very common way of shorting a stock. Apart from my aversion to complex mathematics, as a private trader I have some reservations about the options market because it is a 'made' market.

The options market has Registered Traders and their role is to make a market in certain classes of options. Each Registered Trader is assigned a stock and must provide a bid and offer quote for a minimum parcel of contracts. Registered Traders should not be confused with individuals who are registered to trade options after signing a client agreement form. If you wish to trade options you are required to sign a form acknowledging you understand the market and the risk involved. You register to trade options.

The same applies to traders of warrants.

The Registered Trader makes the market. No matter how we wrap it, a 'made' market is always a manipulated market because it does not reflect the true activity between those who hold stock and wish to sell, and those who want to buy stock.

Chris Tate, writing in _Understanding Options Trading in Australia_, (2nd Edition Wrightbooks 1997) explains.

"Registered Traders are not a public service function, they are either employees of broking firms or individuals working their own account. Their role is to make a dollar for themselves. This puts them in direct conflict with traders attempting to deal in options."

As many options traders discover to their dismay, a 'made' market changes the risk profile substantially, as Tate observes, "it is possible for Registered Traders to continually move the price of the option away from you without any movement in the underlying stock."

Transparent Warrants

Warrants are different in important ways. Trading is totally transparent in the same way as Australian Stock Exchange equity trading. Our sell order for 30,000 ANZ warrants is placed with a broker and entered directly into the SEATS order stream. Behind each buy and sell order already on the screen stands a specific individual buying or selling. We are confident that any spread between the bid and ask accurately reflects the views of those who wish to sell warrants, and those who would like to buy them.

The trading risk profile is different because we are judging the behaviour of a market crowd of traders who think and act pretty much the same as we do. In the 'made' options market we are really trying to second guess the mood of the market makers – the professional Registered Traders – and their agenda is not always the same as that of the general market crowd.

PART III – SHORT BEARS

HUNTING WITH THE BEAR assembles tools, tactics and knowledge in a series of sample trades. More than just hunting stories, they are designed to show how our skills from the equity market are turned into derivative market success. From here it is an enticingly small step into full options trading and Chris Temby provides an expert introduction into HEDGING THE MARKET. Others, uncomfortable with derivatives, wish to apply short-trading techniques to ordinary shares. It is possible in Australia, but it is not easy. Colin Nicholson, President of the Australian Technical Analysts Association, shows the steps in Chapter 14, SHORT BEAR EQUITIES.

PART IV – GRIN AND BEAR IT

Bull markets allow us to develop bad habits so we end up with THE GOOD, THE BAD AND THE BEAR. Bull market conditions hide trading mistakes so we often confuse good outcomes with good planning. Trading survival depends on making rapid contact with reality, discarding inappropriate habits. Sometimes this means

LEARNING TO TRADE AGAIN by more realistically factoring in the way we learn to live with losses. Bear markets bring many more of them and they will kill us unless we limit them quickly.

This ability goes well beyond the mechanics of money management. Success is a mind game so we explore the limits. RULES TO TRADE BY define how our mind game is played.

In writing this book I faced a dilemma created by readers of my previous books, and by new readers of this one. Previous readers, quite reasonably, don't want a full scale repeat of material contained in earlier books. They want to move on, exploring new applications of techniques as well as new material.

New readers, quite reasonably, want an explanation of techniques which are new to them, such as the count back line and the multiple moving average. These have all been covered in full in previous books.

Personally, I dislike buying new books that include great chunks from previous books by the author, or which rework old ground, so I do not write books in this way. I have solved this dilemma by including a summary of previous material, such as the count back line. It gives the new reader a working knowledge so the trading application that follows is fully comprehensible.

There are many references to others books for readers who do wish to explore particular issues at greater depth. Many are by other writers and traders, but some include my earlier books, _Share Trading_ and _Trading Tactics_.

Trades are completed in isolation, but books are the product of assistance from many people. This includes readers who send e-mail through www.guppytraders.com many of whom feel uncomfortable around bears. In particular this book owes thanks to the preliminary readers, John Shepherd and options trader, Bill McMaster, who ploughed through completed drafts. My mother, Patricia, hacked through the manuscript, weeding out convoluted arguments and poor spelling while I went fishing. My wife, Marion, says reading final proofs doesn't get any easier, but admits I am getting better with apostrophes! Just as in trading, any errors are my own and occur despite the best efforts of my editorial assistants.

Our focus is on the way the tools of technical analysis are applied in bear markets. While the bear is strong it is their playground. Our survival, while never guaranteed in any market, is more precarious than ever. Traded with skill and discipline, the private trader can turn the average ugly brown bear into a golden bear.

In _Share Trading_ and _Trading Tactics_ we looked at some ways to run with the bulls. In this book we take a close look at ways to hunt with the bears.

Good Hunting!

Daryl Guppy Katherine, NT. June 2000

PART I

LONG BEARS

CHAPTER 1

BEAR NECESSITIES

D espite the dramatic destruction of capital which they cause, bear markets are not easily recognised. When the market, or market segment, topples slowly it takes some traders a very long time to understand what is happening. They blame slow moving incremental downward price moves, suggesting the shift is so subtle that even experienced traders like themselves are caught unawares.

When Australian markets rolled over slowly at the beginning of 1994 in response to US bond market moves, the majority of fund managers were ill-prepared. In 1996 the Australian Gold Index staggered into a prolonged two-year slow collapse, catching thousands of investors on the wrong foot for over two years. The slow, shambling bear won – again.

Armed with another handy excuse, these same people claim when a market collapses quickly it is so fast that no-one reacts in time. When the Thai baht walked off the currency cliff edge in 1997 many fund managers were caught totally unawares. A ripple effect spread throughout Asia with the force of a large earthquake, catching them and other investors unawares a second time. This time the speedy bear won – again.

As private traders we need tools to identify these different bears very quickly. When the bear swipes prices downward it is better if we are out of the market, or at least, out quickly with a small loss. To avoid a substantial reduction in capital – in our trading capital in particular – we assemble a range of analytical tools to deliver warning signals early enough to save us.

To be fair, we have speed and size on our side. This trading edge contributes to our survival and to our better performance. Unloading a few thousand BHP shares is much easier than the institutional task of selling several million into a falling market.

As a first step towards survival we need to define the type of bear we are dealing with. Although all bear markets attack by swiping prices down they vary in impact across markets, market segments and individual stocks.

These variations deliver our survival strategies.

WARNING SIGNS

When the fisherman casts a lure from the bank of a northern river he looks for likely snags where the big barramundi lurk. He is also alert for warning signs, particularly floating logs moving upstream; for tree trunks with legs stranded on the mud banks; and at worst, the fishy smell of rotting flesh.

Man-eating crocodiles don't clean their teeth.

When the private trader casts for opportunity in the market he is alert to the general market feeling. The first sign of the bear is a sense of market euphoria. The entire community, the financial press, brokers and others all seem convinced the sharemarket will continue only upwards. There are three important groups of signs confirming this dangerous, capital-induced high.

The first is garrulous taxi drivers, and others, prattling about their involvement in the market and the beauty of margin lending.

A 1998 survey by National Financing Management found 30% of investors had only one stock in their portfolio. Nearly half of them had been in the market for less than three years. Almost 9% of new investors had some level of borrowing to fund their portfolio.

The second group of signs is captured in a range of over-optimistic headlines in the financial press. When they proclaim "Southcorp, overpriced but worth it," they unwittingly sound an early warning signal. The same 1998 survey found 73% were not nervous about the possibility of a market correction.

The third group firmly asserts, "Things are different this time." Those who have never experienced a bear market are the most inclined to this. In the survey, over a third believed share prices would keep rising the following year in 1999. Presumably they believed things were different because the market levers were jammed in the up-position.

The range of explanations marshalled in support are always interesting. In one sense they are right. Things *are* different this time because market collapses are never the same in detail. Only the underlying general widespread reduction in capital remains the same.

These are groups of warning signs, and towards the end of this chapter we look at some ways to react to these portents. Our concern below is with the mechanics of the bear attack because it seems unbelievable such a large and lumbering financial animal can move with sufficient speed to maul an entire market of novices and professionals.

INSIDE THE BEAR

A bear market is initially driven downwards by a lack of buyers. This saps the confidence of the market who believe prices travel forever upwards. The trickle of selling becomes a stampede when triggered by some vastly insignificant event. Projected movements of interest rates or inflation some years in the future, as inferred by bond prices have dominated the Nineties. The Y2K bug is another candidate along with the height of President Clinton's zipper and the level of the Russian ruble.

The market is awash with rumours and poor analysis. Eventually some of these turn out to be correct and this is enough to tip the balance. The initial trigger does not have to be significant in itself. What is important is the way it acts on the common market psyche. Quite quickly the crowd rushes for the door.

Bernice Cohen in *The Edge of Chaos* discusses this in greater depth in the context of chaos theory. One of her enduring analogies is a heap of sand at the bottom of an hour glass. As each new grain is added, the pile of sand grows, building a perfect cone. At some point, a single additional grain of sand collapses the cone. The sides cascade. A single grain of sand is insignificant and only later do we assign importance to that particular grain.

But this is the task of analysts and historians. Our task is to recognise when the cone is nearing completion. Our trading survival depends on it. Not all bears are the same so we provide a recognition guide below. Each of the four types of bear are traded differently so accurate recognition is the first step to survival.

FAST BEARS

Houses built on sand, and markets, are notorious for rapid collapses. Lack of market confidence starts the fall, but this is not sufficient to explain the crazy speed of the collapse shown in Figure 1.1. For a better explanation we turn to some purely financial matters and the starting point is found in the enticing advertising that appears as the market cone nears its peak.

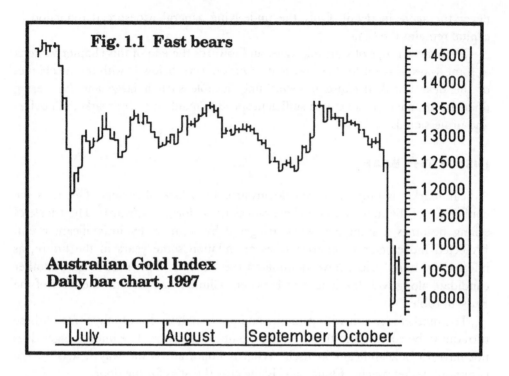

Fig. 1.1 Fast bears

Australian Gold Index
Daily bar chart, 1997

July | August | September | October

14500
14000
13500
13000
12500
12000
11500
11000
10500
10000

"Turn the upstairs into a share portfolio," is snappy advertising copy, and sometimes a prelude to personal disaster. It takes an important step beyond the normal understanding of margin lending because it suggests borrowing against the family home to buy shares carries the same level of risk as buying a block of flats.

Margin lending to trade the market is packaged in several ways. The first of these is the share mortgage loan. A bank loan facility is used as a revolving line of credit but the lender can demand repayment if there is unusual market volatility or after ten-days notice if, for instance, the bank reduces the facility amount or wishes to terminate the agreement. Traders are required to make a selection from an approved list of equities. A typical margin lending approved securities list includes around 150 equities, ranging from Advance Bank and Boral to Great Central Mines and Sons of Gwalia.

The security value, decided by the lender, is an agreed percentage of its current market value. For instance Advance Bank and Boral could be rated at 70%. Others, such as Great Central Mines and Sons of Gwalia may be at 50%. The list, and valuations, will vary in size depending on the lending institution and it changes regularly.

Generally the loan balance accrues interest on a daily basis, every day of the year. The rate is determined by the lender from time to time and interest is due for payment monthly in arrears.

This is not a fixed rate loan, and rates vary according to the reference rate published weekly in the newspapers. The rate moves in the same way as any other loan rate and is loosely tied to Reserve Bank rates. As the bull market nears its peak rates are low reflecting the historically low interest rates that always precede bear markets.

In essence, margin lending allows you to borrow additional cash based on the value calculated from the stocks you purchase. In an important sense this is no different from borrowing to buy your first home. An asset, the home, is used to fund borrowings on the same asset. This can still be a painful experience as home borrowers found in the '80s when interest rates soared.

The second of these borrowed bears turns the upstairs into a share portfolio and is a beast of a different ilk. It may develop into a large and very angry bear. Here, one asset class – the upstairs – is used to finance activities in different asset classes – shares, or even some derivative products such as approved warrants. In both cases the investor uses borrowed money, and like any loan it must be serviced. The borrower believes it will be serviced by capital growth as the shares increase in value, or perhaps it becomes self-funding through dividend yield. The financial markets are busy developing as many combinations as possible because there is money to be made in selling these products.

The same frenzy of new financial products, and old products in new packaging, was seen in 1929 just as the Roaring Twenties reached its crescendo. The products appeared in time to finance the South Sea Bubble and Mississippi trading monopolies just before they collapsed in 1720.

Reach further into history and the products were developed originally as part of the 1630 tulip boom when otherwise sane people paid huge sums for tulip bulbs. Perhaps the first formal futures contracts offered to impatient speculators were towards the end of 1630 to trade as-yet unborn tulip bulbs. The cautious speculator traded option contracts on real bulbs. Options trading sprang into being again to facilitate financing the Mississippi Trading Company in 1720. Instalment warrants and margin loans were baptised with the South Sea Bubble in the same year.

The number of investment trusts, or mutual funds, exploded in 1929 and before collapsing, gave birth to the 'fund of funds' concept. These leveraged instruments returned in 1987 to help fund leveraged buy-outs and deal in junk bonds.

The only new things under the financial sun are all too often a new crop of ill-informed buyers. The tiny ripple created by a decline in market confidence sends share prices south.

Those using margin lending are faced with a margin call. They must put up additional cash, or sell some of their shares to maintain the balance between what they have borrowed and the value of the underlying security – the shares they have bought.

The mechanics of the margin call conceal the terror.

The value of the unused loan balance and the marked to market value of securities purchased with the loan is calculated each day. If the market value of the portfolio is $20,000 and the lending ratio is 70% then the security value at the end of the day must be at least $14,000. A buffer amount, usually 5%, but sometimes up to 10% is also included in the calculation.

The trader need take no action if the sum of the loan balance and any outstanding settlements is less than the sum of the portfolio's security value and the buffer amount. In a bull market this is a comfort.

Should the portfolio's security value and buffer value fall below the loan balance plus any outstanding trades, a margin call is made to reduce the loan to below the security value. This is done by paying cash, pledging further approved securities, or selling shares within 24 hours. Suddenly the share portfolio is very cold comfort. Fail to act within 24 hours and the lender is usually entitled to sell your shares for whatever the market is willing to pay. The lender may take other action required to bring the loan account into order. Just what was the hard property asset you pledged?

Some traders choose to sell shares rather than add more cash to a market they are already losing confidence in. These new sales add to downward pressure. Those who turned the upstairs into a portfolio do not always face these margin calls. Their problems are delayed for a while because their debt is linked to a different asset class. Eventually, with rising interest rates, they need more cash to service the loan and to their horror they discover the value of their borrowed property – the shares – is declining in a very public manner. If they have the courage they calculate the exact devaluation using the daily closing price printed in the newspaper.

In all the market collapses analysed by Cohen, and by Kindleberger in *Manias, Panics and Crashes*, it is the inability, or unwillingness, of borrowers to meet margin calls, or to continue to fund the cost of their borrowings, that accelerates the bear market. A margin call is like throwing petrol onto a campfire. The result is no longer friendly and before too long we are running ahead of real or imagined flames.

PROGRAM BEARS

In the historical analysis which inevitably follows a market collapse, such as that of October 1987, newspaper columnists and later academics, try to find a scapegoat other than just plain old greed. In 1987, and at various times since, the finger has been pointed at program selling. Somehow it is always so much easier to blame someone else than to accept responsibility for our own fear.

The essence of program selling is that trades are based on signals from computer programs. There are three classes of program trading.

The first is a sophisticated arbitrage approach trading a balance of market index futures and the physical shares in the index. These are complex arbitrage trading strategies designed to take advantage of the price difference in two markets. Program traders buy or sell an actual basket of stocks against an equal dollar value position in stock index futures when they believe the actual stocks are under- or over-priced relative to the index futures.

The second is portfolio insurance and requires the systematic sale of stock index futures as the value of a stock portfolio declines. This reduces the risk exposure. It mirrors a number of warrant trading techniques where warrants are used as insurance protection. One of these strategies is discussed on Chapter 13.

Simple or complex, the buy and sell orders are usually entered directly from the trader's computer to the market's computer system. Orders are filled by automatic matching with the Stock Exchange Automated Trading System (SEATS), by floor traders on the New York or Hong Kong Stock Exchanges, or by screen quote matching on NASDAQ and Australian options market.

The third are program trading signals generated as a result of propriety trading software. Institutional traders use propriety trading systems mixing a variety of fundamental analysis approaches, and sometimes technical indicators. These systems often generate the same signals at about the same time and so we see a flood of institutional buying for Telstra or AMP.

All these sound diabolical, but we personally do this every time we act on buy and sell signals generated by our Ezy Chart or Metastock charting software when two moving averages cross over. Perhaps our computers are not linked directly to the Exchange, but a lapse of a few seconds is usually insignificant in the general market melee.

Think more carefully about the equation. Program selling is automatically initiated when prices fall to a specified level. This implements good stop loss techniques and we have recommended this previously as a primary money management technique for survival.

Individual traders, and anyone who has tried to sell in a falling market, know this scapegoat theory has one significant flaw. Just when we want them most, there is not a buyer prepared to take our stock at the price we want. Program selling places sell orders in the market. There is no compulsion for buyers to purchase the offered stock. Program selling has a dramatic impact on a falling market, only when buyers already lack the confidence to buy. Program selling itself is initiated when buyers have already started to desert the market, causing prices to fall. The few buyers remaining are overwhelmed by an avalanche of selling. They do not need to bid up to obtain stock.

The collapse of the Thai baht and the Indonesia rupiah in 1997 shows the same relationship, although in this instance between a currency and currency traders. Linda Lim, a Singaporean analyst, points out the obvious. Financial market traders operate competitively. At times they do tend to move in sync, but this is only because they are all responding to the same underlying economic fundamentals.

The trader does not move prices. Crises move traders, and trading programs, to act. The better trader anticipates looming problems and takes an early position. The collapse in the price of ANZ Bank following US trade sanctions against India and the 1998 riots in Jakarta was not caused by traders taking put warrant positions. It is hardly a conspiracy between you and your computer that caused you to sell ANZ before it tumbled.

Dangerous fast bears like to drive entire markets, as in October 1997 or in some currency markets in 1997. They do strike quickly, but better traders are forewarned as the market accelerates up to the cliff edge. By understanding, in broad terms, the factors contributing to the speed of fast bears we select appropriate trading responses to either protect our capital, or add to it.

Fast bears also drive individual market segments, such as gold in 1997, and individual stocks like Burns Philp. The impact of margin lending and margin calls is not as pronounced in these areas. Here the collapse is driven by falling confidence accelerating when buyers leave the market segment either through fear, or more usually, to chase more attractive returns in other market segments.

SLOW BEARS

Bears are large, lumbering animals and surprisingly well camouflaged. In wildlife documentaries the fast bear swipes quickly in the water, catching fish in its paw. The big, slow bear uses his weight to shake a tree until it slowly topples to the ground where he collects the honey. This bear is just as dangerous, but perhaps a little more cunning.

The driving force is still a fall in market confidence but now we deal with disappearing buyers. This steady process pushes prices down in an orderly fashion. There are no big falls. Each new close is about the same as the previous day, but just slightly lower. Small rallies occur, just enough for us to keep bullish faith alive.

The rallies lock traders into a steadily deteriorating positions as shown in Figure 1.2 by the Straits Times Singapore weekly market index.

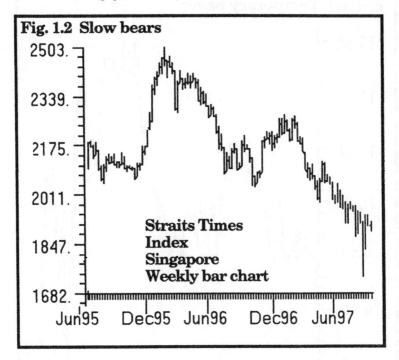

This slow, steady decline is most easily identified over a period of weeks, and is usually blindingly obvious after the event. The slow bear is defined by the absence of buyers. Buyers are not necessarily overwhelmed by sellers as in a fast bear market. Instead they quietly exit, leaving other market participants holding scrip.

We trade these slow bear markets in significantly different ways. These are trend-following techniques rather than momentum-based trades used with fast bear markets.

TEMPORARY BEARS

This special breed of bears hibernates for much of the financial year. They emerge for about six weeks of activity, usually around October and into the first few weeks of November each year. Individual stocks like ANZ Banking shown in Figure 1.3 are hit hard. Most times the growl is much worse than the bite, but when temporary bears team up with fast bears every 30 years or so, the result is devastating.

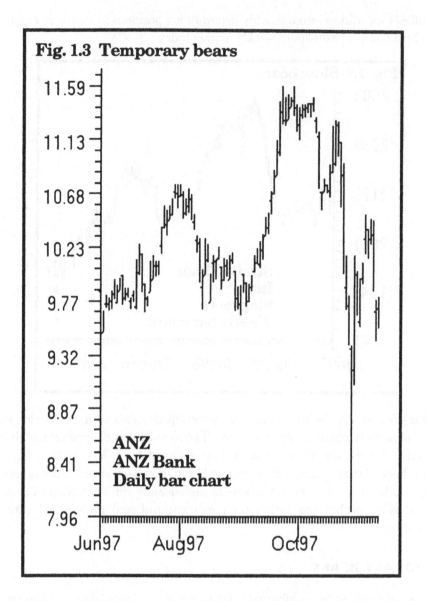

Fig. 1.3 Temporary bears

ANZ
ANZ Bank
Daily bar chart

Temporary bears provide some very specific trading opportunities. For the brave-hearted, annual trading from the long side the last days in October does provide some bargain priced entry points. Our focus is on bear trading tactics, so later we look at short-side trading tactics to use this brief, but regular phenomenon, to maximise profits and protect us in case the temporary bears combine with a fast bear team.

WORKING WITH BEARS

Our challenge as traders is to work with all bear markets. We have three distinct choices:

1. Get out of the market and stand aside.

2. Trade defensively near bull market tops.

3. Trade the bear market using a mixture of techniques.

The choice made by most is to get out of the market with whatever they can salvage. Those who exit early near the top of a bull market have the comfort of cash, but the disappointment that they missed out on the last exciting up-ticks of the dying bull market. Cash is a nice compensation and ought not be dismissed lightly.

Good traders exit before the top, standing aside, or out of the market, for weeks or months, until a definite new market direction is established. Many adopt specific defensive strategies involving short-term rally opportunities and momentum based trades. In a bear market they re-enter using a range of techniques discussed in the following chapters. Good traders aim to survive and thrive in all market conditions.

Traders who have never been attacked by a bear before should spend several months standing aside, observing the market, and developing techniques for trading in this new set of circumstances. Paper trading the new market conditions is an invaluable survival aid. This book provides some starting techniques.

Others less fortunate are caught holding stock they are unwilling to sell. The lucky ones are forced to sell to meet their margin calls. The unlucky ones hold the same stock years later, waiting for the price to recover. Either way, many private traders, punters, novices and unsuspecting participants in the market courtesy of their superannuation fund, are removed from active market participation.

This has two significant impacts on the character of a bear market.

IMPACT ONE

Bear market trading activity is dominated by the professionals trading full time for the institutions. They have no choice. They must be active in the market and fiduciary responsibilities mean they are active in only a small segment. This is broadly defined as the blue chip stocks. Private traders working in bear markets must shift their attention to these stocks. Forget the speculatives, ignore most of the mid-range and mid-cap stocks. Opportunities do exist in these areas, but they are hampered by the lack of liquidity. There are few buyers, and many sellers.

Survival depends on being able to trade the opportunities the institutions have identified, and in a bear market this means mixing it with the professionals.

IMPACT TWO

The other significant impact is the way any rally is initially destroyed by a great mass of sellers. At each upward leg of the new developing bull people who have been holding stock for months, or years, return to the market trying to capture the best prices.

Having finally made up their minds to take a loss they swamp each new rally. This factor is more significant when trading the very end of a bear market as it emerges into a new uptrend. For those trading resource and Asian markets when the bear has finished its feast, these considerations help decide realistic profit targets.

DEFENSIVE TRADING

Near the top of a bull market we trade in a defensive fashion. The objective is to take maximum returns while limiting our risk. Traders do not fully believe the strength of each new rally, but they are attracted to the potential profits. The most effective means of trading these tops is to use derivative trading instruments, such as warrants. Many of the techniques used are equally valid for trading the following bear market when it arrives.

For traders, it is ironic and particularly useful, that the last stages of the bull market spawn the very derivative instruments that make it profitable to trade the ensuing bear market. The new instruments are developed to entice people to trade the bull market, but they also provide the private trader with the means to survive the bear market.

One objective of defensive trading is to reap the last profits before leaving the market in favour of some other asset class, such as property. Others trade defensively to add to their trading capital, and to fine-tune their techniques in preparation for more specialised trading used in a full scale bear market. These are options we examine in more detail later in this book.

Private traders can work effectively with the full bear market. Our objective is to trade the market actively using a combination of familiar, and unfamiliar techniques. We can trade the bear from the long side. We trade it more effectively from the short side, and although it is possible to do this with ordinary shares, it is difficult to find a willing broker and work through the ASX regulations.

More effective short trading is achieved in the derivative markets using warrants and options. These financial instruments also provide enhanced longside trading opportunities in falling markets. We examine both.

Survival for the private trader depends in important ways on defining just how we fit into the overall scheme of things. We are guppies in a market ocean full of sharks and other fish. When there are plenty of fish in the ocean we feed with comfort and relative safety. When the little fish are all eaten, or when they leave our part of the ocean, we look for our meals amongst the sharks.

In a bear market the sharks predominate. When we trade these markets these are our adversaries – the full-time institutional traders, experienced private traders, fund managers, banks and the hedge funds. Like it or not, we do trade on their terms, but not on their scale. Survival goes to the quickest.

CHAPTER 2

BEAR RALLIES

Despite doom and gloom, traders are still able to take money from falling markets using quite ordinary plain, vanilla, trading techniques. This requires good discipline and rigorous stop loss control. In this sense it is no different from trading in a bull market, but when the bear bites, it bites hard. Less skilled traders wash out quickly, sitting uncomfortably on rapidly accumulating losses.

In a bull market the market pays for your mistakes. Carried by the general enthusiasm for stocks, there are usually many willing and naive buyers who pay above current prices to get a slice of the action. Poor trading survives in the flow of new and inexperienced money into the market.

In a bear market, we pay for our mistakes. With less participation from the general public, the active traders tend to be smarter than the average punter and less inclined to chase rainbows, pots of gold at the end of wildcat drilling programs, or test tube miracles in obscure laboratories. When the company price does not perform as expected, these traders dump stock vigorously. The slow are left holding expensive, but increasingly worthless, shares.

A bear market decides who has trading skill and who has not.

We tend to think of a bear market as a uniformly falling market, but all aspects of market activity are present. Some stocks still trade in sideways consolidation patterns, while others buck the trend, pulling in new business.

In a most obvious sense, a bear market is good for insolvency experts and the suppliers of essential services with a non-elastic demand. All retailers feel the pinch, but those in the grocery sector do better than those selling whitegoods, or luxury items. Everybody has to eat.

In this and following chapters we look at three strategies for trading ordinary shares from the long side – buying low and selling high – in falling markets. These bull market techniques modified for falling markets include:

1. Trading stocks performing counter trend, including breakouts.

2. Trading stocks in consolidation bands and, taking a step towards more complex strategies

3. Trading from the price retreat to the resistance level.

Under very specific circumstances, and if you are able to find a willing broker, it is possible to short trade ordinary Australian shares and this is considered in Chapter 14. Here we ignore the possibility in favour of more accustomed long side trading tactics based on buying low and selling high.

TRADING STOCKS PERFORMING COUNTER TREND

Good things do happen in bear markets, even from the long side. In the sustained All Resources downtrend in 1998, the mid-cap mineral explorer East Coast Minerals increased its price from a low of $0.14 to a year high of $1.35. This 864% return brought a smile to many bear traders, and although exceptional, it serves as an extreme example of good returns available in the bear market gloom.

The longside trader has two main counter-trend trading strategies. The first is breakout and spike trading, and the second is true counter trend trading.

We look at an example of each selected from the All Resources 1998 bear market.

BREAKOUTS

Price spikes are a special variety of trend breakout. They result from a moment of madness where the crowd over-reacts to what is otherwise pretty ordinary news. Mining junior, Cluff Resources ran more than 260% on what were, in retrospect, pretty ordinary drilling reports. Carpenter Pacific, took off on a 400% run based on little more than anticipated drill results. In each case the result was far in excess of that expected on the basis of the news alone.

Spikes are an unplanned bonus when we trade breakouts. It is like fishing in the colder months in the Northern Territory of Australia. Using recent fishing maps we plan to fish for threadfin salmon, but when a barramundi strikes unexpectedly out of season we quickly change tactics. In a bear market, we want to trade these moments of madness, either in anticipation, or more dangerously, by jumping on board when the spike first starts.

For many buyers, the spike is an open Tattslotto ticket to riches, but for the trader, the spike offers a clearly defined opportunity with increasing risk.

Previous price history gives the bear trader an edge both in setting profit targets and managing any spike activity. Unlike a price spike in a bull market which moves into uncharted territory with new highs, the spike in a bear market starts from a low point, reaching towards established chart points. The weekly chart of Bendigo Gold in Figure 2.1 shows this clearly.

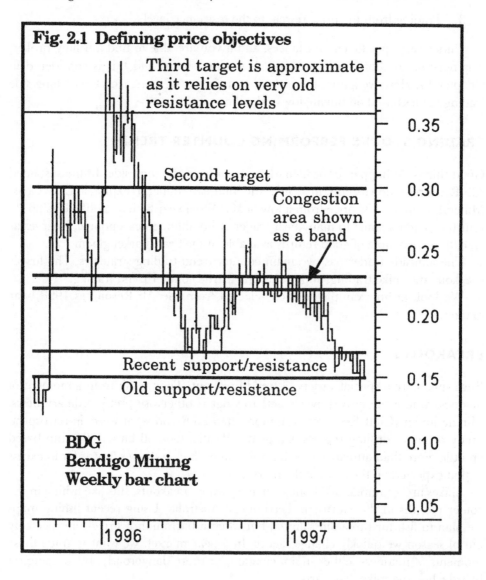

Fig. 2.1 Defining price objectives

Third target is approximate as it relies on very old resistance levels

Second target

Congestion area shown as a band

Recent support/resistance

Old support/resistance

BDG
Bendigo Mining
Weekly bar chart

0.35
0.30
0.25
0.20
0.15
0.10
0.05

1996   1997

In real life we use the daily bar chart to select potential trading opportunities. Weekly charts are used to set trading targets. In this example we reverse the process, starting with a weekly view to set targets first.

Working upwards from the bottom of the chart, we note an old support, and more recently, a resistance level at $0.17. Should we look even further back at the price action in 1995, we find another old support/resistance level at $0.15, with an ultimate congestion area low at $0.12. These three figures – $0.12, $0.15 and $0.17 – provide the calculation framework for any trade.

Support and resistance areas are plotted across the extremes of price moves spanning several days, weeks or months. Congestion areas form when prices stop moving up or down and spend time in a tight trading range with highs and lows close to each other. Identifying and plotting these features are fully covered in *Share Trading*.

Moving up the Bendigo Gold chart we see price congestion towards the end of 1996, spending many days trading around $0.22 to $0.23. This resistance level sets a potential profit target as we expect any steady price move to pause around this level as sellers enter the market.

This basic chart analysis relies on the two most predictable of human emotions – greed and fear. Plotting lines on a chart does not dictate future price action any more than the notations on last year's fishing map mean the fish will be in the same spot this year. When the tides and underwater structures are favourable there is increased probability of catching fish.

The line plots on the Bendigo Gold chart show levels of increased probability as current disillusioned stock-holders gather for the sale. Many people bought Bendigo Gold around $0.22 in late 1966 expanding the share register with new names. Many rode the price down to $0.15, losing on paper over 30%. When prices claw back to $0.22 it delivers a break-even opportunity. This fishing map works because this location, this structure, attracts fish. Traders reasonably expect heavy selling at this level.

With reduced certainty, we apply the same analysis moving further up the chart. This is grandad's much older fishing map, and seabed conditions may have changed. The line at $0.30 extends from the support/resistance areas in 1994, again in late 1995 and early 1996. These targets are sketched guidelines ready to finalise with hard edges as new price action develops.

Grandad's map could be right, but only fish will tell!

These line plots build the outline of a trading plan to capture a potential breakout in a falling market segment. The plan is constructed following the steps outlined in *Trading Tactics* and when completed has five conditions:

🐟 Entry at $0.16 in anticipation of a downtrend breakout.

☞ Stop loss is a close below $0.15, with an expected pause on long-term support at $0.11 with a likely exit at $0.12.

☞ First profit target, $0.23, or 43%

☞ Second profit target, $0.30, or 87%

☞ Expected time for completion eight to twelve weeks, based on the 1996 price rise.

This trading plan is not designed to capture a price spike, although based on past history of the stock the trader is alert to this possibility. We intend to fish for threadfin salmon but are also prepared for other game fish. Sounds too good to be true in real life? This spike trade example uses analysis made in real time and details actual returns.

The daily chart, shown in Figure 2.2, carries forward the weekly chart conclusions into a daily context. Now the chart shows how Bendigo Gold hands traders an opportunity to hook into a spike trade. Clearly both profit targets are hit by a single price spike with a slight pause at the first target level of $0.23.

This trade was prepared on the basis of a much longer time horizon – eight to twelve weeks. The trend breakout targets are still valid, but they have been achieved more quickly than anticipated. In an important sense we were prepared for the spike because we used weekly charts to establish profit points. Our concern is to manage this trade.

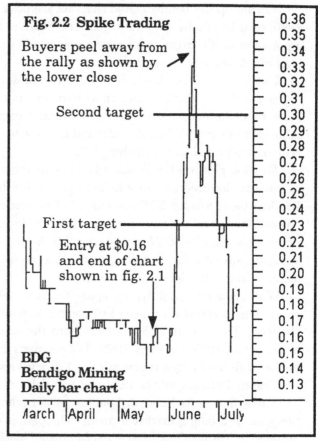

Fig. 2.2 Spike Trading

Buyers peel away from the rally as shown by the lower close

Second target

First target

Entry at $0.16 and end of chart shown in fig. 2.1

BDG
Bendigo Mining
Daily bar chart

March April May June July

0.36 0.35 0.34 0.33 0.32 0.31 0.30 0.29 0.28 0.27 0.26 0.25 0.24 0.23 0.22 0.21 0.20 0.19 0.18 0.17 0.16 0.15 0.14 0.13

SPIKE TRADING

The spike traders, those who jump on board when the spike first starts, use slightly different techniques to manage the same trade. This fishing story is a blow-by-blow analysis of Bendigo Gold, but trading survival depends on understanding how knowledge and speed combine to reap profits and minimise risk.

The first leg of the spike closed at $0.23 with few trades at intermediate prices. Prices paused here for two days, tempting spike traders. Only traders using real-time screens are able to clamber on board this rocket.

Traders looking to enter the next day have one key question: What is the balance of the market? Depth of market provides the answer. Spike traders look for many buyers at, or above yesterday's close, and only a few sellers. The ideal order line is shown in Figure 2.3. Then they buy at market and monitor the price during the day against price targets from the weekly charts.

Fig. 2.3 Ideal order line for spike trading

Buying pressure in the order lineup. Buy at market.

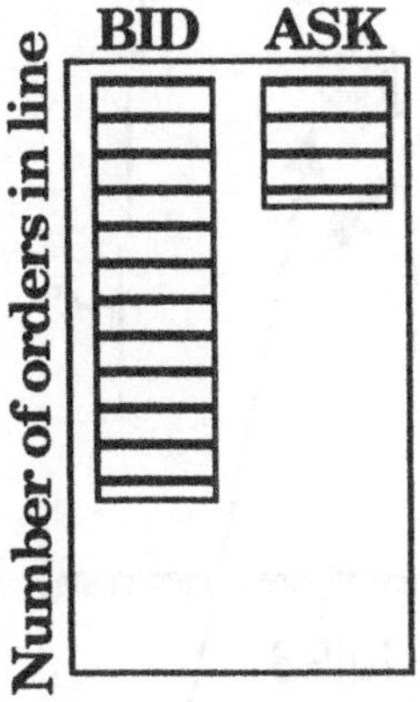

Number of orders in line

BID   ASK

When buyers start leaving the market, spike traders sell at market, taking the nearest bid price. The danger is when buyers peel away from nearby price levels. Perhaps on the open there were nine buyers at $0.34, but by 1 p.m. there are only two buyers left, even though prices have pulled back to $0.33.

This suggests buyers are leaving the stock and momentum weakens.

Only when buyers bid higher, chasing just a few sellers, is the spike trader comfortable. Then the rally has the power to drive the price spike further. He places a sell order at the next profit target based on the weekly charts. In a bear market blue sky does not exist. Rallies tend to be capped in line with previous resistance levels. The spike trader uses these levels to set indicative exit points, knowing momentum is unlikely to travel much beyond them.

This is different from a bull market. Then, the only key is momentum, as prices move into uncharted areas. The bear leaves little room for greed. Often just a few sales take place at the target point and better traders are comfortable with an 87% return. Beyond $0.30, the next resistance level is at $0.37.

The spike trader uses it as a reference point, but exits at the open of $0.31 as this is the best price possible as volume diminishes and sellers start to lower their asking price. This is a 93% return, but carries increased risk of stranding as buyers desert the market quickly.

Spike trading opportunities exist even in the deepest gloom. In mid 1998 the Kuala Lumpur market looked to be on the edge of death, yet spike trading gave good rewards. Malaysian counter, Hap Seng in Figure 2.4 shows how with just a little analysis these rallies are identified and traded.

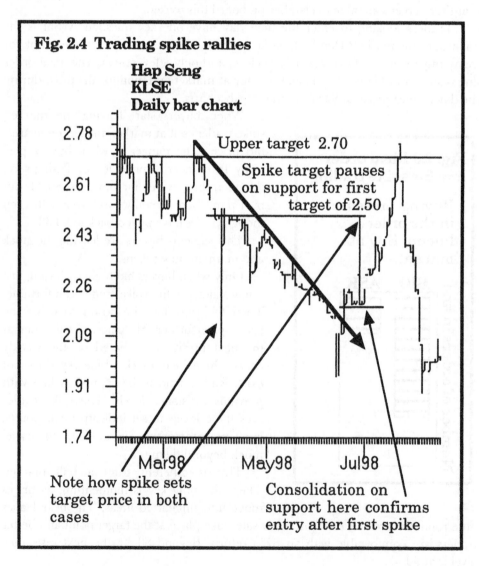

Fig. 2.4 Trading spike rallies

Hap Seng
KLSE
Daily bar chart

Upper target 2.70

Spike target pauses on support for first target of 2.50

Note how spike sets target price in both cases

Consolidation on support here confirms entry after first spike

The first clue is the rally and rest pattern developed in late June. Prices paused around 2.19, even after the spike through to 2.50. Eager buyers pushing prices higher are a bullish sign of things to come. Why pay well above market when a little patience collects stock at lower market prices?

Smart traders took this signal, jumping on board at 2.19. The first target, based on old support levels, and on the height of the initial spike, was 2.50 for a 14% return. The second target, based on old resistance levels, was 2.70 for a 23% return. An exit anywhere in this region is a good trade. Traders backing a new trend break were still holding Hap Seng at 2.00. Spike trading doesn't pretend to be anything other than a short-term trade, usually over days, but sometimes over two or three weeks.

KEY LESSONS

Sound chart analysis identifies trading opportunities in any market condition. In stocks with a history of characteristic price activity, spikes, island days, heavy resistance levels, etc. additional trading opportunities do arise. It is unwise to build trades around specific characteristics such as spike activity as they are difficult to forecast in a precise time frame. Traders are prepared for the opportunity, but realise profits are capped by previous resistance levels.

When I fish in the colder months of the dry season the big fish are cold and sluggish. I bait the hook for threadfin salmon, but I am always prepared for barramundi. In a bear market we equip ourselves to deal with small 'calf', rather than bull rallies, but we need to be prepared for the unexpected.

These trades are not isolated events. About 5% of stocks show these characteristics. The 1998 Australian Resources sector bear market included those listed in Figure 2.5.

COUNTER TREND

Counter trend stocks are less common, with around 3% to 5% rising when the rest of the general market is going down. Severe down days in late August 1998 had stock falls outnumbering rises four to one. We are interested in the exceptions. Unlike breakouts and spikes, early identification is not as vital. These are trend trades in a traditional sense, but they push against an entire market. This is dangerous fishing, so we take greater care, surrendering some profit potential in return for greater certainty.

All trades taken from the long side in a bear market are monitored every day. We cannot assume the up-trend will continue. Even in a good counter trend, a bear market is unforgiving, and mistakes can be expensive.

Fig. 2.5

CFR	GVM	RGR
CPC	LEG	SED
GIR	PRE	SPX
GSR	RBK	TAI

The selections are based on weekly charts and list only the major spikes, or most noticeable trends. Many other stocks gave similar, but reduced opportunities. The list excludes the real wildcat spikes that come out of nowhere and which are not preceded by any useful chart signals.

When all looks lost and conditions are desperate, Harrison, owner of the colt from Old Regret, tells the assembled Snowy River riders, "No use to try for fancy riding now." In bear markets there is less room for fancy trading. We look for robust tools to pry profits from the market. Exponential moving averages make excellent pry bars.

When the bear rolls over, not all stocks are pulled down at the same time, or as quickly. We use this opportunity to play with the leading downtrend stocks to develop a more suitable trading approach and find a set of averages which work. A 10 and 30 day exponential moving average (EMA) provided particularly useful trading signals in the resources bear market of 1998.

It was also useful in the Malaysian and Singaporean bear markets. The standard 7 and 21 day EMA combination was less useful, giving too many whipsaws, shaking traders out of profitable trades too early and in turn, sapping trading confidence.

By working with the early loss leaders – those stocks leading the downhill charge – the best combination of moving averages is found and tested against other stocks joining the general market decline. This robust tool is not designed for subtle or early application. We want confirmation this moving average combination does define downtrend stocks, and when satisfied, we look for the reverse conditions.

If one set of conditions defines a downtrend, then the same set, in reverse order, defines an uptrend with about the same degree of robust certainty. We cannot expect counter trends to become extended trends. The ticket to ride the counter trend is open, but the exit is carefully monitored against pre-set financial objectives. Here the market works against us, not with us, and we forget this at our peril. Adding to the risk is the type of stock most likely to move counter trend. When the gold sector fell in 1997 the leading miners collapsed first. The institutions sold them down, and the general public took the hint and left as well.

At the very opposite end of the market, the speculative gold explorers, all but the most optimistic traders abandoned the market. Volume dried up when money was transferred elsewhere. These characteristics belong to every bear market, be it just a sector, or an entire market. The first objective is to avoid being caught with the last parcel of scrip. The second is to trade in more active market segments.

Active trading cash stays with some mid-cap issues, and we look here for counter trend stocks. Volume and liquidity remain a problem so we calculate the average daily volumes traded. We buy only this many shares, or less.

This improves the exit. Attempting to sell very large positions is difficult as buyers disappear just when you want them most.

Yinnex, a small gold miner, (see Figure 2.6) dramatically outperformed the 1998 Australian Gold index. The robust signals from a 10 and 30 day EMA, confirmed the Gold index turned down in March. By May, major gold companies started a steady fall. Using the 10 and 30 day EMA crossover as a search criterion, Yinnex signalled a buy on the pull-back to, and rally from, the 30 day EMA line.

This is the initial alert raised when the stock is selected from an Ezy Analyser, or Metastock Explorer search based on the moving average crossover points. Appearing on this list is one step but we need confirmation of the strength of the counter trend and this comes from the multiple moving average (MMA) indicator.

CONFIRMING COUNTER TRENDS

Our concern here is to explore how the MMA is used rather than to explain its construction in detail.[1] The MMA consists of two groups of averages and uses fractal repetition of convergences to identify points of agreement about value. We readily understand the signal generated by two moving averages – when the crossover takes place we enter or exit the trade. This crossover also signals a moment of agreement about the value of the stock across two different time frames.

---

[1] See *Trading Tactics* for a full discussion of construction and rules.

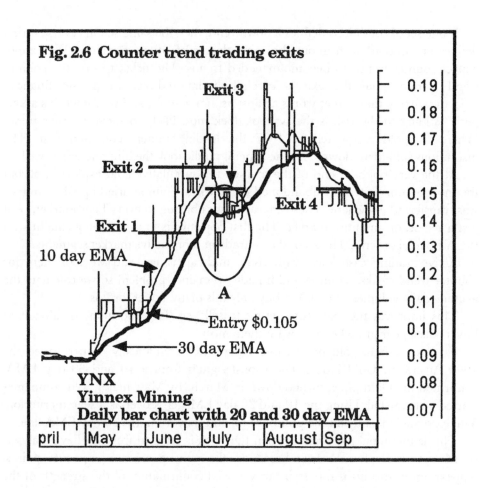

Fig. 2.6 Counter trend trading exits

Exit 3
Exit 2
Exit 1
Exit 4
10 day EMA
A
Entry $0.105
30 day EMA
YNX
Yinnex Mining
Daily bar chart with 20 and 30 day EMA

0.19 0.18 0.17 0.16 0.15 0.14 0.13 0.12 0.11 0.10 0.09 0.08 0.07

pril | May | June | July | August | Sep

When this moment of agreement is spread across several short-term time frames – 3, 5, 8, 10, 12 and 15 day exponential moving averages – we observe many convergences in this short term group. Such widespread agreement about value often precedes a violent disagreement about price. If price and value were both the same there would be no need for the market. We buy stock at a good price because we believe the value will go up. Value is what we think a stock is worth. Price is what we pay for it. As soon as we acquire stock at $1.00 we immediately value it at a higher price intending to sell for no less than $1.20. This creates a disparity between value and price.

Using just a short term group of averages is useful, but it does not identify major trend changes. The short term group tracks the inferred speculative activity of traders. We use the same technique with the long-term group of averages – 30,

35, 40, 45 and 50 day exponential moving averages – to track the inferred opinions of investors.

When both groups agree – when they converge and crossover – we brace for a major trend change. This is the condition we look for in applying the MMA to longside trading opportunities. A bear market demands caution so we wait for the pattern to develop further, entering on the retracement rather than on the indicator breakout.

In particular we look for confirmation of an existing trend as shown in Figure 2.7 for Yinnex. Here the short term group of averages bounces above the long-term group. We have increased confidence in the strength of this trend. We need additional confidence because this trend is moving in the opposite direction to the entire market sector.

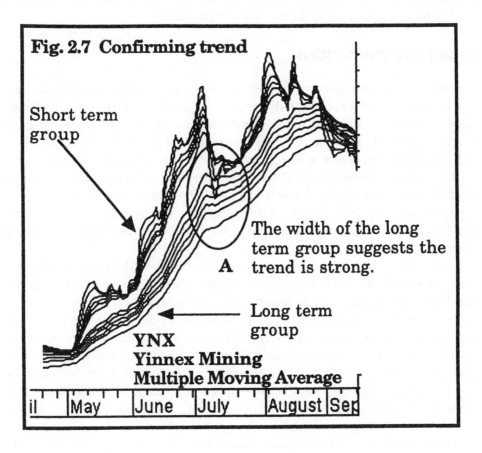

Fig. 2.7 Confirming trend

Short term group

The width of the long term group suggests the trend is strong.

A

Long term group

YNX
Yinnex Mining
Multiple Moving Average

il | May | June | July | August | Sep

Bear markets favour pretty ordinary analysis tools that deliver strong unequivocal signals. Trading from the long side we cannot take the risk with anything more sensitive. The novice thinks he needs to take a greater proportion of available profits because profit levels are reduced, so he looks for tools to signal an early entry in anticipation of a trend break.

Trading near the trend breakout point was never an exact science. Now the consequences of error are magnified. Waiting a little longer builds certainty, adding to profit in the pocket in difficult times.

Selection of these counter trend stocks is made using a first search based on the moving average crossover. Candidates are confirmed using a multiple moving average display. Once found we approach the candidates with more caution, looking for a few days of activity to prove the strength of the trend.

The last thing we want to do in this market is chase prices.

STOP LOSS CONDITIONS

The two moving averages provide both an entry and a stop loss condition. Each day the entry price is recalculated to match the current 10 day moving average value. Two weeks after the initial Yinnex trading signal, an entry is made at $0.105. It hurts to surrender 16% potential profit available between an early entry at $0.09 and the later entry at $0.105 but this is the price of greater certainty.

The stop loss conditions are initially established by the current value of the 30 day EMA line. Should prices fall below this level the trade is abandoned.

As discussed in detail in both *Share Trading* and *Trading Tactics*, the nominated stop loss price is matched with entry position size, so no more than 2% of total trading capital is at risk.

In managing this trade we continue to use the 30 day EMA value as a stop loss point, even once the trade becomes profitable. Alternatively, a trailing stop loss based on count back line calculations is equally appropriate.

In trading this counter trend we need to avoid the exit time lag inherent in any moving average crossover technique. Although we are content to surrender potential profit on the entry in return for greater certainty when the trend is in place, we cannot let this happen on the exit. In a bull market, an exit based on moving average crossovers uses this as an indicative signal rather than an absolute. Often price rallies back towards old highs, letting the trader lock in additional profits despite the lagging exit signal.

This is less likely in a bear market. Once price falls it has the full weight of the market behind it, and it is unlikely any rallies will hand back a reasonable part of the foregone profits. Although we trade this individual stock with its trend we are trading against the general market trend so it is prudent to lower our profit targets and run at the first sign of danger.

This is defensive trading.

SETTING PROFIT CONDITIONS

Yinnex offers four potential exit points, working from left to right on Figure 2.6. The first are set on financial targets. This is not a mid-cap stock so in return for the additional risk we would normally look for 50% to 100% returns. Although 100% would be pleasing, a bear market forces lower profit expectations. This suggests 50% is pretty good and 30% is quite adequate.

Price does spend some time at $0.135 giving ample opportunity to collect these profits as shown by exit line 1. Good trade management shoots higher because price does not fall below the 10 day EMA line. Additionally, the value of the line continues to increase and remains well separated from the slower 30 day EMA line.

This is confirmed with the multiple moving average chart, and the same time period is marked on Figure 2.7.

The separation between the groups of averages, and the width of the long-term group suggests this counter trend is still strong. Shooting for a 50% return with an exit at $0.16 is a reasonable expectation and exit line 2 shows the result.

Traders using advance sell orders based on the financial target are taken out of the trade in late June. Do they need to kick themselves because prices run through to $0.18 and later $0.19? This self-punishment must give many people a great deal of satisfaction because so many indulge in it. This is a fruitless exercise in a bull market and positively dangerous in a bear market.

At the core of trading activity is the management of risk to achieve financial objectives. We ask the market to provide us with a living and only after we have traded for quite a while do we realise the enormity of this request.

The amateur trader flushed with success from the bull market looks at Yinnex and he just knows he could have picked up an exit at $0.18. In retrospect is looks easy, but in real life the sudden dip to $0.12 tests the mettle of the amateur.

What happens to those using other exit techniques? Traders protecting open profits using the count back line technique take their exit at $0.15 for a return of 43%, shown as exit line 3. Those using the 10 and 30 day EMA crossover in this example achieve the same result seven weeks later, shown as exit line 4.

KEY LESSONS

Trading from the longside in a bear market leaves no room for pigs – those who want every last bit of profit. Superficially counter trend trading resembles a standard trend based trade.

Unlike trend breakouts and spike trades considered above, some counter-trend trades move into blue sky. There is no previous chart history to provide a guide for profit targets, so these trades are micro-managed against a background of disaster. We do try to lock in the maximum profit, but better traders exit while the balance of probability is in their favour and the market is liquid.

Sometimes the market will be kind enough to give additional profit – three opportunities to exit at $0.18 with Yinnex. Thankful, the trader dips his hat and offers his stock to the pigs who buy off him in anticipation of even higher highs. At worst, he has ample opportunity to sell at $0.16, still bringing home the bacon with a 50% return.

BEAR SURVIVAL

When we trade the bear market from the longside, trying to take profits from buying low and selling high, we abandon many of the fancy tools found in Metastock, SuperCharts and technical indicator encyclopedias. Survival depends on rapid identification, sound confirmation and defensive trading to lock in pre-defined profit targets. It is not quite the cut and thrust of the bull market. It is a slash and bash approach that ignores the less obvious opportunities.

Traders who used the bull market to develop real trading skills have a better chance of survival than those who rode the profits to exhaustion. It is not easy for the bull to thrive in a bear market but it is possible when he trims the profit targets in individual trades.

Opportunities to trade rallies are limited. Spikes are more common than breakout events. What look like breakouts from downtrends are powerfully limited by previous resistance levels. Real uptrends are scarce and must be traded with caution. This small group of opportunities makes lean pickings for bulls whose trading repertoire is accustomed to greener pastures.

While many stocks are bashed to the ground and gutted, others lose momentum and drift sideways. A few of them provide unexpectedly good trading opportunities. They are not spectacular enough for the real bull market trader but with steady 10% and 15% returns they should not be ignored. We look at these survival stocks in the next chapter.

CHAPTER 3

BEAR SURVIVAL

G enerally we do not enter the market expecting to lose money. We accept the possibility of loss as part of a sound money management plan, but we demand a profitable bottom line over time. This bullish outlook fits naturally into the standard 'buy low and sell high' longside trading approach. Many traders find it difficult to break out of this mindset to sell high before buying low. This is not always a problem in a falling market unless this bullish attitude pushes the trader into unrealistic trades.

This natural optimism sometimes traps the trader into one view of price charts. BHP traded at $20.00 in 1997 so when it trades at $13.00 in 1998 these traders see 53% profits some time in the near future as price climbs back to old highs. At the beginning of a new bull market this natural optimism is an advantage because it supports risk-taking, and by using past price history, establishes reasonable profit targets.

At the beginning of a bear market this same natural optimism locks the trader into losing positions, or encourages an early entry into short-lived rallies. From a high of $20.00, BHP looked attractive at $17.00, mouth-watering at $15.00, almost pornographic at $14.00 and just a worn-out old strumpet at $11.30. We cannot afford to buy multiple positions in BHP at every bargain point on the way down. By shifting bull market optimism into a bear market the trader blinds himself to the reality of the market.

To trade falling markets from the longside we harness this optimism in a defensive way, reducing profit objectives, using nearby profit targets, limiting time in the market and paying much closer attention to trading opportunities that were too unexciting to notice when the bull roared. These are found in stocks moving sideways.

Fishing stories are interesting only to the person who caught the fish. Finding the best fishing spots interests all fishermen. Here we look more closely at an example of a trading band approach to find the best fishing spot. We avoid unnecessary detail because we want to show the processes of evaluation. The key factor distinguishing these trades from similar trades in a bull market is the way profit-taking is aimed at the congestion areas, where volume provides the security needed to fill orders and make the exit possible.

DON'T FEED THE BEARS

The price action shown in Figure 3.1 is enough to put any bull trader to sleep. The directors of junior miner, Federation Resources, no doubt had grand plans, but the market was less convinced. Who wants to be in a gold stock when the Reserve Bank sells gold for a pittance? The news is always bad in every bear market so within reason we ignore the news and concentrate on understanding the mood of the crowd as shown in the price chart.

We cannot expect major opportunities, so we hunt for the small ones, trading them with extra care. Starting in October the trader picks up one, and later, two strong trading signals. The first is the development of the upward sloping triangle, complete with an early breakout. The second is the establishment of very broad consolidation bands and these allow us to stay with Federation for an additional three trades.

The upward sloping triangle develops from the low in October. Buyers believe this stock is going somewhere, so they clamber on board at slightly higher prices on each price retracement. This builds the sloping trend line, and each new retreat and rally reinforces the validity of the line.

This pattern is bullish, and in a bull market we would project it forward into time to establish a new long-term uptrend. It is foolish to do this in a declining sector, although, as shown with Yinnex in the previous chapter, counter trends do develop.

Not all upward sloping triangles develop into new uptrends but they do provide short-term trading opportunities. By using the length of the triangle, shown as line a-a, traders project possible upper and lower price targets. The starting point for this calculation is based on the upper horizontal line.

Look for price action filling the gap between the upsloping trend line and the upper target line. This gap is usually closed over several days, each one higher than the other. Sometimes a single day provides this reference point.

With Federation Resources the conditions are filled in mid-November. Taking this starting point the upsloping trend line is projected forwards to complete the triangle, shown as the thick horizontal line in Figure 3.1.

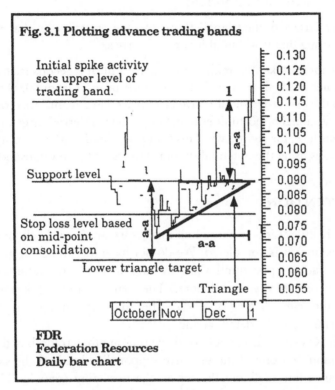

Fig. 3.1 Plotting advance trading bands

Initial spike activity sets upper level of trading band.

Support level

Stop loss level based on mid-point consolidation

Lower triangle target

Triangle

October | Nov | Dec

**FDR
Federation Resources
Daily bar chart**

Project this line upwards to give an indicative target at $0.115, shown as line a-a. The lower target is at $0.065. All a-a lines are the same length. These are indicative features, and they are firmed up using a point and figure chart for confirmation. In particular we look for confirmation of resistance at or above the projected profit target. Resistance below the target makes it less likely the triangle projection is accurate as prices are likely to stall early in any rise.

These triangle projections are completed early in the development of the triangle, and clearly suggest $0.115 as a target. In a blinding rush of enthusiasm prices raced to this projected level in late November, providing us with valuable information when prices collapsed back to the trend line. The way the trend line holds encourages an entry at $0.09 or better for three reasons:

↪ The single price spike sets an indicative target with a potential 27% return. This is a good return in a falling market. Even a 22% return from an exit at $0.11 is satisfactory.

↬ This price spike builds on a bullish chart pattern – the upsloping triangle. We look to trade the dominant pattern rather than the spike. A few buyers, perhaps better informed than many others, believe Federation Resources is worth at least $0.115.

↬ The upper surface of the triangle formed by the resistance level at $0.09 is not so strong that it will inhibit later price rises.

Please do not mistake this analysis for a perfect fit. It is reconstructed from my trading notes at the time. The first small trade takes us from $0.09 to $0.115. Although the exit order should have been placed in advance this trade does provide additional opportunities to get out at our preferred target, trading at or beyond this level for eight days. This action sets up the other trading opportunities using the potential support level and the new consolidation level.

FOCUS ATTENTION

This is a handy little trade and in a bull market we are more likely to move on to better pickings once it is completed. We do not have this choice in a bear market because good trading opportunities are few and far between. Naturally we like to stay where success has visited before. The same reasoning keeps fishermen returning to the same fishing spot day after day. We have a lot of faith in repeatable events – but the details change.

Federation Resources is capable of delivering another trade based on support and consolidation, but only if the tentative support line holds at the same level as the old resistance line, defining the top of the upsloping triangle. The stop loss conditions are set at $0.08, around the mid-point congestion area in November. This also matches old minor support levels in September. These levels are projected forward into time, and Figure 3.2 shows how subsequent price action behaved.

For the second trade we do not place a buy order in anticipation. We need to see the market independently confirm our analysis. We must avoid becoming the market ourselves, buying at $0.09 and in so doing, setting the price tick that confirms our analysis. This neat trick is fatal.

Validation is established by the market. Our activity impacts on the market but it is not an independent reflection of the market. We wait for guidance from other market participants, content to follow, rather than set the pace. There are times when we are happy to be market-makers, setting the highest or lowest tick for the day, but this is only in response to trading signals initiated by the market on the previous day. Our trading should never initiate our own trading signals.

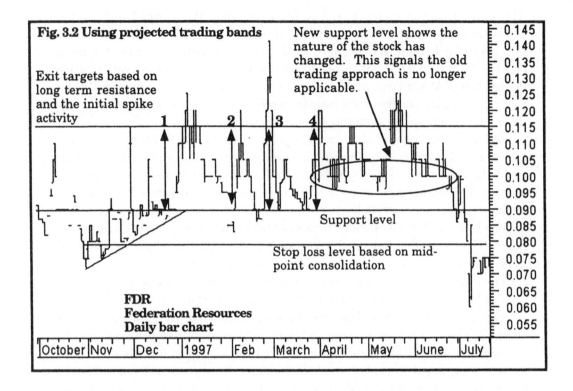

Fig. 3.2 Using projected trading bands

New support level shows the nature of the stock has changed. This signals the old trading approach is no longer applicable.

Exit targets based on long term resistance and the initial spike activity

1   2   3   4

Support level

Stop loss level based on mid-point consolidation

FDR
Federation Resources
Daily bar chart

October | Nov | Dec | 1997 | Feb | March | April | May | June | July

0.145
0.140
0.135
0.130
0.125
0.120
0.115
0.110
0.105
0.100
0.095
0.090
0.085
0.080
0.075
0.070
0.065
0.060
0.055

This means we miss the next Federation trade unless we log on to a real-time screen and notice the price moving above $0.09. As prices retreat towards the target area we should take the time to monitor the market more closely, perhaps ringing our broker two or three times a day, or making use of other quote providers or real-time information delivered by Internet services like William Noalls Ltd Trading System 2.5. The bear market does not hand us opportunities. We have to carve them out ourselves.

The second trade runs from around $0.092 to $0.115. The third and fourth trades repeat the process, with each returning around 27%. Each is shown in Figure 3.2. The fifth trade is abandoned at $0.085 after another entry at $0.09. We do not need to spend time with fancy trend lines and oscillators to know the party is over. In the film *Jurassic Park* the approaching dinosaur makes the puddles ripple. Federation Resources ripples before it succumbs to the bear. In the preceding months prices did not drop below $0.095 so this sudden series of trades below the old support line signals a rapid exit before a close below the original stop loss at $0.08.

DEFINING BAND ACTIVITY

This style of trading snatches crumbs from the table. We proceed with caution, accepting smaller profits in return for less time in the market. Holding the support line is crucial because the pressure is always downwards. At times this means chasing the price a little but this is acceptable if the chase remains within strictly defined limits. When large profits are on offer, a cent or so is unimportant. When profits are smaller and the trading environment more dangerous, a cent sometimes defines the difference between success and survival.

Although the consolidation, or resistance, level may be broken this is not a bullish signal. One of the standard longside trading band approaches uses any upside break as a signal to stay with the trade, perhaps even adding to a position, as the bullish market encourages and nurtures resistance breakouts. The strategy of buying new highs is successful.

In a bear market spikes above consolidation levels are like nails sticking out of a board. The temptation to bash them down is too strong. The trap is set for greedy traders because only a few sales take place at these spike levels.

The trap is sprung when prices hurtle below the consolidation level towards the support level. This does not always allow for a dignified exit.

The series of Federation Resources trades could be improved using a sell target of $0.12. This is a feat more easily achieved in retrospect than in real time. Had the trader shot for this level there would have been a reduced probability of filling the sell order, based on analysis made at the time. The second and fourth trades in the series just tipped $0.12 with only a few sales, although the last trade did give exit opportunities a few weeks later. If the second trade had been missed through greed, the total return from Federation Resources series would have been seriously reduced.

SLIM PICKINGS

By setting precise conditions, defining and refining them, as a series of trades develop, we protect ourselves from our own greed. At times we do return to the same stock and the same style of trades and they do provide a reliable source of income in a hostile environment. This market allows no room for complacency so the chart must be closely analysed for clues to changed conditions.

When conditions change, defensive trading strategies take us out of the trade quickly. This is the core of survival for the longside trader in a bear market. Those who are not fleet of foot get flattened. Federation later went to $0.06, flashed to $0.16 and crashed to $0.04, leaving many squashed traders underfoot. By June

1998 Federation Resources had changed its spots, rendering old trading approaches obsolete. Our trading survival depends on noticing the change and acting appropriately.

The bear trading message is clear. Greed is not good when trading from the longside. By reducing profit targets and trading defensively the trader builds better returns in the face of adversity. The final bear trading techniques available to committed longside traders rely on rapid defensive trades coupled with tight stop loss conditions. This is dancing with the bears using trend lines and multiple moving averages.

Trading from the longside will not make a fortune in the bear market, but it can deliver a steady respectable income by trading carefully defined opportunities. This is a great comfort, particularly when the same market is destroying the fortunes of others.

Bear market survival depends on taking advantage of steady trading opportunities. Spectacular returns are unlikely, so a series of conservative trades based on limited profit objectives is a more useful approach. These strategies are successful where stocks have steady liquidity and an appropriately wide trading or consolidation band. Stocks that appear to be going nowhere – neither up nor down – do provide trading solutions.

CHAPTER 4

DON'T FEED THE BEAR

Fear is reputed to clear the mind but a bear market seems to encourage a growth of woolly thinking. This snarled knot blocks the way to effective solutions and survival strategies. Much of this woolly thinking has a single common strand. We believe we can buy protection without effort or risk. Variously described as a flight to quality or investing in real companies with real products for the long term, we are encouraged to believe that quality will always win.

It is an interesting view because it consoles the investor in a bull market when he compares his returns with other possible higher returns. The same view provides consolation in a bear market when his blue chips do not fall as fast as other more volatile stocks.

When the NASDAQ tumbled in April 2000 there was a certain amount of worry amongst investors and some traders. A lot of commentators took almost unseemly delight in dancing on the grave of Dot Com stocks. Having predicted the end of the bubble for so long they were relieved to have finally got it right even though most Dot Com stock charts showed the bubble had burst eight weeks earlier. The commentators promoted the value of a defensive portfolio. This is an investment style and different from the defensive trading techniques mentioned in Chapter 1 and elsewhere.

These defensive strategies are built around the idea that quality is somehow a magic charm against risk. The core assumption is that quality stocks will retain their value despite changes in the wider market. What we expect from quality, and what we expect from the behaviour of our portfolio are two different things. In our portfolio we want an effective way to manage risk, and there is no escape from the need to manage risk aggressively rather than passively.

The protective or defensive aspect of quality can be misleading. By the end of April 2000 many high tech and Internet based stocks had lost a lot of value in just a few days. In contrast, the defensive quality portfolio had lost around an average 25% of original purchase value over the previous three to six months. For investors who bought near the recent highs their financial loss was substantial, even if spread over a longer time. Poor understanding of risk permits some investors to accept a 30% loss over six months while being terrified of a 30% loss over six days.

The defensive, diversified portfolio turns out to need just as much active management of risk as any other portfolio selection. Protection in falling markets does not come easily.

DEFENSIVE INVESTING

We all want a defence against falls in the market and many novice traders want it provided at low cost and with the least amount of work. They are good candidates for accepting common, muddled, ideas at face value and only later do they understand just how much these ideas can cost in real losses. The muddle includes defensive portfolios, diversification as a guaranteed antidote to risk, and a confusion about the way size and quality combine with risk management. We need to briefly unpick each strand individually from this woolly thinking if we are to make better use of these concepts to survive a bear market. If we fight the bear with fuzzy thinking we get slaughtered.

The first strand is connected to the idea of counter cyclical investing. This defensive investment approach means investing in those sectors that perform well in bad times. When economies stall there is still demand for food, alcohol, tobacco and other basics. These sectors are believed to defend investors against a general market or economic decline. As we show in the next chapter, just selecting a strong sector is not enough. Traders must also find the strongest stocks within the sector because not all are winners. Sector analysis is not a solution. It is a first step to finding a solution.

This is forward defence. It means capturing capital gains while others are losing. It is an aggressive strategy requiring active risk management. In really bad markets there are just a few winners so it makes sense to do more than just throw cash at a general sector and hope that some of it sticks to a winner.

DIVIDEND TAKE ALL

Although the NASDAQ chart in early 2000 shows a sudden change in direction it does take longer for the market to catch up with the fall. Markets, and large stocks, have a momentum beyond the last traded price. This shows up in dividend payments which are calculated well in advance of the ex-dividend trading date. A company may have suffered a mortal wound in the crash, but is still committed to dividend payments previously announced to the market. Other companies put a brave face on events and maintain dividend levels to improve market confidence and shore up the share price. Dividend compensation is a second strand meshed in the woolly thinking about defence and survival.

For those who intend to hold the stock for a long time the dividend provides a welcome bonus. This is a defensive benefit. In a period where there is little change in prices or the value of the portfolio the dividend stream compensates for the lack of capital gain. For some investors the dividend stream forms the basis of their investment strategy. They are most likely to shift capital from the sharemarket to bonds and other interest bearing investments as rates rise. Their investment in blue chips comes at a cost of lost capital because selling their blue chips crystallises the loss. For the very wealthy this may not be a problem as their investments are spread over non-related sectors including property and interest-backed instruments.

For the rest of us, the decline in blue chip capital is a problem. The dividends are the only compensation for a stalled share price. The defensive strategy turns into a something closer to holding on for dear life because the alternatives are too dreadful to contemplate. At best we hope that companies will continue to pay dividends at the old rate.

In a real bear market these company tactics are unsustainable. In a short-lived bear market they provide an opportunity for unexpected benefits for fast traders. They buy distressed blue chips at low prices and capture high residual dividends. At the end of a bull market these dividend returns can be impressive. This is a trading strategy in itself but it generally lasts around two turns of the company reporting season.

This is sometimes implemented as a form of dividend stripping where shares are bought just before they go ex-dividend and then sold as soon as they do go ex-dividend. A variety of taxation laws apply to the practice and the exact impact depends on timing and intent. Tony Compton in *Shares, Derivatives and Taxation* covers this complexity in more detail and with authority. This is recommended reading for traders considering these strategies.

This is a rearguard defensive action. The real danger is that the battle has been lost so our small victories are not enough to turn the tide in our favour. At times like this a dividend is just a small mercy.

DOES SIZE COUNT?

Popular opinion wants to believe that quality and size offer some inherent protection against calamity. Many believe they were protected from the NASDAQ inspired market fall because they invested only in quality blue chips. Names such as Southcorp, Lend Lease Woolworths, National Australia Bank, and others were frequently mentioned. These people believed that quality protected them against market falls and the volatility of the high tech sector. This naive belief is common and forms a third strand in the knot of woolly thinking. While it is true that many of these stocks did not show the same downside volatility as the speculative stocks, it is not true to say that this is a protection against market loss, or a lowering of risk.

The main impact of size is to slow the impact of change. It takes a long time to stop a road train towing three trailers. It takes a long time to change an uptrend in NAB into a downtrend — or does it? In a few short days in 1999 NAB fell from $30.21 to $24.50. This was a 19% fall. In just a week the uptrend which had been in place for seven months clearly turned to a downtrend. Big stocks do fall, and they can fall quite quickly. Size does not slow them down when they fall off the cliff. And when they reach the bottom it can take a long time to get up.

Recovery is usually much slower, even in a generally bullish or rising market. Three, old large blue chips provide an example. Both BHP and MIM were once considered an essential part of any blue chip portfolio. It took BHP two and a half years to recover from its 1997 highs. MIM turned into a basket case and two and a half years after its 1997 highs, recovery still does not look realistic as it plunges towards $0.75 again. After six years Burns Philp is not within seeing distance of its 1994 highs.

Some argue these examples are not relevant because we would no longer class them as large or blue chip stocks. While this is true it also begs the question of just when investors were advised to delete them from their portfolios. Was it at their highs, or closer to their lows? Generally sell recommendations are not as timely or as enthusiastic as buy suggestions.

We have been selective with these examples because we want to show that size by itself does not offer protection. This defensive approach huddles behind a wall believing the bulk of the structure is strong enough to withstand the new economic forces. Sometimes it does work.

WALLFLOWERS

Some traders believe in chivalry so they come to the rescue of distressed stocks. This is bargain hunting — one of the major bear traps discussed in Chapter 5.

One of the most dangerous forms of this approach is focused on wallflowers. These are the lonely and unloved stocks. While the rest of the market has been going up these stocks have been going down. By a perverse twist of logic some see these losers in a strong bull market as attractive choices in a bear market. The usual explanation, or excuse, is that they are fundamentally sound companies like Mayne Nicholas.

Apparently the only problem with these stocks is that their share price has been languishing. Some commentators claim these wallflower stocks are attractively priced. If we accept that buying a wallflower stock is sensible just because the price is low, then we fall into the bargain hunting bear trap.

The Mayne Nicholas weekly chart shown in Figure 4.1 is enough to cause even a novice investor to pause for thought. There is no reason to expect this downtrend to change into an up trend just because the down trend has been in place for so long. In a bear market there is even less chance of recovery as investors and traders are looking for strength, not weakness. Inviting wallflowers into our portfolio in a bear market is not a good idea. Once they start to blossom we can join the crowd in bidding for their attention.

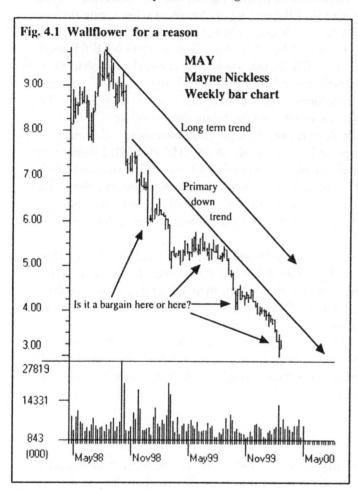

Fig. 4.1 Wallflower for a reason

MAY
Mayne Nickless
Weekly bar chart

Long term trend

Primary down trend

Is it a bargain here or here?

From a charting and technical perspective we have some doubts about the value of wallflowers no matter how good their fundamental story may be. They are being ignored by the market for a reason. It is safer for our portfolio if we let others discover the reason for the languishing share price. Traders are interested in the way the crowd is encouraged to actively consider these basket cases. When crowds gather, action happens, and trading opportunities arise. If enough of a crowd assembles, then investment opportunities might also arise.

Our profits in a bear market do not come from the defence of stocks in distress. The market doesn't care about our chivalry or about our good mannered approach to wallflower stocks. In a bear market we should worry about capital protection and profit. It sounds hard-nosed but the market is even harder.

DIVERSIFICATION AND VOLATILITY

When markets fall to their knees diversification is suggested by many analysts as an antidote to risk. It is perhaps the central strand that draws together the knot of woolly thinking because it combines ideas of size, dividends, low price volatility and cheapness. Volatility is a slippery concept and we discuss it more fully in Chapter 8. Here we use the common understanding that captures the probability of a large price rise or fall in any short term period. A quality stock might decline just a few percentage points during the days' trading but a speculative Dot Com might fall 15% or more in a single day. This is volatility. We love it when applied to price rises but it makes us gasp when prices fall.

Diversification approaches suggest a core of ten or so quality stocks will protect the investor from the volatility of the market. One typical group includes Telstra, Fairfax, National Australia Bank, Woolworths, Foodland, OPSM, QBE Insurance, Leightons, TAB, Australian Gas Light, North Mining, Western Mining and Woodside. These are stable stocks with less volatility than their Dot Com cousins. At one time News Corp may have been included in the list, but its volatility in early 2000 has eliminated it.

Volatility has more than one measure and although the probability of a substantial daily price fall with this group of stocks is small it does not mean there is a reduced risk of a price decline. This low volatility can translate into a painful slow decline in value a shown in Figure 4.2. These are the important details used to assess the validity of any claim about defensive investing strategies. It is not enough to protect against loss. We should also aim to make money.

This list of quality stocks is hardly a candidate for a diversification award. Although they are drawn from different sectors — insurance, commodities, retail, and telecommunications — they are all blue chip stocks. That is, they are all large, well established, heavily traded and well capitalised. They live up to the description of quality. The problem is that there is no diversification in the essential characteristics of these stocks. Like a genetically modified crop where all the plants are exactly the same, they are all equally vulnerable to a single disease. The weeds have better survival chances. This is not what diversification is about.

Diversification is more effective if it includes different levels of volatility, different sectors and a varied mixed of return horizons and rates. This may include short-term trades, long-term investments purchased at low prices, trades with high profit potential and trades with steady accumulation from stable uptrends. This type of combination truly reflects the idea that some of the portfolio will be up while other sections are down. It may provide some protection through diversification.

Fig. 4.2 Defensive or offensive returns?

	High	Low	Fall	
NAB	29.66	20.19	31.93	FROM MAY 99
WOW	5.85	4.69	19.83	FROM JULY 99
TLS	911	700	23.16	FROM DEC 99
FXJ	6.17	4.95	19.77	FROM MAR 2000
FOA	10.23	7.22	29.42	FROM JAN 2000
OPS	2.98	2.33	21.81	FROM DEC 99
QBE	7.97	6.78	14.93	FROM FEB 2000
LEI	6.39	4.4	31.14	FROM SEP 99
TAB	3.04	2.24	26.32	FROM NOV 99
AGL	10.59	7.68	27.48	FROM AUG 99
NBH	3.88	2.67	31.19	FROM SEP 99
WMC	8.69	6.25	28.08	FROM JAN 2000
WPL	12.19	9.43	22.64	FROM JAN 2000
AVERAGE LOSS			**25.21**	

Full diversification includes a spread of capital between equity, property and fixed-interest markets but our focus is on the stock market.

The suggestion that investors use a core of ten stocks like the list above as a defensive strategy is often really just a repackaging of the idea that size offers protection. Experienced market participants observe that BHP and MIM, once solid blue chips, are no longer included in this list. At some stage in the depths of the bear market in metals they were quietly dropped from brokerage and investment recommendations. They disappear when prices are at their lowest and this is not helpful for those who bought at higher prices on previous brokerage advice.

An effective defensive strategy must provide many options, including attack, retreat and holding the fort. Using volatility is part of the solution to survival in a bear market.

NO MEAL FOR THE BEAR

All these strategies spring from the same knot of woolly thinking. Our objective in this chapter is to encourage traders to critically think about the information that is provided from a multitude of sources. Uncritical acceptance of Dot Com recommendations is just as financially damaging as an uncritical acceptance of the need for ten core quality stocks.

We discuss these approaches only to highlight the most basic rule in the market. A loss is a loss no matter what sector it takes place in and no matter what time frame it is measured over. A slow reduction in capital is less frightening than a fast reduction but at the end of the day the outcome is the same. A quick glance at a chart of price activity will do more to manage risk and protect profits than a passive selection of a diversified portfolio or quality stocks.

When we take analysis at face value we sometimes find there is no value. It always pays to verify market commentary with your own chart-based analysis.

Survival in a bear market requires a higher standard of analysis and a conscious desire to independently verify what others are saying, no matter how well qualified. Come to think of it, these are exactly the same skills required to survive in any market. We do not want to become a meal for the bear, but with care we can profitably dance with the bear.

CHAPTER 5

DANCING WITH BEARS

A part from the odd catastrophe, markets tend to collapse in an orderly fashion. The rules of technical analysis are not thrown out the window. Nor are they temporarily suspended just because the world is turned upside down by falling prices. The old rules are good rules and they provide the last group of trading strategies from the longside. These strategies are enhanced using derivative instruments, but for this chapter we ignore them. They are discussed in more detail in the next part of the book.

Our bear trading focus is still on taking longside trades, buying low and selling high; but now this style of trading is very short term, usually spread over two to five days. This nimble trading carries severe penalties if we get it wrong. In major stocks with good liquidity the returns are usually limited. The liquidity makes up for this by improving the chances of an exit at the target price. Better returns may be available in mid-cap stocks, but liquidity is more erratic. It is all too easy to be stuck with unwanted stock, or the remains of an incompletely executed exit order.

This dance does not accept greed as a partner. The entry rules require judgement, but the exit rules require real discipline. These trades take advantage of the greed of others. Their misjudgment cannot be ours. Bear markets are hard on bulls, so we do not push our luck.

RALLY TO RESISTANCE

This strategy turns a straightforward observation into a profitable trading strategy. The key is appreciating the way a straight edge down trend line acts as a resistance level.

Our first port of call is to find a low flier, and Western Mining Corporation (WMC) in 1997 is a good example of a sustained bear market. From the high in June the only direction of price was down.

The chart in Figure 5.1 shows the initial trend line, plot A, and the final trend line, plot B. The initial placement of a trend line is always tentative.

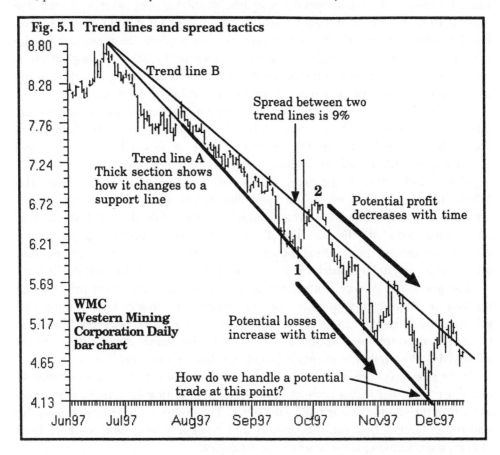

Fig. 5.1 Trend lines and spread tactics

Trend line B

Spread between two trend lines is 9%

Trend line A
Thick section shows how it changes to a support line

Potential profit decreases with time

WMC
Western Mining
Corporation Daily
bar chart

Potential losses increase with time

How do we handle a potential trade at this point?

Jun97 Jul97 Aug97 Sep97 Oct97 Nov97 Dec97

As price action develops over days and weeks, it is lifted, usually further to the right, when the initial placement is disproved by new price action. Trend line A was initially accurate because it defined the first six weeks of the decline. When a new high was made in August, the trend line was tentatively moved to position B. This line plot is confirmed by later price action.

The placement of a trend line is valid when several price extremes hit the trend line and react away from it. In plotting the trend line we aim to include the bulk of price action as confined by the extremes. In a downtrend we use the highs because the trend is defined by the failure of prices to close above old highs. The reverse applies in an uptrend, so then we plot the new lows.

The more times the trend line is approached, but not broken, the more valid the trend line is in defining the trend. Valid trend lines are at the core of this bear market strategy. We could spend some time discussing why such a plotted line appears to have such an impact on market behaviour, but it is out of place here. Readers who want to refresh these explanations or explore the reasoning for the placement of trend lines will find a full discussion in *Share Trading*. What is important for this strategy is the persistence of this phenomenon, and the trading opportunities it offers using two important characteristics of the trend line.

The first is the way the trend line represents a changing valuation over time. The market believed WMC was worth less and less, as 1997 hammered commodity prices back into the ground. This is a rational devaluation and proceeds in an orderly fashion, inviting traders to the dance party.

The second is the role the trend line plays as a resistance or support level. The WMC chart shows both roles. The upper line B acts as a resistance level. Prices approach the plotted line and retreat from it in an almost predictable fashion. This has nothing to do with the line. The plot on this chart has no magical properties. All it does is define where we expect the market to pause. Our long-term intention is to use this to signal potential trend changes when price closes beyond the line.

The lower line A, was plotted first as a resistance line but when prices broke through in August this purpose was invalidated. It changed its nature and subsequently defines the support level for WMC. Although support trend lines can be used in downtrends, it is unusual to see the coincidental development shown with WMC. We would not normally project this line as a support line.

Perfect examples are perfect in retrospect, but in real time they are tentative so in August the trader leaves both trend lines in place waiting for future price action to confirm the validity of one line or the other. The observant bear trader notes the way prices bounce between the support and resistance level, and as these lines diverge, starts thinking about trading opportunities.

SPREADS

How much return is enough to compensate us for risk? It is a difficult question at the best of times, but in the worst of times it is amazing just how little we are content with. The expanding width of the two trend lines provides bear traders ready calculations of reward. They also cap risk.

The September spike, believed to be a broker's error, is a good starting point.[1] The spread between the lower trend line and the upper line is over 9%. This marginal return is made attractive by steady liquidity. Good volumes are traded each day, so not only can we get an entry, but we can also make an exit at our preferred price.

A trade entered at $6.06 (point 1) as prices pull back to the lower trend line has a maximum exit at $6.76 for nearly 12% return (point 2). Do we take it?

The answer is no, and this defines the core difference between a breakout trade taken with bullish optimism and our dance with the bears. We do not expect this rally to develop into a breakout leading to a new uptrend. We explore the way we reach this conclusion later in the chapter. Our trading judgement cannot afford to be clouded with the prospect of a trend breakout making new highs. This dancing bear trade is based on limited objectives defined by falling profit targets.

When the trade is entered at point 1 the maximum reasonable expected profit is defined by the upper trend line. With every new day this line moves down, taking our profit target with it. Each day our potential profit is reduced because the market consistently revalues WMC at lower prices.

In a bull market we watch speculative bubbles created as prices race ahead of the pack, pursued by the inexperienced and greedy. When prices retreat to the upward sloping trend line we see an entry signal. The bear depresses prices and the market is just as prone to over-reaction. With WMC the level of over reaction is defined by the lower trend line. When prices plumb these depths we look for a rally – not to a new bullish high – but to the resistance level determined by the upper downtrend line.

SPREAD MANAGEMENT

This style of trading, of dancing with the bears, observes seven rules.

☞ The maximum profit is defined by the upper trend line.

☞ The maximum profit decreases daily, using the last trend line plot as the calculation value. If the upper trend line value was $6.63 on day one of the WMC trade, it will fall to $6.62 on day two.

☞ Enter when prices touch the lower trend line. Returns are always limited so do not reduce them further by paying high entry prices.

---

[1] The opening buy appeared to be a data entry error keyed at $7.27 rather than at $6.27 which was a cent above the previous day's close. As the remainder of the day's trading clustered within a 10¢-range it is a fair assumption the first bid was a mistake. We ignore this as a potential exit for this reason.

↪ If unfilled, the entry price is revised downwards every day so it matches the new value of the lower down trend line. Traders looking for a WMC entry in mid-November lowered the buy price from $4.65 to an ultimately successful $4.21 as prices finally hit, and bounced off the lower trend line.

↪ The stop loss point on entry is defined by a close below the down trend line. The market pressure is downwards and any slip is likely to be fatal. Other stop loss measures, such as a count back line trailing stop loss are inappropriate in this dance.

↪ Every trade is revalued every day and when the potential return, defined by the upper trend line, reaches an unacceptable low level, the trade is closed. This allows the trader to lock in small returns as he is not distracted by the hope of higher closes above the upper down trend line.

↪ The stop loss protecting us from complete stupidity is at breakeven. Remember the balance of probabilities is for prices to continue lower and any rally is knocked on the head by the upper trend line. These trades do not have room to breathe. This style of trading requires discipline and patience. It also asks for independent verification.

DANCING PARTNERS

It takes two to tango so we verify this enticingly simple trading strategy by using the multiple moving average (MMA). It is far too easy to convince ourselves that every new rally is a breakout so the multiple moving average indicator acts as a brake on this ambition.

The multiple moving average indicator consists of two groups of moving averages. The short term group includes a 3, 5, 8, 10, 12 and 15 day average. All are calculated as exponential moving averages.

The behaviour of this group delivers inferred trading signals. When the averages converge it suggests an agreement about price and value. Such agreement cannot last, so we anticipate a change in market direction as the gap between value and price grows. The key feature is the way the group compresses just prior to a trend change. It represents trading activity.

The second group of exponential averages – 30, 35, 40, 45, 50 and 60 – are the long term group. They show the same behaviour as the short term group, compressing just before significant changes in market direction. We use these as a proxy for investors.

For traders the key usefulness of the MMA indicator is when both groups are combined. Then we see the long term group acting as a fractal repetition of the short term group. When major trend changes develop both groups of averages compress and cross over each other. This is a major trend trading signal and we explored the application of this in *Trading Tactics*. Here we want to apply this indicator in new ways to refine the way we dance with the bear.

We have suggested the trader ought to be satisfied with the profit targets defined by the down trend line, but like all traders, we also want to ride any significant trend break. Getting on board a trend reversal early positions us for better than average profits. We are not alone in hunting in these areas. So a key question is when to hold on to the trade as part of a trend reversal, and when to abandon it because there is a high probability the down trend line will limit profits.

The potential trade from the December low of $4.13 in Figure 5.1 encapsulates the dilemma. The MMA in Figure 5.2 resolves it.

The long term group of averages is widely spread, suggesting little agreement on value. The long term group provides inferred information about the way investors view Western Mining. Few of them are convinced WMC is going anywhere but down. Even as the rally develops the long term group remains unmoved. The averages in the group do not start to converge and nor do they start to turn up. This verifies the likely impact of the straight edge down trend line. We reasonably expect prices to pull back once the down trend line is hit.

COMBINED INDICATOR MANAGEMENT

This simple visual relationship keeps the longside trade, and the profit targets, in perspective. We set profit targets with a higher level of confidence rather than hoping for a breakout trade and shooting for the stars. We use five rules to apply the MMA in these trades.

⚡ When the long term group is widespread, the downtrend line sets the profit target.

⚡ When the short term group is at its widest point, an entry is signalled. This is usually confirmed as prices touch the straight edge down trend line. Where a lower down trend line cannot be drawn with confidence we use the turning of the three and five day average lines as the entry signal.

⚡ When the short term group compresses, an exit is signalled. This is usually when prices hit the upper trend line, but the MMA does give useful early signals of rally failure.

⚡ The down trend is weakening when the short term group of averages begins to penetrate the long term group, before falling away again.

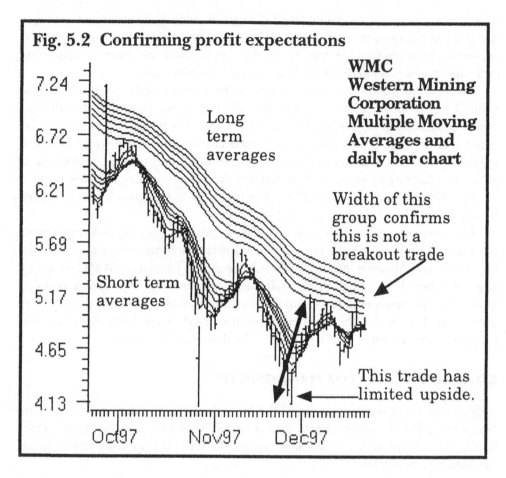

Fig. 5.2 Confirming profit expectations

WMC
Western Mining
Corporation
Multiple Moving
Averages and
daily bar chart

Long
term
averages

Width of this
group confirms
this is not a
breakout trade

Short term
averages

This trade has
limited upside.

7.24 · 6.72 · 6.21 · 5.69 · 5.17 · 4.65 · 4.13

Oct97   Nov97   Dec97

↪ When the long term group begins to narrow, and the short term group pushes through, and retreats to a lesser extent than previous rallies, the downtrend nears reversal. This is the breakout signal opening the gate to the bulls.

Bulls are resilient creatures, perhaps typified in the film *The Life of Brian*. Nailed to the cross, Brian sings, "Always look on the bright side of life". Bullish traders, pilloried by sustained price falls, keep looking for any breakout to restore their fortunes, plus a little extra.

Resources giant Rio Tinto (RIO) (see Figure 5.3) completes the picture of a rise from the ashes. The MMA places the trader firmly with the developing trend, while allowing him two early trades to build capital. In this example the compression of the short term group of averages is used to signal the entry points. Trade 1 has limited objectives defined by the behaviour of the long term group.

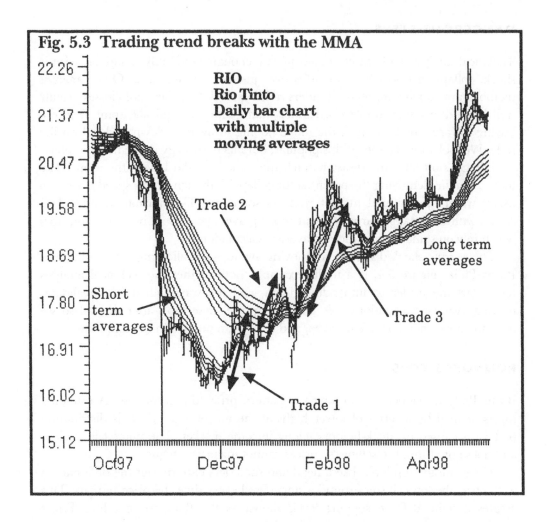

Fig. 5.3 Trading trend breaks with the MMA

**RIO
Rio Tinto
Daily bar chart
with multiple
moving averages**

Trade 2

Short
term
averages

Long term
averages

Trade 3

Trade 1

Oct97   Dec97   Feb98   Apr98

Trade 2 is fuelled by hope as the long term group of averages both converges and turns up. It takes a long time to stop a fully-loaded road train – a truck towing three trailers -- and turn it around. When market heavy-weights fall they too take time to turn around. Rather than backing and filling, they rally and retreat giving traders a number of opportunities to get on board the trend change.

Trade 3 gets the all-clear from the bull as both groups of averages converge and turn up, finally crossing in February. First, we treat this as a counter trend trade using the techniques covered in Chapter 2. Later we manage the subsequent breakout trend trade into a new bull market uses a different range of techniques discussed in _Share Trading_ and _Trading Tactics_.

DANGEROUS STEPS

Technical analysis tools rarely react quickly enough to identify a sudden seismic shock, collapsing prices 30% or 50% over just one or two days. Other analysis methods are equally impotent. Traders holding stock face inevitable losses usually well beyond any stop loss levels. Rather than getting out quickly, some hold on, buying towards the bottom of the move hoping to average down and sell on the rally. We look more closely at this popular, but failed, strategy in the next chapter.

Life goes on after the disaster much the same as it did before the event. The tools useful in identifying the potential for collapse – though not its speed – are also useful when the stunned market resumes something like normal trading. This comes with one major warning about moving averages and all of those indicators which rely on some form of moving average calculation.

The seismic shock disfigures all moving averages, invalidating their usefulness. Burns Philp, Figure 5.4, is a useful example, both of the way technical analysis tools alert the trader to impending doom, and the way such a fall invalidates moving average calculations. We do want to use these tools after the fall so we need to know when it is safe to do so, and if they can be used in the same way.

ROUNDING TOPS

Burns Philp developed a rounding top pattern prior to the collapse. A rounding top is defined by a series of lower highs at the top of a trend. This distribution pattern is caused by stock-holders selling into the market. The market is weaker, and does not absorb the selling, so prices cannot make new highs.

The rounding top looks like a head and shoulders pattern, but the difference is in the way the lows cluster around a single level every time the price retreats. This creates a quite definite support level, shown as the thick straight line. Prices consistently test this level, but when they bounce up they do not create new highs. The price action is difficult to define with straight edge trend lines, but is easily described with an arc.

This pattern usually develops slowly but sometimes the collapse of a rounding top can be quite sudden, so cautious traders sell into the rallies on the right hand side of the pattern. This tells us a significant section of the market is uncomfortable about current price levels. The big money is withdrawing from, or unwinding, positions in the stock. With few buyers they are forced to drop the asking price.

This is essentially a price pattern reflecting a relationship between price and value so we would expect the multiple moving average indicator to deliver some useful signals. When applied to Burns Philp, Figure 5.5, the relationships confirm

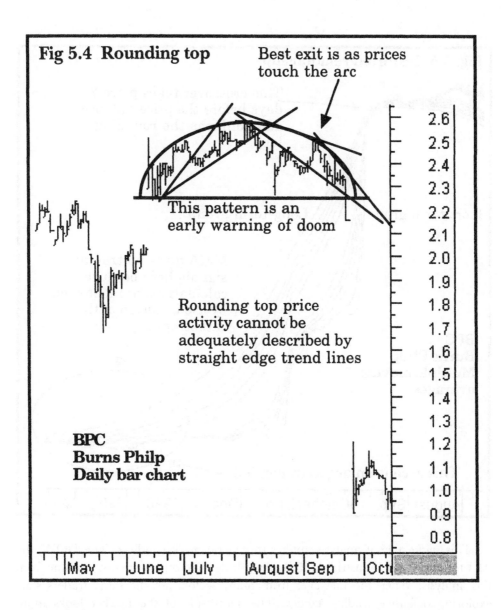

Fig 5.4 Rounding top

Best exit is as prices touch the arc

This pattern is an early warning of doom

Rounding top price activity cannot be adequately described by straight edge trend lines

**BPC
Burns Philp
Daily bar chart**

May	June	July	August	Sep	Oct

the distribution. Although the chart price scale is distorted by the fall from $2.60 to $0.30 the MMA still shows clear warning of a significant trend change in August and September. If the development of the rounding top was not enough to alert traders then the convergence of the long and short term groups of averages sounds extra warning bells.

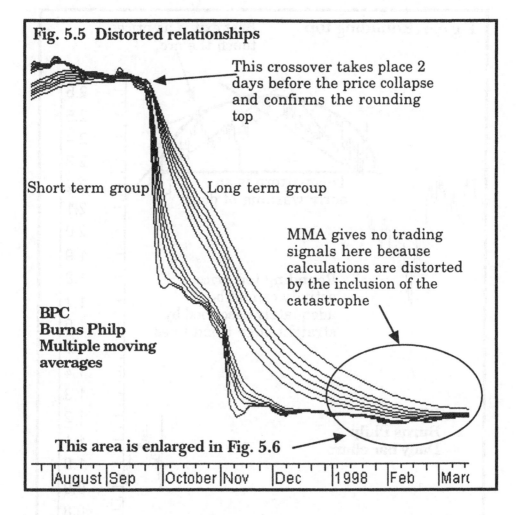

Fig. 5.5 Distorted relationships

This crossover takes place 2 days before the price collapse and confirms the rounding top

Short term group   Long term group

MMA gives no trading signals here because calculations are distorted by the inclusion of the catastrophe

BPC
Burns Philp
Multiple moving
averages

This area is enlarged in Fig. 5.6

August Sep   October Nov   Dec   1998   Feb   Marc

This same style of analysis applies to general market indices. The DOW, the All Ordinaries, All Industrials, the Banking Index and others are not immune from this analysis. When the messages from many sectors are the same traders start exploring defensive trading tactics. The short side of the market looks more attractive.

The MMA chart also illustrates the shortcomings of all indicators based on moving average calculations. When the values change dramatically the moving average plot is distorted. Burns Philp fell 45% in a single day from $2.20 to $1.20. This large fall impacts on every average, creating a distortion that does not accurately reflect the position of today's price against yesterday's. Nor can it accurately plot tomorrow's price because the average still includes price data that is well out of range.

The shortest group of averages starts to deliver valid messages as soon as the catastrophic events drop out of the exponential moving average calculation series. The three-day moving average is valid on day four. The 10 day moving average is valid on day eleven. With the MMA, the 60 day moving average is valid on day 61 – twelve trading weeks after the event. Prudent traders wait at least another month before using the MMA to dance with the bears.

SCALE QUESTIONS

When the impact of distorting price data is removed the Burns Philp multiple moving average builds a useful trading picture. The chart price scale in Figure 5.6 includes only the post-fall action. The MMA values are displayed more clearly and without the distortion of the fall.

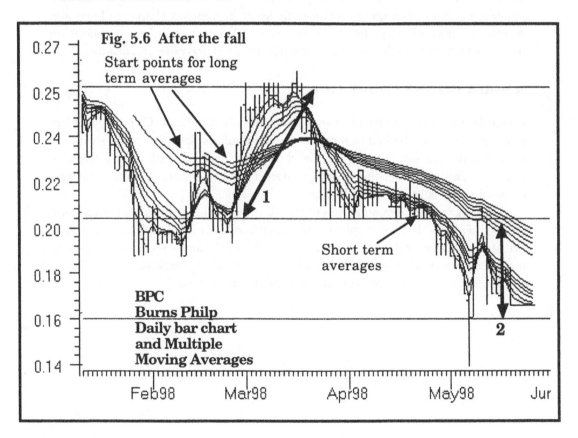

Fig. 5.6 After the fall

Start points for long term averages

Short term averages

BPC
Burns Philp
Daily bar chart
and Multiple
Moving Averages

The chart signals two trading opportunities. The first from $0.21 to $0.26 for a 23% return. The second returns 31% for a trade from $0.16 to $0.21. Both trades are longside rally trades taken in a falling market.

The starting point for the longest of the long group of moving averages is shown on the display. Because the data selection does not include the previous very high prices it is able to adjust moving average price behaviour to suit the scale of the new sideways movement. This reveals quite ample trading opportunities not shown on the previous MMA chart that included price data from before the fall.

Although partly obscured by the MMA overlay, the underlying bar chart also shows the benefits of the scale adjustment. When the scale includes old price activity at $2.60 the current trading activity is apparently reduced to a narrow line. This hides real opportunities. The new scale shows an active trading band and exploiting these narrow bands was discussed in Chapter 3.

In adjusting to the new trading reality we are both patient and aware of the way the landscape changes to suit new patterns of price behaviour. These sideways patterns provide opportunities already discussed in previous chapters. They also provide a dangerous temptation to average down. This particular bear trap deserves more attention because like the modern land-mine, it is pervasive and deadly.

A WALK ON THE SHORT SIDE

Longside traders do survive in bear markets, but life is difficult. Opportunities are few, and returns are limited in ways not found in bull markets. For traders with the mental agility to take a walk on the short side, bear markets offer interesting returns. Like all better-than-average market returns, these trading strategies demand better skills to handle the higher level of risk.

The risk/reward equation is enhanced when these analysis techniques are coupled with the leveraged returns available from associated derivative markets. We step into this world in the next part of the book and explore some ways to make long side trading approaches more effective in falling markets.

But first we examine the land mines planted in bear traps.

CHAPTER 6

BEAR TRAPS

Bear traps come in many shapes and sizes, all individually personalised to fit our particular mix of fear and greed. The most successful trap of all is sometimes introduced by our broker, or by well-intentioned financial advisers. Sometimes we stumble into it all by ourselves and think we have made an amazing discovery. No matter how disguised or dressed up, its real name is averaging down and it is best avoided. It is a pit trap − a large, deep hole concealed by a flimsy cover, in the middle of which is placed a bait.

The bait is a simple, friendly concept based on mathematics and our desire to recover from damaged positions. Because we approach the market so frequently from a mathematical perspective it is easy to fall into a purely numerical trap. We use figures to analyse fundamentals, numbers to record price and volume, and charts to display the progress of price and the relationships between calculated indicators. It seems natural to turn to numbers for another solution when we are in trouble.

Every market number is a measure of crowd sentiment. Crowds oscillate from passive indifference to extremes of emotion, colouring the numbers with psychology. Purely mathematical solutions, although elegant, are only tenuously related to the real world of buying and selling. In theory, averaging down looks attractive on any spreadsheet, but in practice the numbers are hammered by the market crowd.

Avoiding this trap is easier written than done. Our challenge is first to understand why the trap works, and then consider which of our earlier strategies turn this understanding to our trading advantage.

DIGGING THE HOLE

This pit trap is constructed in soft ground. There is a lot of digging to do so it is easier if the bear finds an emotional soft spot. Some bears are very aggressive, striking suddenly and unexpectedly, decimating trades taken in good faith and for sound reasons. Good traders know the correct reaction to these attacks – sell now, sell quickly, sell as close to the nominated stop loss point as possible and stand clear of the falling market. This is sound trading discipline, and if we followed it there would be little need to talk about other ways of recovering from bear attacks.

In the real world we get caught. Prices tumble well below our stop loss levels. In these apocalyptic conditions the old rules are temporarily thrown out the window. In this emotional soft spot we dig the trap ourselves, encouraged by the belief trading survival depends on the price we pay for stock rather than the price we get for it. Others call it bargain-hunting or bottom-fishing.

The strategy suggests we leave our original position open so we do not sell the stock purchased at $7.00, even though the current price is $3.00. Instead we wait until the stock gets even cheaper, and so the reasoning goes, because the stock is very cheap at $1.00 it must be an even better buy than it was at $7.00. A few brokers are fond of covering their mistakes this way.

So we buy more to lower the average price paid for the two parcels of stock. In very simple spreadsheet mathematics the average price is reduced to $4.00, $(7+1)/2=4$.

Too many assumptions? Obviously yes, as the exact figure depends on how much cash is allocated to the second trade and the brokerage paid. Yet we have all been tempted by this scenario and without thinking much beyond these simple mathematics, we are encouraged to buy more stock because it is so cheap. I suspect the bear laughs as we dig the pit trap even deeper.

Common sense and mathematics suggests the average down approach works, so why does it so often fail in a bear market? Part of the answer, and the trigger for the trap, is found in the nature of the people who find the strategy appealing.

THE FLIMSY COVER

Plain common sense tells us when the average price is lowered then the profitable exit target is also lowered. It is a persuasive idea with dogged logic. Its widespread popularity provides the flimsy cover for the financial pit we helped dig. This cover is weak because it removes the emotional content from the numbers.

The market reflects the hopes and fears of all participants. Most of them think in much the same way and trading profits come from knowing when to run with the crowd and when to stand aside. Our own instinctive reactions as novices provide a ready reference point to the thinking of the wider market.

Three numerical reference points are immediately established when we buy stock. Later they become emotional reference points. How we rank them distinguishes good traders from the rest. Some traders note the points formally on a spreadsheet, and ways to do this are explored in *Share Trading* and *Trading Tactics*.

Reference point one is the purchase cost. This is printed indelibly on our bank statement and the contract note.

The second reference point clusters around the profit objective. For experienced traders this is an exact figure, or set of exit conditions. For the novice and many others, it is a vague notion defined by the words "great wealth."

The third, and for us the most significant reference point, is established by the fear of loss. A small group of good traders know exactly where this level is, and define it as a stop loss.

A much larger group prefers not to acknowledge this at all, but they know beyond a certain level the paper loss is so great that they will not sell. They are victims of their emotions – driven by greed and held back by fear. They weave the fragile cover for the trap by embracing the concept of averaging down. Ironically, their reactions make the strategy less likely to succeed because of the way they use the three numerical reference points to band together for emotional protection.

These emotional huddles appear as price congestion, or consolidation areas. On a chart of price activity they show up as a tight trading band perhaps a few cents wide. This sideways movement persists for several weeks, or sometimes months. The stock no longer trends and buyers take the opportunity to purchase new positions or add to old positions. These areas are particularly significant when accompanied by good volume.

In this huddle we know many new stock-holders are added to the share register. Just like us, they all develop two reference points based on the entry cost, to calculate profit and loss. But unlike us, many take additional positions based on lower cost when the price collapses.

When prices do rise, sometimes months or years later, these people react in quite predictable ways. These provide new trading opportunities for traders, and better recovery strategies for existing stock-holders.

Put quite simply, when a large number of people buy stock at $7.00, many buy again at $1.00 as it bounces along the bottom of the chart. Assuming they allocate the same number of dollars to each purchase, then the average down break-even point appears to be $4.00. Traders watch the order size on the screens. The dollar value of orders often remains the same even though the order size changes. At $7.00 the order size may have been around $7,000 for 1,000 shares. At $1.00 the order size often grows to around 7,000 shares, still committing $7,000 to the trade.

These people build their own trap before falling victim to it. They believe they will make a profit from the lower average price which is now $1.75, ($14,000/8,000=$1.75). But time erodes their resolve and months later when prices do recover to around $1.75 they overwhelm the market with "break-even" selling. Price runs into seemingly impenetrable resistance, encouraging more average down selling because stock-holders are frightened prices have stalled. The only profitable traders are those who trade this specific crowd reaction.

We cannot say with certainty the hundreds of people who purchased shares at $7.00 are still holding their shares when the price falls to $1.00. We can infer from price action that many people do hold earlier share parcels. The more definite the consolidation pattern, the stronger the inference. Consolidation delivers an important message. Many shares change hands at about the same price. This means many people are making profit and loss calculations from about the same starting point. These areas acquire emotional significance.

Nor can we say with certainty the new buyers at $1.00 already hold shares purchased at $7.00. It is a fair assumption that quite a few will be existing shareholders because the belief in the benefits of averaging down is so widespread. Again, this inference is often supported by subsequent price action.

Readers familiar with concepts of support and resistance understand this analysis leans heavily on these concepts, with one key difference. Under normal circumstances we look for resistance levels to cap a price move and this is often around old consolidation levels. This bear trap shifts the goal-posts to spring the trap, rendering the straight average down approach a loser.

BAITING THE TRAP

We all approach the market with our eyes open so why do so many of us fall into this bear pit with its tissue thin disguise? Good traps use irresistible bait. A handful of cash in the middle of the trap cover is too obvious. A better bait is random returns. The complete mechanism is discussed in Chapter 15. Here we examine the way the mechanism works in this particular trap.

Although it is true poker machines do make losers of most players and smoking sometimes triggers cancer, it does not prevent people from playing poker machines and smoking. We all know of some big-time poker winners and life-long smokers who never developed cancer. The averaging down trap is baited with similar random success stories and sweetened with the help of some genuine skilled players.

Quite unintentionally skilled players sprinkle money around the trap area – an almost irresistible bait.

The average down approach is sometimes very successful when applied intelligently by people with long time frames and deep pockets. These include fund managers like Peter Lynch and Warren Buffett. They invest for the long haul. They do not buy on the margin, using funds borrowed from a brokerage or a bank, so they face no unexpected repayment schedule. With sound personal and business reputations, many people lend them money at no charge, content to wait upon investment and dividend returns alone.

As a private investor the strategies used by fund managers will also work for you if the same basic conditions apply. These include full ownership of all stock with no borrowings: the ability to wait three or five years or more for the stock to perform: no requirement to draw on those funds for any other purpose; access to additional debt-free cash to buy even more of the same stock at lower prices. A prevailing bull market is also very helpful.

And, most importantly of all – complete faith in your ability, or the ability of your fund manager, to make the correct selections.

These winners, no matter how unlike ourselves, add the glitter of dollar notes to the bear trap. All that remains is to attract a victim.

SPRINGING THE TRAP

The victim enters the trade expecting to make money. Because he does not act on his stop loss conditions, he ends up managing the trade to save money. The switch from making money to saving money also implies a major psychological switch and this gets the trader into trouble.

The victim assumes prices will return to old high levels. He wants to believe prices will claw back to $7.00. Chastened by the previous collapse in price and still smarting from the need to screw up courage to buy again at the bottom for $1.00, most settle instead for an exit around break even, defeating weak beliefs. If our inference is correct we would expect to see a wave of selling around $1.75.

Market reality supports these conclusions. A quick glance at Figure 6.1 shows this inference in action with AMX Resources, with congestion areas around $0.49 and sustained selling around $0.40. We examine this in detail below, but at first sight the average down trap is fully sprung and claiming multiple victims. Break-even sellers are victims because the cash tied up in their two trades should have been better used elsewhere.

Real trading is never as neat as the text book examples so our challenge is to use these inferred reactions to understand the behaviour of the market. By waiting for price action to develop we get confirmation, and once received, we have a choice of two bear trading strategies.

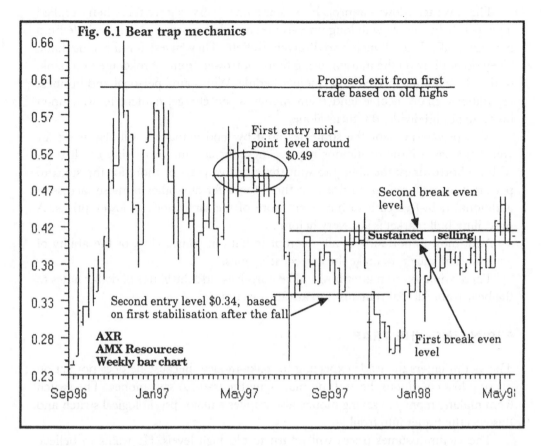

Fig. 6.1 Bear trap mechanics

The confirmation key is the new consolidation area. The positioning of this depends upon two different types of calculation. We make the calculations in advance because they set preliminary profit targets. We could wait for price action to provide the results for us, but we miss the first recovery opportunity.

Price consolidation – this new resistance level – plots the perfect balance of fear and greed. Fear that traders will not get their money back, and the greed that entices them to hang out for just a little profit above break even. The precise level depends on how the balance is calculated, either using dollars or numbers. We use a weekly chart of AMX Resources to explore both solutions. They provide both the explanation for the failure of average down approaches and for the success of other trading techniques.

Both examples use the congestion level over three months from April to June, around $0.46 – $0.52 as a starting point. For the sake of simplicity we make three assumptions in this example.

Assumption 1

For calculation purposes we use the mid-point of the congestion area – $0.49.

Assumption 2

The first parcel of 40,000 AMX Resources, excluding brokerage, costs $19,600. Profit objective is 22% based on previous peak highs at $0.60.

Assumption 3

When AMX Resources stabilises after the price collapse in July, the entry price suitable for an average down approach is $0.34.

In assessing any recovery strategy in bear markets we note in large letters on our trading screens. "The first loss is the cheapest." It is only when we ignore this advice that we even contemplate average down strategies to rescue old positions.

DOLLAR EQUALITY

To avoid the bear trap we need to know how it works and we do this by duplicating the calculations made by less experienced traders. Most traders adjust position size on the basis of the amount of cash available. This is clear in the depth of market order stream. Buy orders at one price are pulled out of the order line and re-positioned at a higher bid price, but for a lower quantity. The order size is cut to fit the trading capital available. It is often called dollar cost averaging.

This dollar approach works when it comes to averaging down. We spent $19,600 on the first AMX Resources parcel. How many new AMX Resources shares are available for the same money at $0.34? We add a second parcel of 57,600 additional shares to the 40,000 first purchased at $0.49. Figure 6.2 shows the resulting average down calculation.

How accurate is this $0.40 break-even figure? Only time tells, but initially the calculation helps define a potential emotional resistance level.

We make these calculations more accurate by analysing the average order size at $0.49 and $0.34. We look for the dollar value of average orders at $0.49 to see if this matches the dollar value of average orders at $0.34. If it does, then we know many investors have based their average down calculation on dollar values, spending about the same amount for each parcel of shares. From this we project their break-even point and establish the new resistance level to any rally.

Some refine this calculation further using turnover analysis to match the number of shares purchased at $0.49, less those traded on the way down, with the equivalent number of shares being purchased at $0.34. This totals the volume

Fig. 6.2 Averaging down — same size dollar approach

	Quantity	Price	Total cost (no transaction costs)
First purchase	40,000	0.49	$19,600
Second purchase	57,600	0.34	$19,584
Average price	**97,600**	**0.40**	**$39,184**
First target sale	97,600	0.49	$47,824
Return unreasonable greed			22%
Second target sale	97,600	0.44	$42,944
Return reasonable greed			**9.59%**

traded in the nine congestion weeks around $0.49. Subtracted from this is the volume traded during the collapse to $0.34. The result is a guide to the ratio of new and old shareholders.

Not all traders need such complex accuracy. The market will confirm or reject the validity of their price projections.

IDENTICAL PARCELS

It hurts paying out the same dollars twice for the same company at a significantly lower price. The spreadsheet calculations do not easily transfer into real cash transactions. Rather than matching dollar positions, other investors choose to match position, or parcel, size. Their calculations deliver a different break-even figure.

With 40,000 AMX Resources shares in hand from the first purchase they choose to double the size of the parcel to 80,000 at more favourable prices. This hurts less and is a popular approach with lower priced securities. Watch for it with speculative shares, warrants, options and other derivative instruments by comparing average order size at different times.

The calculations for AMX Resources using this approach are shown in Figure 6.3. The new emotional break-even price is $0.415.

Fig. 6.3 Averaging down — same parcel size approach

	Quantity	Price	Total cost (no transaction costs)
First purchase	40,000	0.49	$19,600
Second purchase	40,000	0.34	$13,600
Average price	**80,000**	**0.415**	**$33,200**
First target sale	80,000	0.51	$40,800
Return unreasonable greed			**23%**
Second target sale	80,000	0.46	$36,900
Return reasonable greed			**11%**

These two figures, $0.415 and $0.40, derived from different calculation methods, suggest a band, or consolidation area, may develop as a barrier to upward price movements. Sometimes the barrier is lower, reflecting the full depressing effect of bear markets. We must be prepared to modify the precise targets, but we still anticipate this specific consolidation pattern created in a large part by those who average down. These patterns determine the success, or failure, of our trading approach.

Good trading theory says we exit this losing position by acting on our stop loss. The reality of our contract notes tells a different story. In recovery trading we should avoid decisions based on the most destructive reason of all – it owes us money – because then we trade this stock to get even. If this is the main reason for entering into additional trades then it is worthwhile pausing for a moment.

Emotional revenge trading is the most destructive of all. The market happily takes all you can throw at it, and more, if you borrow money for this vendetta. Blinded by revenge it is difficult to rationally recognise when losses have grown beyond reason. If you feel this way then rush out and rip up a few fifty dollar notes.

You will come to your senses much more rapidly and for less cost than by using trading as a proxy for your emotions. These emotions drive the average down survival strategies into failure.

UNREASONABLE GREED

Observing these consolidation developments is the first step in building strategies for success. Intuitively many reach for two strategies using the average down approach in a classic, and often unsuccessful way. Because these are so common we explore them briefly to show how they contain the seeds of their own failure.

Unreasonable greed comes in two packages, both using the original profit targets as objectives. Not content to survive the market collapse, these traders want to spit in the face of the bear. These are unwise strategies, but revenge is a powerful motivator. We look at them only to illustrate the dangers. Hopefully you will not see yourself reflected.

The first package mixes greed and hope. The objective is to make about the same profit, around 20%, from the combined trade as the trader anticipated from the original trade. The spreadsheet extract in Figure 6.2 summarises the calculations for traders using same dollar size parcels.

The average down price of each share is now $0.40 so even a simple rally to $0.49, the original entry level, gives a 22% return. This is about the same as the trader originally wanted from this trade, so it doesn't seem to be an unreasonable request, let alone unreasonably greedy.

Change the calculations for traders using equal parcel sizes and the target rises to $0.51. It is even less probable but emotional traders are blind to reason. Figure 6.3 gives a spreadsheet summary.

These simple numerical calculations make these approaches so superficially appealing. Even when brokerage is included, the calculations are barely dented in the eyes of the desperate novice because he believes he makes a profit from calamity.

In the real world prices do rally and eventually after many months they may climb back to the old highs. But this is a bear market and these objectives require a reversal of the downtrend and a break past several key resistance levels. In prevailing market conditions these are improbable events.

The unreasonable greed approach, although showing a good return on paper, is the least effective strategy in practical terms. The strategy is enhanced when a purchase is made at the extreme low. Although it sounds logical and clever, and is quite clear on the chart, it is much more difficult to achieve in real time. When we rely on extraordinary events to deliver average returns we mix a lot of hope with our trading cash. Faith can move mountains but it is not so good at moving markets.

Combining the spreadsheet and the chart shows how unrealistic this approach is. Despite this many succumb to the temptation, attempting to disprove the theoretical results with real money. Others rationalise, believing if they lower their expectations averaging down will still work.

The origins of this fantasy are in the speed and simplicity of the spreadsheet. We set the trap when we forget the emotional content of the numbers. Very rarely does the strategy come to fruition in the market without the addition of substantial additional capital.

REASONABLE GREED

This grows out of the break-even approach. The trader makes a weak promise to himself that when the price reaches his break-even point, $0.40, he will sell and exit the total position with dignity. Some traders actually do this. Others develop creative excuses for staying in the trade to collect a modest return.

Prices do reach the break-even level around $0.40 but having recently thrown another $19,584 into the gaping jaws of the bear, ostensibly so he can make a break-even exit at $0.40, the trader really would prefer to collect a return for his efforts. The trader convinces himself a rapid rally is a sign of strength so this new dynamic trend is likely to continue. This confirms his preferred option of remaining in the trade for a modest return. If the trade takes several weeks to reach the break-even point, as with AMX Resources, the trader reasons he ought to be compensated for this additional time and risk.

Either way the indecisive trader sets a modest profit target, often around half of his original expectations. The spreadsheet in Figure 6.2 uses a modest return target of around 10% – just under half that of the original plan.

Those using the same parcel size face a more difficult task. Prices must rise almost back to the initial entry level as shown in Figure 6.3 before even a modest profit is harvested from the market.

This can be a successful strategy if we have the time to play it out in full. In bear markets prices do rally, but we have noted the limits are more often defined by existing downtrend lines and consolidation areas than by any desire by the market to reach our modest profit objectives. After seventeen agonising weeks AMX Resources prices do touch $0.44 taking the first trader out for a 10% return. This strategy is more effective in a bull market when prices are generally moving upwards. It is less effective in bear markets although it does provide a clue to more useful strategies.

Greed compounds the failure of these average down approaches because it establishes exit targets without reference to demonstrated, or likely, emotional crowd behaviour. By accepting the restraints imposed by the market we can turn these strategies into winners.

Averaging down is sometimes a successful strategy if greed is controlled. At best it returns some profit. Most times it comes in at break even. This is the first, and least desirable choice of bear trading strategies for rescuing fallen positions.

BIRD ON A WIRE

The market is not our friend, although it may walk by our side for a considerable distance before dropping behind and attempting to knife us in the back. Some strategies incorporate this average down behaviour into other better trading approaches. We turn to more aggressive trading strategies to rescue us from these positions, making particular use of trading bands. Profit is a nice bonus, but it is not the only measure of success.

Describing how a trap is constructed, showing how it works and where the bait is laid is not particularly useful if we have already fallen into it. It is useful to understand why averaging down strategies are so prone to failure because they provide the conditions necessary for our successful recovery.

These conditions are essentially the way many people make financial and emotional calculations that establish the new congestion or resistance levels. When sellers cluster at known levels we place our own sell targets there to improve the chances of trade execution. The calculations made by others help define the position of trading bands because those who flock together are often plucked together.

Recovery means hard trading using the techniques discussed in Chapter 3. The Federation Resources example relied on multiple trades based on movements between support and consolidation bands. Had these levels been established as a result of averaging down activity we could use this knowledge to trade successfully. Recognising the trap is the first step to avoiding it. When the market suggests many investors are averaging down the opportunity exists to make good use of the new consolidation levels as sellers cluster on the line like birds on a wire.

Averaging down is a less-than-average solution to rescue and recovery. More often than not it is a bear trap, sucking the trader into sending more cash to his broker. There is no single average down solution. Each solution carries its own risks and the one you choose will reflect your particular attitudes towards risk and the market. The selection of solutions available reflects your trading ability.

Very clearly the best approach is to avoid having to choose any of these options. Taking an early loss is the most cost-effective response to falling markets. Like all traps, this bear trap is best avoided.

PART II

BEYOND THE BEAR

CHAPTER 7

DERIVING SATISFACTION

Equity trading opportunities, and profits, are often very slim in falling markets. Derivative instruments offer traders ways to leverage these small opportunities into much more significant and satisfying returns. They are also great opportunities to turn small losses into substantial, or even catastrophic losses!

Some derivative trading combinations are complex and generally more suited to institutional trading. We avoid these in favour of straightforward offerings, and even then, our main focus is on warrant trading. Much of what follows is also applicable to options and to a lesser extent, futures. We explain the differences when appropriate. Derivatives offer the trader the opportunity to take small longside trading opportunities – those identified in Chapter 3 – and develop them into superior returns. The small profit trades taken from a rally upwards to the dominant down trend line shown in Chapter 5 are multiplied by using leverage.

More importantly, derivatives trading provides the most convenient way to trade the short side of the market, effectively selling high and buying low. This option is available with fully paid ordinary shares but the mechanics of the process are difficult and not widely available. Chapter 14 looks at this more closely. Derivatives provide an easy way to hunt side by side with the bears.

We start this second part of the book with market observations and leave the theoretical models until later. When we do look at the theory we use it to account for practical reality. If you wish to delve into the theory first then the heavy work begins in Chapters 9, 11 and 12.

WHERE IS KANSAS?

Dorothy, the star of *The Wizard of Oz*, is swept from Kansas into a strange new world. Equity traders are shoved into the world of derivatives with one terrific bear paw swipe. We do want to understand this new world from the perspective of an equity trader. What follows is not a detailed study of options, warrants and futures. We aim for a working knowledge because at heart we are still equity traders. Readers who find this taste of derivative markets to their liking will find many signposts along the way for additional reading.

Derivatives go by many names and come in three major styles – options, warrants and futures. Not all carry the same level of risk. Understanding the differences, summarised in Figure 7.1, gives us a way of selecting the most appropriate instrument to trade the market as we see it.

Fig. 7.1 Defining derivatives

	Options	Warrants	Exchange traded options	Futures
What it does	Raises additional funds for the parent company	Hedges Institutional risk by 'renting' out part of their portfolio	Repackages risk to make profits for Registered Traders and Institutions	Transfers risk from producers and processors to speculators
Created by	A company	A financial institution	Registered Traders and Brokers	A financial market place
Obligations	The right to buy or sell, or to do nothing, at an agreed price at a set date in the future.	The right to buy or sell, or to do nothing, at an agreed price at a set date in the future.	The right to buy or sell, or to do nothing, at an agreed price at a set date in the future.	The obligation to buy or sell at an agreed price by a set date in the future
Market	Direct market matching of buyers and sellers	Direct market matching of buyers and sellers	Market set by market makers	Market set by market makers

Many writers refer to the underlying security when explaining derivatives. This is all very good until we consider advanced derivative products like index warrants. Index options, swaps and Over-The-Counter (OTC) instruments are not securities. To cover all the possibilities we use the term 'parent' to encompass whatever the underlying security or financial instrument may be. And in the same way parents amused small children with shadow pictures on the wall before TV took over the task, we consider derivatives in a similar fashion.

All derivatives are like shadows, flickering against a wall, reflecting and magnifying the activity of something real. Without a real parent company, an operating business, a bushel of wheat or bale of wool, there is no shadow. No matter how lively, or frightening, the shadows are created by an underlying security, or parent. The derivative has no life of its own.

Shadows rely on substance – derivatives rely on substance. We understand the shadows better when we know they have been created by fingers and hands to project the illusion of duck or a rabbit, or when they are reflected through the elaborate fretwork of Indonesian shadow puppets in a *Wayang Kulit* play for credulous children. Adults do not mistake the shadow for the real thing. Traders should not mistake derivatives for the substance that created them.

The derivatives, or shadows, are created by an individual company – an option; by a third party – a warrant or exchange traded option; or by an industry market-place – futures. No matter how they are created and packaged we describe them with the generic term financial "instruments" to distinguish these derivative shadows from the substance – equity shares or commodities – on which they are based. Later we want to make some further distinctions, but for this introduction the generic term is adequate.

IT'S NOT KANSAS, TOTO

For accomplished equity traders stepping into the world of derivatives for the first time it is a little like playing *Dorothy in The Wizard of Oz*. Although we know it is not Kansas, we are not too sure just where we are. Warrant price charts look the same as equity price charts. The same technical indicators seem to apply. The market mechanisms for trading are similar and yet something is not quite right.

In the distance we see the glow of the yellow brick road and perhaps a franchise sign reading 'options.' Getting from here to there looks complex and dangerous. Later we consider three trading styles – the speculative trader, the premium, or warrant price, trader and the conversion trader. The relationship between them is shown further ahead in Chapter 11, Figure 11.7. These are the groups we trade with and against, but first we draw perspective on the new world by comparing it to the old. In this case by looking at it from the long side – buying low and selling high – with one foot in the secure world of equity trading and just a couple of toes testing for a firm footing in the new world of derivatives and virtual reality.

Stand back for a moment to consider the essentials of equity trading activity using a sample trade in a stock called PaRent Stock Ltd (PaRent Stock). We buy a known price now and we hope to sell at a better price at an unknown time in the future. Our intention is to buy PaRent Stock Ltd for $1.00 and sell at $1.20.

This simple transaction has one major problem and we solve it with hope. We do not know the price will get to $1.20, but we hope it will. The time frame is fuzzy. Ideally we hope to sell PaRent Stock within a few days, or weeks, but in practice it might take months, or even years, before the price hits $1.20. Obviously sooner is better than later, but time is not an absolutely vital factor in the trade. We can wait if we have to. There is always tomorrow.

We can, and do, complicate the picture a great deal more, adding layers of fundamental and financial analysis, worrying about brokerage and trade execution, and fiddling with timing and investment objectives. But if we strip trading back to bare essentials it is about buying a known price and selling an unknown price at an unknown time in the future. We try to discount the impact of these unknowns by using sound analysis, better tools, brighter brokers and high performance investment funds.

The key factors here are the relative positions of price and hope. We buy PaRent Stock at a known price and follow it with hope – hope of selling at a desired price and at an unknown time in the future.

Wouldn't it be great to read the future when we buy PaRent Stock? When PaRent Stock does go to $1.20 it would be magnificent to be able to turn the clock back, pick up PaRent Stock shares at $1.00 and then immediately sell them at $1.20. Traders can do this, but forget using the pages of psychics listed in the back of *New Idea* to help. Derivatives give us the opportunity to lock in past prices.

Derivatives allow us to buy, and sell, the future. With derivatives we have the choice of buying PaRent Stock at $1.00 by a set date in the future no matter what the current market price of PaRent Stock is at the time. Or we can sell PaRent Stock at $1.00 by a set date in the future. We lock in buying or selling prices in a way not possible with ordinary shares. For the moment we stay with buying the future. If the future is as bright as we hope it will be and prices rise, we can buy PaRent Stock at less than the current market value. Immediately we sell PaRent Stock at current market price to lock in a profit – guaranteed. We complete this neat trick using a "call" – the derivative equivalent of buying low and selling high – to complete a familiar longside trade. We 'call' on the supplier to deliver PaRent Stock shares at a previously agreed price.

Dorothy sets off to find the yellow brick road, taking one step at a time. In the new world of derivatives so many steps are similar to the equity world, and some steps look even more secure. Being able to buy at a known price in the future appears to make everyday trading much more certain. When we take the first step in this direction we discover the power of leverage.

The ancient Gods gave mere mortals the secret of fire and we have been burning ourselves ever since. Later they gave traders the power of leverage and we self-immolate with glee. When we take a bath in this market – lose money – it is like sitting in a tub of petrol and lighting a cigar because the outcome is disproportionate to the trigger event. Leverage provides the explanation. It is sometimes cited as the tenth wonder of the world, right after compound interest. Before we harness its power we need to understand what drives it in this particular market segment.

CALCULATING VALUE

Fully paid ordinary shares, warrants, and options are all traded on the Australian market, but the differences between them provide a range of opportunities, risk and reward. This is important in a bull market, but in bear and sideways markets, these differences are crucial in deciding the size of returns. Fully paid ordinary shares – the parent – are the basis for all calculations of derivative values. The shadow is always linked to the parent.

We are interested in the leveraged relationship between four reference points:

1. The current price of a share

2. The future nominated share price, or exercise price

3. The current price of the warrant or option

4. The time left before the warrant or option expires.

There are formal mathematical methods of solving equations for this in the options market.[1]

We are more interested in understanding the relationships without too much of the mathematics. Several trading tactics emerge from these equation. One helps traders to identify under or over valued options. Another permits the comparison of options series based on the theoretical fair value of each. For our purposes these are intriguing approaches, but they are not why we are interested in using options or warrants.

The fictional PaRent Stock trading opportunity provides a useful nutshell to explore the process and relationships. We start with options, the godfather of warrants, and gradually introduce the more complex aspects.

OPTION INSTRUMENTS

We begin with a company PaRent Stock option issued by PaRent Stock Ltd. Equity traders know them as bonus sweeteners with share issues or as a cheap way to buy additional shares on a partly-paid basis. Most of them end up as scrap paper because we do not have to buy new shares if the share price is low. These options are designed to raise additional funds for the company. They attract the conversion traders.

Consider just a single share, before we move on to complicate the discussion with the real world. The option buyer has the right to purchase a single share in PaRent Stock at a predetermined price, say $1.00, no matter what the current market price of PaRent Stock. He must exercise this right by an agreed date, for example 30/6/99. After that date the option expires. If the option is exercised the company gets the exercise amount and issues new fully paid shares.

This is no different from the half price hamburger offer from a fast food chain valid until the end of June. Once the offer expires we cannot take the voucher to the store in August and expect a half price hamburger. To get the discount hamburger we must exercise the offer by the due date. Just like an option, we are not forced, or obligated, to get the half price hamburger at all. This is the meaning of fine print in the options literature – we have the right, but not the obligation to exercise the option. Quite simply it means we have a choice. We can change our mind. We cannot get our money back, but we do not have to pay any more.

Very little in the market, or the hamburger store, is free. The option buyer must pay a premium for the option. For $0.10 we get a contract that says we can buy a PaRent Stock share for $1.00 before a set date in the future. The hamburger store is a worse deal because generally we must buy a full meal just to get the voucher.

My nearest hamburger store with these half price meal vouchers is over 300km away. This is a long way to go for a hamburger even if it is discounted. If I don't get to Darwin by the due date my meal voucher is worthless, but all it cost me was the price of the first meal. If we don't exercise our option to buy a PaRent Stock share at $1.00 by the due date, then we lose at most only the $0.10 paid as a premium.

Is the PaRent Stock option worth a trip to the bank? The current price of PaRent Stock when the option expires provides the answer. If the current PaRent Stock share price is $0.80 it is one trip to the bank we forget about. Our option contract says we must pay $1.00 for the PaRent Stock share. Why do this when we can go straight to the ASX market and buy the share for $0.80?

How much do we lose? Had we purchased a PaRent Stock share instead of the option we would now face a paper loss of $0.20. We paid just $0.10 for this option so the penalty for getting the direction of price wrong is much smaller. We lose just $0.10.

We do note in passing that this reduces risk. We all buy assuming the price will go up. When it goes down we take a loss, again assuming we exit according to good money management rules. Had we paid $1.00 for 10,000 shares we would face a loss of $2,000 when the price slides to $0.80 and even greater loss if the price continues to fall. Buying 10,000 options each worth $0.10 costs $1,000. The maximum penalty for our error buying options is $1,000 no matter how low the share price falls. We will look at this in greater detail in Chapter 8.

If the hamburger store has a special offering 60% off list price then its definitely not worth a trip to Darwin to cash in my half price meal voucher.

It's different if hamburger prices have increased. Now the meal voucher is worth even more. If the current PaRent Stock price is $1.20 just before the option expires we cash in, buying PaRent Stock for the agreed price of $1.00. We can sell PaRent Stock immediately for $1.20, or hang onto the parent shares for even further price rises. When we buy the option we buy the future. This trip to the bank pays for itself handing us a $0.10 profit. Why only $0.10? It costs a $0.10 premium to buy the option so we do not show a profit until the PaRent Stock price hits $1.11. The full cost to us is the cost of the option plus the exercise price of the option. ($0.10 + $1.00 = $1.10).

This yellow brick road bristles with possibilities, not all of which we want to explore in detail just now. The first step on this road feels different from our first steps in the equity world and our initial focus is on this difference.

Generally an option, just like half price meal offers, is near-dated. That is, it has an expiry date just a few months in the future. When we move further into the future, it is distorted by a time warp and that packages risk differently.

EXCHANGE TRADED OPTIONS

Our second step towards the yellow brick road is a small detour. When equity traders talk of options they usually refer to company issued options and this ignores a vast shadow market of exchange traded options. These options are issued by institutions or by options market Registered Traders. Do not confuse these professional market-makers with the registration process on the client agreement form required before you are permitted to trade in this market.

The Exchange Traded Option series is designed to hedge risk and to make money for the institution or Registered Trader. There are some important detail differences between these Exchange Traded Options and their derivative cousins, the warrants, and these are summarised in Figure 7.1. Our focus is on warrants but because warrant trading in many ways resembles options trading we do draw information from the options market.

The most significant differences for our purposes are the options market operation, the way options are created and the options' lifetime. Exchange Traded

Options are traded in a 'made' market. Options buyers and sellers complete trades with Registered Traders acting as market-makers. These Registered Traders are professional traders who aim to make a profit on each transaction for themselves or their firm. At best each Exchange Traded Option transaction includes two lots of profit. The first lot for the option holder and the second lot for the Registered Trader or market maker.

Warrants are traded under SEATS, just like ordinary shares. The broker takes a commission from the trade, but not a trading profit.

The second difference is the way Exchange Traded Options are created. They are issued by an outside party, such as a brokerage, based on existing shares. They have clearly defined contract cycles, or expiry dates, set by the Australian Options Market. Unlike company options, no new shares are created when Exchange Traded Options are exercised. In contrast to warrants, a Registered Trader may offer an unlimited number of options in any series as long as he has the margin cash security, or shares, to cover them.

The third difference is the life span. Generally, Exchange Traded Options have a shorter life span than warrants and expire according to a timetable established by the Australian Options Market. Shorter time period warrants are appearing, so traders always check the time remaining before buying either Exchange Traded Options or warrants.

These differences do matter if your path to the yellow brick road takes you along the Exchange Traded Options detour – from here on referred to simply as options. It is not the route we intend to take and although for the remainder of this section much of what we say is equally relevant to options and warrants we are really interested in warrants. Equity traders feel more comfortable with derivatives traded in equity markets because the SEATS screen has the same dealing transparency. Signposts to additional reading for the more adventurous are included along the way.

WARRANT INSTRUMENTS

A PaRent Stock warrant is issued by a merchant bank or institution. It is designed to hedge the institution's portfolio risk and to make money for the institution, not for PaRent Stock Ltd. The institution usually owns the underlying, or parent, shares and a warrant is a way to 'rent' the shares out. Our risk is packaged differently. We want to trade ordinary warrants associated with listed companies and the All Ordinaries and Gold indices. We ignore the endowment and capital plus varieties.

Who gets our money, or who we take money from, does impact on trading tactics because the skill level of the competition changes. Consider the differences between options and warrants.

An option is designed to make money for the Registered Trader or market-maker. Our risk is that he is smarter than we are. In contrast, a warrant makes money for the issuing institution. At one level we are encouraged to believe our risk is covered by our belief that we can outsmart the institutional issuer by using the 'rent' as a down payment on the parent asset. No prizes here for guessing whom the odds favour. Our risk is usually limited to a single rent payment which is the amount we paid for the warrant – the premium.

Despite this difference in purpose – renting as opposed to helping someone else make trading profits – the mechanics of warrant expiry are much the same as options. Warrants tend to be long dated with expiry dates one to two years or more in the future. The fall of the axe is delayed. Whether this is an asset or a liability is not clear cut. Extra time too often lulls the warrant trader into a sense of false security. It depends on our trading style and the way we manage risk in this new timeframe.

The hamburger offer gave us the opportunity to assist in the growth of the store even if it was only by eating their products. The warrant market sells a third-party service, so we leave the hamburger chain for the fishing tackle shop next door.

Fishing lures are attractively coloured. My preference is for tiger striped yellow lures, or speckled green bullet-head mullet look-alikes. My son likes the glitter of sliver with bold red and yellow. North Australia's premier game fish, the barramundi, cannot tell the difference because they see the world in black and white. The lures in every tackle shop are designed to catch fishermen first and the management knows how to cast a bait and set a financial hook.

My local tackle shop is run by a professional fishing guide. When he stocks his shelves he has fishermen in mind, but when he goes fishing he has fish in his sights. Much of his income comes from speculating on the behaviour of fishermen, irrespective of whether the fish are actually biting or not. As derivative traders we make the same distinction because in the derivative markets we are fishing for fishermen – not fish. Our profits come from the trade in lures, not fish. Later this profit gives us the time to go fishing for real.

In many ways warrants are like lures, offering a way to catch fishermen, so by understanding how the lure-buying fishermen are caught we expand our profit.

TRADING BY THE HOOK

Attractive packaging sells. Warrants are often promoted in well meaning newspaper and magazine articles as a way of reserving a larger parcel of shares.

Some warrants take this lay-by approach even further. Buyers make instalment payments with endowment warrants.

Our concern is with the way many people are encouraged to use ordinary equity warrants – those associated with companies – to reserve shares. We do not intend to trade warrants in this way, but this crowd of people helps create a market where we intend to prosper. They are the conversion traders.

Step into their shoes for a moment. Ordinary warrants are very useful if we expect to get the cash in the near future because we use warrants to reserve shares at a set price.

Perhaps we are waiting for funds to clear from the sale of a house. We have $200,000 coming, but cannot draw upon it for another thirty days when settlement is completed. Meanwhile, PaRent Stock is selling at an attractive $1.00 and we worry that in thirty days time it will be $1.50.

Warrant packaging has two attractions. The first is greed. Potential profits from a 50% return – buy at $1.00, sell at $1.50 – are always attractive. The second is an appeal to investment strategies. PaRent Stock is a good candidate for the portfolio and if the $200,000 was available now we would add a substantial parcel at $1.00.

With limited funds warrants allow us to reserve the equivalent of $200,000 of PaRent Stock shares by purchasing the PaRent Stock warrant exercisable at $1.00. The cost of this reservation is the premium, perhaps $0.10 per warrant, for a total of $20,000. This secures us the right to collect 200,000 PaRent Stock shares in the future at a total cost of the warrant, plus the exercise price, ($1.00 + $0.10 = $1.10). Traders will note the potential profit from any move to $1.50 is immediately reduced from 50% to 36% because in effect we pay $1.10 for each PaRent Stock share.

When the house sale settlement is completed, we exercise the warrant and purchase PaRent Stock shares at $1.00 even if the PaRent Stock is selling for $1.50 at that time. The warrant gives us the power to turn the clock back. This is packaged as a very useful investment approach. Traders see an opportunity in fishing with this lure.

This common packaging displays one facet of leverage. Here it is used to reserve – or more formally, control – a large block of shares for very little outlay. When the share price increases beyond the warrant exercise price the warrant-holder exercises his warrant and collects the parent shares by paying an agreed price that, in this case, is below the current market price. He then sells the parent shares on market, clearing the difference as a profit.

Packaged slightly differently, the same lure is sold to poorer fishermen as a way to participate in a more expensive market. This is the second attraction. With limited capital, in theory he can control very large blocks of shares in several blue chip companies. When there is not $200,000 available in the future, this fisherman pretends. His $20,000 reserves a block of parent shares. Perhaps he intends to trade the warrant, or like the house seller above, intends to convert the warrant into parent shares. To the outside observer it is difficult to tell if he can afford to play.

This common packaging uses the warrant as a proxy for the parent shares with the clear intention of converting the warrant into shares. This is the way lures are supposed to be sold. It is a valid trading strategy and the one most commonly advocated by brokers and the institutions who issue warrants. It is also potentially a losing strategy for those still holding warrants on expiry date as many warrants expire below their exercise price.

TRADING WITH THE HOOK

Just like the tackle shop owner, our objective is to understand the relationship between the lure and the customer. Some lures are so attractive that no matter where they are displayed, customers seek them out. Good retailing puts these at the back of the shop, forcing the customer to walk past other goods. Instead of buying his intended lure, the customer comes away with several spur of the moment purchases. The tackle shop owner boosts trade by understanding the behaviour of his customer. He does not have to believe the lures will catch fish, only that the lures will catch customers.

In examining the warrant market, we are more interested in a second aspect of customer behaviour. In a simple way it works as described below. Later we add additional real life complications, but this is the starting point. Let's step back into the shoes worn by the crowd, returning to the example used above and work through the calculations.

They, or as we are in their shoes again, we, have a PaRent Stock warrant exercisable at $1.00. PaRent Stock is currently selling on-market at $1.50. We have an open profit of 36% calculated by adding the cost of the warrant to the exercise price, ($0.10 +$1.00= $1.10). We could convert the warrant into shares, sell on-market at $1.50 and take 36% profit.

This warrant is valuable property, a little like a sure-fire lure still attached to a 36kg barramundi. This lure comes packaged with the barramundi attached. How much is a new buyer prepared to pay for this warrant knowing he can exercise it immediately for 36%?

Pay more than $0.50 and the total premium cost of the warrant plus the cost of exercising it is equal to the current share price. The profit is destroyed, ($0.50+$1.00=$1.50).

Pay $0.25 and the immediate profit is 20%. Total cost of warrant and exercise price is $1.25 and market price for the PaRent Stock share is $1.50.

Figure 7.2 illustrates the conversion combinations for a single market price of $1.50.

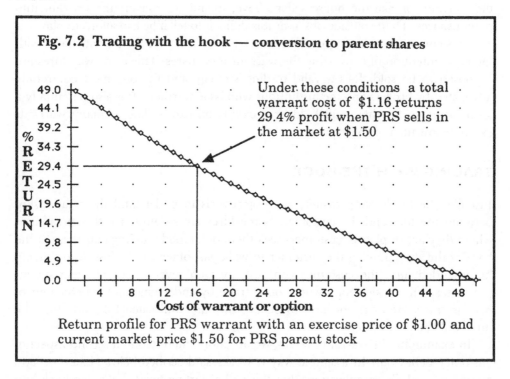

Fig. 7.2 Trading with the hook — conversion to parent shares

Under these conditions a total warrant cost of $1.16 returns 29.4% profit when PRS sells in the market at $1.50

% RETURN (y-axis): 49.0, 44.1, 39.2, 34.3, 29.4, 24.5, 19.6, 14.7, 9.8, 4.9, 0.0

Cost of warrant or option (x-axis): 4, 8, 12, 16, 20, 24, 28, 32, 36, 40, 44, 48

Return profile for PRS warrant with an exercise price of $1.00 and current market price $1.50 for PRS parent stock

Now stretch the imagination for a moment. There is an aquarium in the tackle shop full of live barramundi, each a different size, and each with a different lure lodged in its jaw. Buy the lure and get the barramundi. What great packaging! A crowd of buyers collects and sales are brisk. Just how they behave is considered in Chapter 10.

Stretching the analogy beyond reasonable limits we know the RSPCA will put an end to this packaging fairly quickly. In our trading world the warrant expiry date kills every trade.

Our immediate concern is how this crowd of hopeful fishermen is going to finance our fishing trip by boosting lure sales. It is time to step out of the shoes worn in the crowd to plant our feet firmly on the path to warrant trading.

GONE FISHING WITH LEVERAGE

If our tackle seller is as good at trading as he is at selling lures, he knows where trading profits lie. Lures sell. Lures that work sell better. Lures that come with fish attached sell best of all. The last sell for more than the first, and the relationship in pricing is leveraged.

This is how it works. Look at the lure from a fisherman's perspective. It was originally available at $0.10. Now the lure sells for $0.25 because it has a fish attached. The fisherman sees a 20% return because the lure comes attached to a 20kg barramundi. In trading terms, the PaRent Stock warrant purchased for $0.25 is converted into $1.00 PaRent Stock shares and sold on-market at $1.50 for a 20% return as shown in Figure 7.2. The conversion crowd is happy.

The tackle seller has a different perspective. He bought the lure for $0.10 and sells it to eager fishermen for $0.25. Just buying and selling this lure offers 150% return so the fisher of men profits more handsomely than the fishermen. This is our trading advantage as warrant traders. We do better as premium traders when we buy and sell the warrant price, or premiums, as shown in Figure 7.3. This is the power of leverage at its most awesome – and its most dangerous. From this tackle shop example we step back onto the yellow brick road.

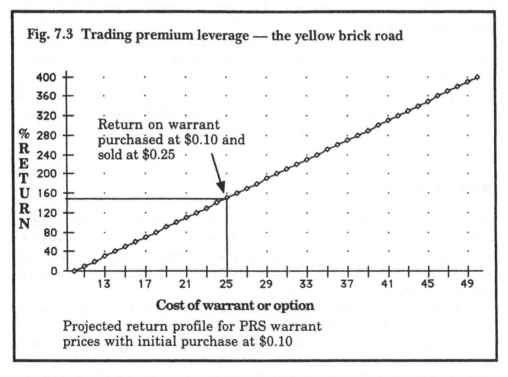

Fig. 7.3 Trading premium leverage — the yellow brick road

Return on warrant purchased at $0.10 and sold at $0.25

Cost of warrant or option

Projected return profile for PRS warrant prices with initial purchase at $0.10

Warrant premium trader or equity investor using a lay-by derivative? The answer decides the way we approach warrants and other derivatives. The investor uses warrants as a lay-by system to reserve fully paid ordinary shares. The intention is to convert the warrant into shares and hold the parent shares for a long time, collecting dividend income as well as any capital gains.

These traders look for the conversion advantage, in our example, taking a reliable 36% profit in PaRent Stock by turning the clock back to purchase parent shares at yesterday's prices.

Derivative premium traders take the money from selling the lures – a 150% return – and move on, perhaps moonlighting as a fisherman on some lazy Northern river.

It is this leveraged section of the yellow brick road we want to follow and although this high wattage return attracts us, as we explore this territory more closely we run the risk of being dazzled by other warning lights related to intrinsic value, volatility and time decay. We look at each of these in more detail as they appear on our horizon.

Derivatives provide leverage and flexibility. The leverage enhances longside trading opportunities. We use 'call' instruments to effectively buy low and sell high. This enhances many opportunities that are otherwise too small to trade profitably. Derivatives are a powerful weapon in a bear market, magnifying the slim edge into a true trading advantage.

We use only half the power of these weapons if we ignore derivative flexibility. They provide us with a convenient way to short the market – to sell the future. Before moving further down the yellow brick road we pause to see how we could walk on the short side. We may choose not to use this flexibility. Ample returns are available just from trading calls but selling the future adds depth to our market analysis. Short trading extends the period when cashflow is available from the market.

WHAT A VIEW!

Step back into the world of equities for a moment. If our market view is that prices are going to fall, then we can ask our broker to borrow stock and to sell it into the current market. We guarantee to replace the stock within a set time frame, perhaps two months. Our objective is to use the proceeds from the sale to buy the stock back at a cheaper price.

The risk, and it is substantial, is a price increase, and then we have to pay more to buy the stock back. Risk is compounded because we sell something we do not own.

These are the very basics of short selling and they have been hammered into our collective consciousness as an immoral activity responsible for the 1929 market crash and Depression. We have to discard this notion if we are to make the best use of short trading opportunities. If it provides more comfort for traders who are exploring the idea of short trading, then we ought to have at least a basic understanding of the original equity processes, even though the derivative process is different in important ways. We cannot successfully trade from the short side if we are encumbered with inappropriate understandings of what is involved.

Who would lend such stock for such an apparently crazy deal? Let's start with a high net worth individual with an investment portfolio. With 100,000 BHP shares in his portfolio purchased over many years at various prices, he is not worried by the temporary gyrations of the market. He holds BHP for the long haul. As long as he has 100,000 shares just before the books go ex-dividend he continues to receive a steady income. His objective is dividend flow, not primarily capital appreciation.

In between dividend dates his 100,000 BHP shares do very little. In the old days the certificates would gather dust, but with modern technology, even that task is denied. If he were to lend 100,000 of those shares to his broker between dividend dates, he could effectively rent out his holdings in return for a small fee. He would require a cast-iron guarantee that just prior to dividend calculation time he would have the 100,000 shares returned.

With a fee and a guarantee, all that stands between him and profit is market regulations. The ASX regulations are discussed in Chapter 14, but here our concern is with the reasoning, not the nuts and bolts. In the United States, the regulations assist short trading rather than hindering it. The broker arranges to borrow the shares and passes the fee, an interest rate for the loan and the risk, on to the trader who uses these borrowed shares to sell into a falling market.

In this example, before the borrowed shares are required by the original owner for dividend purposes, the trader buys them back from the market. He delivers them to the broker, who returns them to the high net worth individual. The lease, or rental fees, provide additional income above and beyond the dividend stream.

This is short trading in its original form. Markets have moved on and there are three important additions to this elegant solution to making money in falling markets.

THREE STEPS

The first is where the shares are owned by the brokerage itself, rather than a high net worth individual. As Australian banks have discovered, there is nothing so satisfying as charging fees for services already paid for. This development is not substantially different from the activity of the high net worth individual. The real significance is the transfer of risk from an individual to a company. It makes possible the next development, although in the US it was assisted by the Glass-Segal Act which prohibited banks providing brokerage services.

The roaring twenties was a diminishing personal playground for high net worth individuals. The demand for wider market participation started the mutual fund craze and added the 'fund of funds' approach in the last days before the crash of 1929. It took ten years to recover and the financial landscape changed, cementing the institutions, rather than individuals, as the most significant financial players. Institutions included banks, insurance companies, finance providers and the 'funds' industry. They had existed before, but the post-World War Two period saw the development of much more aggressive propriety trading activity and market participation.

Increasingly profits were wrung from trading activity rather than long-term investment. Growing in size these financial institutions controlled great blocks of shares at any one time. In time they dwarfed private holdings and provided another storehouse of shares that did nothing. Here was an opportunity to take over the role of the high net worth individual. The financial institutions and brokerages began to package leasing deals based on long term shares rusting away in fund portfolios.

This is the last in a long series of small steps into the virtual reality of futures markets and the synthetic instruments traded by Orange County and detailed in Partnoy's book, *F.I.A.S.C.O.*

The first tiny steps were taken in 1636 during the Dutch Tulip mania with the introduction of futures contracts to buy or sell as yet unplanted tulip
bulbs. Such innovative trading was limited by technology. The twentieth century explosion of chip technology rumbled through Wall Street pushing a tidal wave of derivatives ahead of it. We benefit from its effects with the development of derivatives backed by the leasing and buying ability of these financial institutions. The warrants we trade are issued by a handful of banks and brokerages. Their purpose is to make good use of idle assets. Our purpose is to trade them profitably.

A SHORT WALK IN VIRTUAL REALITY

To make full use of all trading opportunities in a bear market we need to get comfortable with the idea of selling first and buying later. As explained in the preface, we all take advantage of short trading opportunities when we buy an insurance policy, pitting a small premium against the potential of a large loss.

When disaster strikes, we expect a pay-out either in replacement goods, or cash, which is a type of virtual reality settlement. We get the value, which is almost the same as getting the goods, but not quite. The market uses the same principles in a more aggressive fashion.

Short trading adds a depth to trading opportunities allowing us to develop more appropriate, and profitable responses, to falling markets. Traditionally short trading has meant physically borrowing shares. Derivatives mean we no longer have to physically borrow shares. Instead we buy 'put' warrants. Now we trade a future commitment where somebody else, the warrant issuer, agrees to 'buy' the equivalent of parent shares at a particular price when we 'put' the warrant to them. This is a brush with virtual reality. The Wizard of Oz had more hidden up his sleeve than Dorothy realised.

Come time to exercise, the issuer must buy the parent share, although from the trader's perspective, the put warrant issuer normally delivers the cash equivalent based on the price specified in the warrant agreement – the exercise price. This removes several steps from the process of physically borrowing, selling and buying back actual parent shares. Instead of scrip changing hands we get the end result – cash changing hands. The 'put' warrant is an agreement made by the warrant issuer to pay a set price when the warrant is exercised. For us, the short warrant trade takes place in virtual reality. The cash we pay, and receive, is very real so to this extent we are not concerned with the issuer's internal mechanics of the trade.

Because we are not required to go through the hoops of arranging to borrow shares it is easy to go short. All we do is select a derivative matching our understanding of the market. When we buy the warrant we enter into a standard contract guaranteeing a profit if the price falls. The inverse relationship between the parent price and the warrant price is confusing. From a trading perspective we are content to know that as long as the purchase price of the warrant is lower than the sale price, we make a profit.

Derivatives allow us to buy or sell the future with the certainty of guaranteed prices. A call derivative lets us lay-by parent shares so we can BUY them later at a fixed price. This is particularly attractive when price increases.

A put allows us to lay-by virtual parent shares so we can sell them later at a fixed price. We SELL the future which works really well when prices fall.

The first step on the yellow brick road finds call warrants and options with an umbilical cord still attached to the parent share. In theory each is exercisable for a parent share. Many options and warrants are exercised and converted in this way.

The second step snips this umbilical cord. In the bear strategies which follow we dispense with the cord, trading derivatives purely for their leverage. We trade the changing value of an agreement – the settlement value of put warrants. It draws upon the principles of share borrowing underpinning the original short selling activities, but the action takes place one step removed in virtual reality.

Financial institutions have embraced the quantitative shift from substance to shadow, taking the third, and perhaps final step into the complete derivative swamp of virtual reality. They move into a mind numbing world of full derivative trading where virtual reality is sometimes the only reality. This world of Over-The-Counter trading is described sensationally in _F.I.A.S.C.O._ It is covered in more detail and with greater understanding in Edna Carew's book, _Derivatives Decoded._ This is a good starting point for those who want to explore this complex world of OTC trading and tailored risk.

Our objectives are more modest. We want to hunt with the bears with a clear conscience. Warrant trading on the short side provides the solution.

THE THEORY COMES UNSTUCK

This yellow brick road needs to be very wide to handle all the traffic chasing these opportunities. Stop here and you only see reward, not risk. True, some equity risk is eliminated, but in its place new risk grows with frightening speed. When everything goes our way the profits roll in, but in the real world, and even the derivative world, events often go against us. The call warrant is not exercised because the parent price falls to $0.80. At worst we lose only the premium paid for the warrant, but the market snatches it from us in an unaccustomed fashion.

Warrants and options give us the opportunity to change our minds at any time. At the extremes we can choose to exercise the warrant, or let it lapse. In reality we can sell the warrant on the market at any time during its life. This trades the warrant premium and is exactly the activity we aim to do better. Our derivative focus is on warrants, although the analysis is also applicable to options. The comments in the following chapters concentrate on extreme outcomes – exercise or lapse – but remember, every point on the return curve offers a different level of reward.

A brief warning note about futures. The futures contract legally commits us to buy or sell at a specified price. We are obligated. The contract obligation does not lapse and the only way we can dispose of the obligation is to shift it to someone else before expiry, or by settling in cash. *Understanding Futures Trading in Australia* by Chris Tate provides a handy introduction to these perils.

It is tempting to take leverage at face value particularly at 150% return as in the lure trading example above. It is a characteristic of derivative markets, but learning to use it effectively is more difficult than this passing glance suggests. Derivative risk has unique characteristics chiselled by leverage, volatility, volume and time. How they work for or against us is explored in the following chapters.

[1] The exact values in this type of relationship are decided in a rather complex equation originally developed to explain the options market. Within broad parameters, these relationships hold true for all derivative instruments. Two mathematicians, Fischer Black and Myron Scholes worked on this problem in 1973, both receiving ever-lasting fame, and hopefully some trading profits. The Black-Scholes Options Pricing Method is designed to calculate the implied volatility or the theoretically correct price. Readers with a very sound knowledge of mathematics can look at the full reasoning of the method in *Trading Stock Options and Warrants* by Temby. Luckily for the rest of us many charting programs; Metastock, Option-Vue, SuperChart, OptionTrader and OptionPro, complete these calculations, give us the answers and leave us with the simpler task of selecting the most attractive result.

CHAPTER 8

PREMIUM TRADERS

When we trade the warrant price, or premium, we go fishing with leverage. At first glance it looks a complete solution because it magnifies small trading opportunities into sizeable returns. In fact leverage is one quarter of the trading equation and those who rely largely, or soley, on it for success run into unexpected disasters. In this chapter we explore the limitations of leverage in real trading before moving on to consider the role volatility, volume and time play in better derivative trading solutions.

Leverage is the initial core attraction of derivative style trading, be it in futures, currencies, options, or warrants. Leverage lulls the novice trader into a false sense of security. For just a little bit of cash, he becomes a market player, taking his chances on a massive reward. As many US advertisements for commodity trading systems coyly note – "There is a risk of loss trading futures". The risk is just as massive on the downside as it is on the upside because futures contracts, unlike warrants and options, must be settled in cash or kind.

Even in a bull market, derivative or leveraged trading, carries specific dangers not encountered when trading fully paid ordinary shares. There are no training wheels, no beginners sections of the market. The moment we buy a single stock, we trade for real. And we are up against the very weakest, and the very best of traders. The disadvantage is even stronger in the derivatives market because many more of the opposing traders are very experienced. As long as we can muster the cash, no other trader in the market asks our qualifications and experience before trading against us.

To use derivatives more effectively we need a better understanding of leverage and our relationship with it. Most of the following discussion is based on trading from the long side – buying low and selling high. Longside trading is easier to understand because the linkage between price and return is intuitively acceptable. When price goes up, so does return.

With short trading the link is reversed. Now we sell high and buy low so when prices go down, return goes up. This is an uncomfortable relationship and makes it more difficult to clearly examine the elements of leverage. We start by exploring each of the observations about leverage from the long side before looking at specific short side applications and examples.

SIMPLE LEVERAGE

One glance at the beauty of simple leverage is not enough because the theory breaks down in some painful ways when it meets market reality. To avoid this pain we revisit simple leverage with actual trading examples drawn from National Australia Bank. The warrant code for this includes the stock code, NAB, and an individual three letter code, wmc for instance, assigned by the Australian Stock Exchange to make a six letter warrant code. We show this in lower case as NABwmc to make it clear when we are referring to the warrant.

If we use the simple arithmetic as shown in the previous chapter, for every $1.00 share in the fictional PaRent Stock we may end up with $1.50. In equity trading terms, for every $1 we commit we take home $0.50. This style of handy return attracts traders to derivatives and other speculative markets, so a quick summary forms the basis for further explorations in this chapter.

Having completed the stock selection, the trading analysis and the financial calculations, we always have a final choice. Our analysis, in this example, has National Australia Bank available for $20.00 and we expect the rally to take it to $23.50. We can choose to buy National Australia Bank at $20.00, or we can by a NABwmc warrant exercisable at $20.00. Our example in this chapter buys the warrant for $1.00. Leverage supplies us with an initially attractive solution.

Assuming we are prepared to allocate $20,000 to National Australia Bank, then at current prices, $20.00, we can purchase 1,000 shares. In return we get fully paid ordinary shares. We owe nothing, are entitled to the full dividend stream, and are under no compulsion to sell for any reason. If we do sell at $23.50 we make $3,500. In bull markets this level of analysis is quite adequate.

The bear sneers at this analysis, encouraging traders to explore a variety of alternatives using simple leverage to snatch larger returns from an unfriendly market-place. By using the same $20,000 we can buy 20,000 NABwmc warrants at $1.00 each. We assume each warrant is exercisable at $20.00 for one National Australia Bank share. Now our capital gets us greater exposure.

We know this is the first impact of leverage. For the same dollar value we control a much larger parcel of National Australia Bank shares. Confident our projections for a rise in the National Australia Bank share price to $23.50 are correct, when the time comes to exercise the warrant we buy the additional National Australia Bank shares for the exercise price of $20.00, and immediately sell for nearly 12% profit, raking in $50,000 profit. Remember the NABwmc is exercisable at $20.00 but we paid $1.00 for the warrant. The combination of possible outcomes is shown in Figure 8.1. This basic strategy entices with two carrots – the cheap cost of entry, and better profits available on exit. And often this does work in the real world in a bull market. Using leverage in this way in pursuit of good profits is a valid investment strategy. It is less useful as a trading strategy.

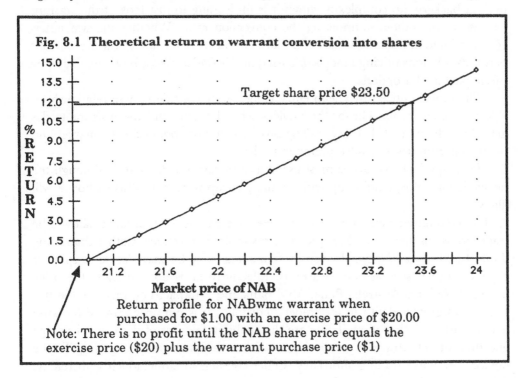

Fig. 8.1 Theoretical return on warrant conversion into shares

Target share price $23.50

% RETURN

Market price of NAB

Return profile for NABwmc warrant when purchased for $1.00 with an exercise price of $20.00
Note: There is no profit until the NAB share price equals the exercise price ($20) plus the warrant purchase price ($1)

FANTASY LEVERAGE

The second impact of this leverage is on the hip pocket and on risk control. Many novice traders would like to buy 1,000 National Australia Bank shares, but lack the capital to do so. One of the fantasy aspects of all derivative style trading is the idea that for just a few dollars the trader effectively controls a lot of shares. This aspect of leverage encourages traders with little capital to trade as if they have a lot of capital.

The fantasy starts with the trader imagining he can get 1,000 National Australia Bank shares which under normal circumstances would cost him $20,000. Reality bites when he scrambles through his passbook savings account and finds only a spare $1,000. Derivatives let him dream on because the NABwmc warrant exercisable at $20.00 is selling at just $1.00. Now our fantasy trader can own, for a short while at least, 1,000 National Australia Bank shares.

People taking this approach have their eyes fixed firmly on the second carrot – cheap entry. This carrot is laced with so many assumptions it seems unlikely many warrant buyers would factor this into their decision-making.

Yet warrant issuers have turned to issuing lower priced warrants, often based on a four to one conversion factor, to improve the liquidity of the market. Taking a peek at background complexity shows it is misleading to just look at the warrant exercise price without considering the conversion ratio. Whether the warrant is converted into one share, or part of a share ultimately determines how the warrant performs. Options pricing models discussed in *The Options Course* by Fontanills show this impact for 1:1 options.

The crowd enticed by cheap entry alone rarely considers these relationships. When leverage comes cheap, the novices see a bargain and the warrant trades actively in the market. Fantasy trading provides cannon fodder for the market and many opportunities for skilled premium traders.

This aspect of leverage is most useful as a means of risk control, although the novice ignores this, loading up with as many cheap warrants as his cashbook will allow.

For committed derivatives traders, leverage in the first instance allows the trader to use limited capital to spread across multiple positions. Rather than using the $21,000 to buy National Australia Bank warrants, he may decide to split his capital between several other warrants. Effectively he is able to trade the price action of National Australia Bank, ANZ Bank and Westpac. Leverage used in this sense gives greater depth to the trader's portfolio. It is not an excuse to fantasise about market participation. These are the enabling features of derivative leverage and they attract crowds. Some in the crowd have a fantasy understanding. To the novice they make trading affordable. Others remain in closer touch with reality. To the professional, they widen the basket of trading opportunities and control risk. For the private trader it is the gathering of the crowd that is significant.

TRADING LEVERAGE

In the previous chapter we suggested the seller of lures makes a greater return than the fisherman who buy the lures to catch fish. Trading leverage lures many different types of traders. We want to avoid the grim wipeouts experienced by many warrant traders so it is helpful to consider the way the same National Australia Bank calculations above blind some traders. Understanding how the crowd thinks helps us to out-think them.

We suggested above that $20,000 would buy 1,000 National Australia Bank shares. For the moment we assume the target exit price is $23.50. This gives a quite respectable return of almost 12% above the exercise price of $20.00.

Leverage dazzles the novice warrant trader when he compares the same leveraged results from the warrant trade profit projections shown in Figure 8.2.

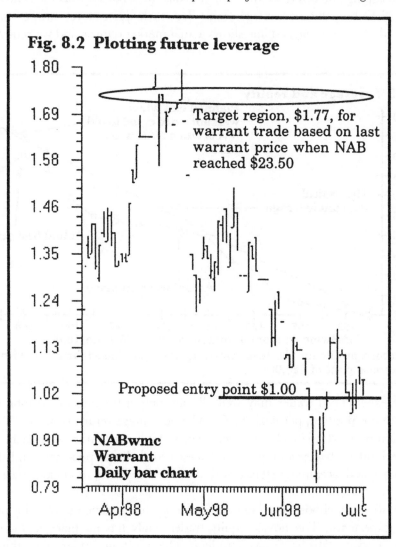

Fig. 8.2 Plotting future leverage

Target region, $1.77, for warrant trade based on last warrant price when NAB reached $23.50

Proposed entry point $1.00

NABwmc
Warrant
Daily bar chart

Apr98   May98   Jun98   Jul98

The proposed warrant entry is at $1.00. Looking at the chart of warrant price history, he notes when National Australia Bank was last at $23.50, the NABwmc warrant traded at $1.77. He thinks it is likely to perform in the same way again, so this warrant trade could lock in 77% return.

The spreadsheet gives all the enticing combinations. If we allocate all of our intended cash to this warrant trade, we turn $20,000 into $37,170. Even the fantasy trader, working with less cash, turns $1,000 into $1,770. We cannot ring our broker fast enough. The theoretical return combinations are shown by the straight sloping line in Figure 8.3. The line has the same slope as the return line in Figure 8.1, but the percentage gains for each price level are considerably enhanced. The lower jagged line shows actual market returns and we return to this later.

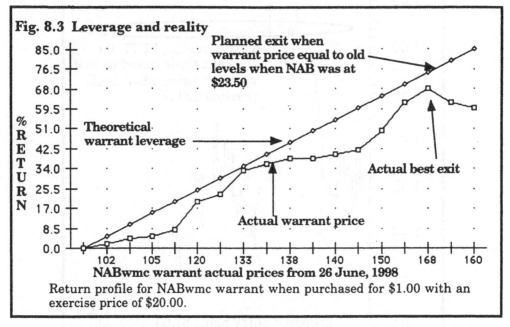

Fig. 8.3 Leverage and reality

Return profile for NABwmc warrant when purchased for $1.00 with an exercise price of $20.00.

The experienced trader may well allocate only a fraction of his total trading capital to this position, perhaps $6,000. The percentage return is still 77%, but the dollar return is $10,620. The novice rejects this conservative approach. In this treasure hunt he believes only a fool leaves with half-full pockets – and the trek back to his bank account is littered with discarded treasure, too heavy to carry any longer.

The way we choose to trade this leverage often depends on our previous trading experience. The novice equity trader really has no place in these more difficult markets. His is fantasy trading. The position trader who thinks the leverage will improve his otherwise poor returns is deluding himself with another fantasy. The survivors tend to be already successful position traders.

THE LEVERAGED TRADER

The derivative trader who has not moved beyond simple leverage has often migrated from speculative equity trading fields. Accustomed to trading junior gold stocks, tiny explorers, gene research companies, bio-tech start-ups and Internet software developers, he trades warrants in the same way. Buy very, very low, and sell very much higher.

He has seen a puff of wind lift low-priced equities much higher while the rest of the market was unruffled. Using these tactics profitably is discussed more fully in *Share Trading*. These tactics are used successfully in trading bear markets from the longside, but for real success they require the one thing that derivative markets cannot deliver – time.

Traders in the warrant markets who make decisions primarily on potential leverage offered by low price warrants have a low survival rate. When they assess a warrant their first consideration is a low price.

This is the final dangerous aspect of simple leverage. With warrants in particular, price size does count. Although National Australia Bank may trade at $21.00, given a choice on price alone, many in the warrant market will choose the NABwxa warrant at $0.85 rather than the NABwmc warrant at $1.00. Not content with the obvious benefits of leverage, these traders want a bargain as well. This bargain-hunting trait is so strong that in a bid to improve the tradability of one warrant series, the issuer announced an on-market four to one split. The impact was immediate. The warrant traded much more actively, even though no other factor changed.

Is the $0.85 NABwxa warrant a better buy than NABwmc at $1.00? Yes – simple leverage says so and novice traders who listen do not very often survive to become full-time traders. The jagged line plot on the return chart in Figure 8.4 shows the real disadvantage of a cheaper entry. NABwxa looks to have many factors in its favour. With a lower exercise price the warrant was already in-the-money. It reached $1.28 the last time National Australia Bank had peaked at $23.50. The theoretical slope remains the same, but percentage returns are reduced to 50%. Real warrant prices, shown by the jagged line, are even worse.

Compare these actual percentage returns with the maximum obtainable in real trading for NABwmc in Figure 8.3. The lower priced warrant delivers 47% while the higher price NABwmc warrant returns 68%.

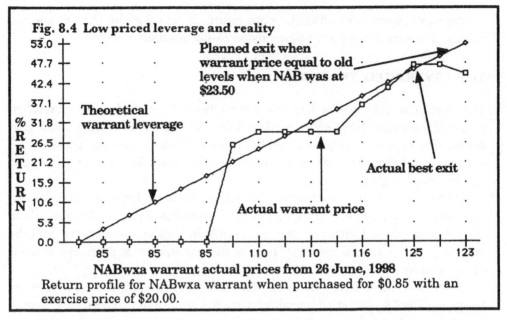

Fig. 8.4 Low priced leverage and reality

NABwxa warrant actual prices from 26 June, 1998
Return profile for NABwxa warrant when purchased for $0.85 with an exercise price of $20.00.

These disparities cannot be explained by leverage alone. Making better use of warrants requires more than just an appreciation of leverage. Although the cheaper warrant is attractive, it is most often a chimera, because the leverage is not always greater. Very few trades based on leverage alone are successful unless there are special circumstances.

A SHORT SEASON

In the natural world the seasons are marked by the migration of birds and animals. In the financial world, October marks the flight of capital. Every October is an anniversary of the 1929, or 1987 crash or the 1997 correction. Despite every indication to the contrary, even in the midst of a very strong bull market, October provides a trip wire.

Predictably, market commentators trot out nervous comments towards the end of September. Columnists prepare the October 1987 Remembrance Day feature pages, complete with comparison charts, anecdotal reminiscences and the 'What were you doing on the day?' recollections of long forgotten traders. And sometime in October the market stumbles, often lurching horribly to its knees. This hardy annual event is traded with leverage alone.

In Australia, we have a regional short-term migration of capital in June. It runs away, frightened by book squaring and the tax man. Falls are not as pronounced as in October, but the price retreat can be traded from the short side, and the following rally in July is traded from the long side. Using just leverage in these specific market conditions enhances returns.

June, and October in particular, are ideal opportunities to short the market using the power leverage alone to maximise the returns. In 1997, National Australia Bank provides a real example of this strategy as shown in Figure 8.5.

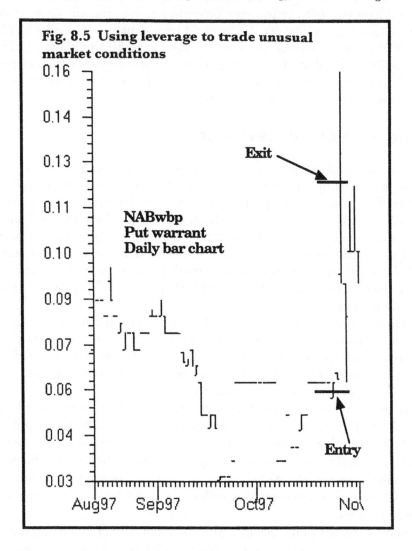

Fig. 8.5 Using leverage to trade unusual market conditions

This very short-term trade is designed to take advantage of a specific market event. The NABwbp warrant was selected because it offered the best combination of price and leverage.

In initiating the trade all other factors are ignored because it is assumed the event would develop its own volume, and its own volatility. By pre-positioning, the trader uses both the brief volatility and volume to maximise the inherent leverage in the trade. The real trade was entered on weakness when nobody wanted to buy the warrant, but it was exited on market strength by selling into volume.

This exhilarating 100% return over three days relied primarily on leverage to take advantage of an unusual event. Could we have done better? Undoubtedly an entry at $0.035 and an exit on the very few sales at $0.16 would have yielded a stunning 357% in 15 days, but trading reality usually delivers less than perfect returns. This trade was entered on the basis of the potential leverage that at any other time has a very low probability of success.

GETTING MORE OUT OF LEVERAGE

Long side or short side, these aspects of leverage work in exactly the same way. A small pile of cash is turned into a large heap. Or, depending on the derivative product traded, it slowly disappears into thin air when the warrant or option expires. We do not have to stay with the warrant until the bitter end and the premium trader sells for a small loss rather than riding the price to the very bottom. Futures and commodity contracts, if ignored until the very bitter end, dig a deep hole capable of swallowing all your trading capital, your assets such as the house and the car, and still leave you in debt. Despite these difficulties, leverage is an attractive package.

Our purpose here is not to recommend one leveraged approach over another. The exact combination you choose will impact on your profits, but more importantly, it will impact on your survival. Going for the big speculative hit satisfies many people. Other traders are satisfied with consistent, smaller profits that use the benefits of leverage in a sustained way.

Except in unusual circumstances, it is not sufficient to base trading decisions on leverage alone. The trader turns to other analysis factors, such as volatility and volume, before selecting the most effective warrant to execute his trading strategy. Although we consider these in separate chapters, in reality they are combined into a single analytical approach. Without an appreciation of our individual attraction to particular aspects of leverage, it is difficult to make full and effective use of volatility and volume.

Archimedes claimed to be able to shift the world if only he could find one spot to apply a lever. We have more modest objectives. We want to use the principle of leverage to roll a large profit in our direction. As we have seen above, the principle is good, but we do need a stick to start the ball rolling.

CHAPTER 9

VOLATILITY AND THE BEAR

everage is an essential survival principle in a bear market, magnifying returns. Because derivatives provide the easiest way to short the market, traders have no choice but to learn to manage leverage on these trades as well. This does create additional risk as small upside rallies rapidly destroy gains from put warrants. Leverage works both ways, magnifying losses as well as gains. In selecting the most appropriate trading strategy for shorting the market and the best derivative instrument, we turn to volatility for additional information.

This stick rolls profit in our direction. It is the second part of the trading equation and it modifies the impact of leverage by assigning a range of probable price action. We nudged volatility into the picture in the last chapter when we projected price targets for NABwbp in Figure 8.5.

As many victims discover, leverage is not very useful without volatility. The National Australia Bank call warrant once available at $1.00 looks less attractive in three months time if the high for the period has been $1.05 and the low $0.56. There are three new factors at work here: volatility, volume and time. Along with leverage they make up the trading equation. We look at them in the next chapters.

Established bear markets settle into a steady decline, and when they bottom out they tend to travel sideways for an extended period. The primary characteristic is limited volatility. The general public withdraws what little is left of the money they had used for investment, or for trading. Quite simply, when we are broke we cannot trade. When we are strapped for cash, we do not feel like trading. The market shrivels while the public licks its wounds. Only the professionals remain, and they have a much better idea of the relationship between price and value. A subdued market lacks volatility, so low consistent volatility coupled with the best leverage available may give better returns than the intuitive equity trader's choice of greater volatility.

Experienced options and derivatives traders have already moved well beyond our discussion of these volatility relationships. They trade in a specialised mathematical world different from ours in many important ways. The most powerful volatility measure in options trading is implied volatility. The concept is designed to answer a specific question – what is the volatility of the option, given the past and current price relationship between the option and the parent stock? The answer determines 'fair price'. Those who wish to explore the details of the calculations will find them in Temby, *Trading Stock Options and Warrants* and in McMillian, *Options as a Strategic Investment.*

Our objective as equity traders wanting to become better premium traders is more modest, less specialised and less complex. Remember, although we are dealing with a bear market we intuitively look for longside trading opportunities. We choose to start with a call warrant example – buying low and selling high – because equity trading means we are familiar with the basic concepts. This reduces any initial confusion in handling new trading instruments because we do not have to turn parent price and profit relationships upside down.

We aim to make good use of unfamiliar derivative instruments to maximise short-term opportunities in falling markets. When trading warrants we are assisted in reaching this objective because the choice of available parent companies is limited. We easily apply volatility techniques to each of the few parent stocks. Using the live charts function in Ezy Chart we regularly search through the parent stocks looking for either long, or short side, opportunities.

VOLATILITY

We need volatility because it gives us a measure of the liveliness of prices. Traders transferring their skills from the arena of penny dreadfuls and other speculative stocks know the deadening impact of prolonged no-trade days and the excitement of sudden rallies on small volume. Their trading skills include a waiting game. Derivatives trading shortens the waiting period. Holding an open derivative position is like holding a hand grenade with the pin removed. The countdown is irreversible and every no-trade day brings the prospect of personal injury one day closer.

At its most basic, volatility is a measure of the way price moves up and down and how often it does this. Beyond this basic understanding things rapidly become much more complicated. To trade bear markets successfully using derivatives we need to make an informed selection of the most appropriate measure of volatility for our trading style. This measure need not be complex. We start by analysing the parent stock before taking a trade in the derivative. The parent drives the shadow.

Here we look for a robust understanding of volatility that is easily understood and applied. As traders garner more experience in these markets they move onto more complex understandings of volatility. The options trader uses Black-Scholes methods and others to calculate implied volatility based on current options price and a theoretically fair value. Trading with these methods shifts the focus towards finding mis-priced instruments.

Our focus remains on simple applications of volatility to initially enhance returns from what are often small and short-lived rallies in a dominant down trend. But even at this level, the consequences of an inappropriate choice are severe because time is not on our side.

This is one search where we can start at the end and work backwards. As traders we know our preferred outcome. We look for trading opportunities where there is a strong probability of active price behaviour and we intuitively start with the range, or distance, between high and low. Later we look at how rapidly they move. Parent stocks may drift sedately, ranging between year highs and year lows over six months or more, or rapidly oscillate, sometimes with regularity, but often with annoying irregularity.

Exactly where we choose to ambush our trading opportunities depends on our preferences as much as any objective criteria for measuring returns. Speculative traders are attracted to low-priced instruments with exercise prices well away from current market prices for the parent stock. They value extreme price ranges. More conservative traders look for warrants moving into-the-money where the exercise price is almost the same as the current·stock price. They value frequency. We need to apply our preferred understanding of volatility so it works for us in the best way possible.

YEAR HIGH AND LOW

The first calculation establishes the potential range of price moves by defining the very top and bottom. It is not a sophisticated approach, but it is a starting point for many traders in the equity markets. For warrant traders the activity of the parent stock drives the warrant so the year high and low figure looks useful.

Because only a few stocks have warrants issued it is a comparatively simple matter to manually rank these selections on a spreadsheet. The figures are found in the *Financial Review*, or *Shares* magazine. In the final spreadsheet column use a formula to determine the percentage gain from the low to the high. The results for all stocks with attached put warrants is shown in Figure 9.1. This table makes no distinction about the direction of change. Commonwealth Bank consistently increased its price during this period while BHP lost value. We use this approach even if the parent stock has consistently lost value during the year because we are interested in the total variability of the moves, not the direction. When the column is complete it is sorted from highest to the lowest gainers. Later the results are sorted into candidates for shortside or longside trading.

Fig. 9.1 Year high and low figures for all stocks with put warrants attached August 1997 to August 1998 ranked by % change

Stock	Year High	Year low	Difference	%
AMP	45.00	18.53	26.47	142.85
News Corp	13.65	5.76	7.89	136.98
WMC	7.67	4.15	3.52	84.82
Santos	7.47	4.11	3.36	81.75
Woodside	13.40	7.42	5.98	80.59
Macq bank	15.60	8.75	6.85	78.29
Boral	4.48	2.71	1.77	65.31
Mayne Nick	9.86	6.00	3.86	64.33
Normandy	1.91	1.18	0.73	61.86
Westpac	11.45	7.10	4.35	61.27
C'wlth Bank	20.75	13.70	7.05	51.46
ANZ	12.04	8.00	4.04	50.50
Qantas	3.18	2.13	1.05	49.30
Brambles	35.45	23.80	11.65	48.95
Amcor	9.09	6.14	2.95	48.05
Rio Tinto	22.35	15.20	7.15	47.04
St George	10.85	7.40	3.45	46.62
BHP	17.50	12.30	5.20	42.28
Coles Meyer	8.05	5.92	2.13	35.98
Tab	2.85	2.16	0.69	31.94

NOTE. The AMP year high was set on the first day by an enthusiastic broker. He later resigned as AMP closed at $22.88 on the first day of trading. This figure is misleading, but a computer scan does not show this. It is vital to inspect all computer search results by looking at the price chart.

As a very broad measure, this list provides a basis of comparison for returns possible from all stocks in no matter which direction they are travelling. In theory, an 80% price drop in a falling parent stock is made profitable using a short trade. An 80% price gain in a rising parent stock is locked in with a long trade.

In cold hard print we are inclined to dismiss this simple ranking process as inadequate. In the comfortable warmth generated by broker and analyst reports it is exactly this type of calculation that encourages investors to buy BHP at $12.00 because it is historically cheap with an upward potential of $20.00 or more to previous highs. In the fevered heat of novice trading with penny dreadful speculative resource stocks, these calculations project today's dismal Giants Reef Mining price of $0.02 upwards to its glory days at $0.27.

In the derivatives market this approach buys BHPwmb call warrants at $0.01 because they are cheap. And cheap equates with leverage when previous BHPwmb highs have been $0.43. These speculative warrant traders often lose money waiting for the previous highs to return because the clock always winds down to the expiry date.

These volatility calculations are valid but they are not a good place to stop when applying leverage. Although on one measure of volatility we would prefer a stock with a 90% difference between its low and high, on many other measures such a stock does not provide trading opportunities. It is not useful if the price spiked to a low of $10.00 for three days, rose rapidly to $19.00 over the next three weeks, then stayed there for the last six months. It is less useful in a bear market when prices collapse dramatically, and continue at base level lows for extended periods.

One move a year might be fantastic, but we can go broke waiting for it to happen. Our measure of volatility needs to include the frequency of these price moves.

A STANDARD OF DEVIATION

When we select stocks on the basis of year high and low performance we establish, in a very broad way, the maximum historical variability of price moves. Effective trading needs a measure of the frequency of those moves and a measure of the probability of prices reaching the extremes. The concept of standard deviation provides both those measures. Fortunately we can skip the mathematics because most charting software is equipped with indicators to measure and plot these conditions.

Later we show how these indicators are used to identify conditions prior to a sharp move, how they are used to augment stop loss calculations and to identify active trading candidates. Standard deviation is not always an old friend as some American Presidents have found. We should renew our acquaintance with the concept to better understand how a Bollinger band calculation uses standard deviation.

Standard deviation is a statistical measure of volatility noting the extremes of market activity and relating them to an equilibrium point. This is where prices have clustered for most of the time. To make the calculation we define a time period we wish to study and the price element.

Elementary statistical analysis tells us around 67% of future price movements should be contained within one standard deviation of the mean price. Around 95% of price movements should be trapped within two standard deviations. Before you rush off to trap 95% of future price movements, pause for a moment to consider the short-comings of elementary statistical analysis.

It is OK for politicians to get it wrong because they are only using taxpayers' money. We use our own cash, so we apply elementary statistical analysis with more caution than politicians, as suggested by Figure 9.2 with a Fosters Brewing daily bar chart. All three Standard Deviation Channels, A, B and C, use the same starting date. The upper and lower bands are all calculated two standard deviations away from the trend based, in this case, on the close.

We note two defects at first glance. First, the linear regression trend line uses the close for its base calculation. Second, as the trend develops these plotted standard deviation lines are increasingly less relevant to the limits of price moves.

Trends are part of the problem, not part of the solution. The theoretical model of standard deviation assumes random and trendless data. As soon as a trend develops these 67% and 95% values are not as accurate. This doesn't invalidate their use, but it does introduce a note of caution. Additionally, the accuracy of a standard deviation calculation is supposed to improve in a direct relationship to the number of data points included. The results do change as the time period lengthens from A to C, but only the most optimistic trader labels them an improvement.

There is a danger when traders plot a Standard Deviation Channel. Inevitably they make a subjective selection of the time period and usually apply it to strongly trending data. The Standard Deviation Channel tool in Metastock uses a linear regression plot to incorporate the trend and this makes the subjective choice of the data series critical. Incorrectly chosen points invalidate the standard deviation projections and so deliver false messages about volatility. Too often the result is damned lies, statistics and charts.

As with most market analysis we have a choice between the simple and the more complex. The more complicated is useful when it yields better than a marginal improvement in results. Some trading techniques use very complex volatility models with great success.

This are discussed in detail in *Buying and Selling Volatility* by Connolly, *Options: Trading Strategies that Work*, by Eng, and *Technical Analysis for Trading Index Warrants* by Temby, amongst others.

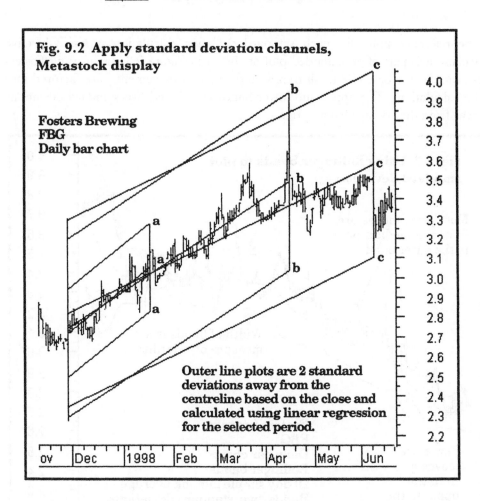

Fig. 9.2 Apply standard deviation channels, Metastock display

Fosters Brewing
FBG
Daily bar chart

Outer line plots are 2 standard deviations away from the centreline based on the close and calculated using linear regression for the selected period.

Many traders, like the ANZ derivatives desk in 1998, sometimes find complexity gets in the way of profits. As private traders, it is useful to stay on the side of simplicity unless there are compelling reasons for taking more complex paths. The results of a Standard Deviation Channel do not look helpful.

BANDS ON THE RUN

American trader, John Bollinger comes to the rescue with his Bollinger bands that, when used properly, do help the trader to buy champagne of the same name. Bollinger modified the concept of standard deviation to fit a moving calculation based on a more objective measure of the equilibrium point over time. Rather than selecting just a single linear regression trend or starting point, his bands are plotted continuously around a moving average drawn through all historical price activity.

The reference point for each standard deviation calculation is less subjective because it is part of an extended plot as shown in Figure 9.3, again using Fosters Brewing as the base chart. All trends, and sideways movements, are factored into the calculations. The upper and lower bands are plotted two standard deviations away from the 20 day median price.

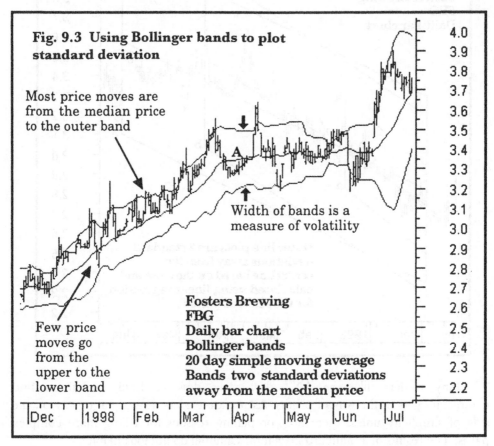

Fig. 9.3 Using Bollinger bands to plot standard deviation

Most price moves are from the median price to the outer band

Width of bands is a measure of volatility

Few price moves go from the upper to the lower band

**Fosters Brewing
FBG
Daily bar chart
Bollinger bands
20 day simple moving average
Bands two standard deviations
away from the median price**

Dec | 1998 | Feb | Mar | Apr | May | Jun | Jul

Price data is delivered as an open, high, low and close combination. On any single day we can establish the average, or median, of price activity. This is reached by adding the high price and the low price together and then dividing by two.

Observation verifies these bands do include around 95% of the total price action above and below the median line. Although this is not a precise measure it is robust enough to give us confidence to use the bands as a measure of the range and frequency of price movements. This rescue package takes us back to our original focus: to establish a reliable measure of volatility useful in identifying and ranking trading candidates by range and frequency.

But first read the invisible warning message printed with these bands. Wider bands mean greater volatility. In trading terms this tells the trader 95% of future price action, up or down, will be contained within the upper and lower bands. This is equally balanced either side of the median line so the price range from $3.37 at point A in Figure 9.3, to $3.50 is most likely to catch 95% of this up-move. This represents a 3.8% return in dollar terms.

But – and this is the 'but' responsible for financial cancer – any price collapse from the median line captures 95% of the potential price move at $3.23. This translates into an even larger 4.2% dollar loss.

Despite these warnings, these measures of volatility do help us determine how effective leverage is likely to be, and how achievable. The direction and strength of the trend switch the balance towards one direction. For the moment we note the warning because we return to the downside of the volatility and leverage relationship in the next chapter.

How reliable are these projections? Reliability improves with longer data spreads and these are achieved by changing the time period calculation from 20 days to 60 or 120. Beyond a certain value, the results begin to lose reliability. Check the appropriate values with an eyeball assessment of the plots. Look for around 95% of price action to fall within the bands. If it doesn't, then the time period is too long or too short.

FREQUENCY BANDS

Returning to our second task we want to use Bollinger bands to establish the frequency of moves between the bands. We want to identify active trading candidates. A simple year high and year low analysis of the Comex Continuous contract for Silver gives values of 430 and 740. This sets the range parameters for moves between extremes showing apparently ample room for profit unless you bought contracts after February.

When we apply a Bollinger band analysis to Comex Silver as shown in Figure 9.4 we get a better idea of the frequency of volatility. The bands we use to judge the frequency of moves now enclose 95% of extreme price action. This is a much more useful measure of the frequency of price movement. Using the movement between the median price and the upper and lower Bollinger bands, we find a total of four moves from the median to the upper band.

A comparison with the Share Price Index (SPI) continuous contract traded on the Sydney Futures Exchange shows seven up-moves in Figure 9.4. The SPI is a more volatile instrument than Comex Silver because prices range more actively within the bands. This measure of volatility includes frequency.

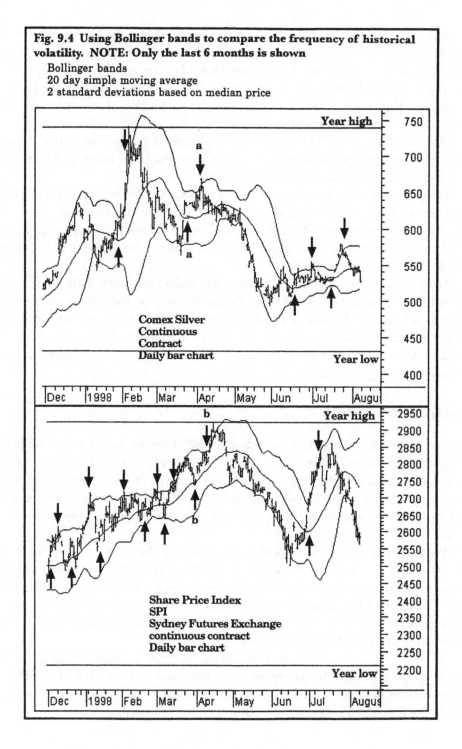

Fig. 9.4 Using Bollinger bands to compare the frequency of historical volatility. NOTE: Only the last 6 months is shown
Bollinger bands
20 day simple moving average
2 standard deviations based on median price

Year high

Comex Silver
Continuous
Contract
Daily bar chart

Year low

Share Price Index
SPI
Sydney Futures Exchange
continuous contract
Daily bar chart

On this level alone we conclude the SPI offers more longside trading opportunities because it has greater historical volatility and frequency. However, leverage changes the assessment. Comparing the two trades, a-a and b-b, from the median level to the upper band we find that the SPI returns a 3.6% change against the Comex Silver change of 8.1%. The occurrence or frequency of volatility must be weighed against the leverage offered, and as we examine in the next chapter, the available volume.

This basic analysis does ignore many factors. Standard deviation analysis does not handle trending markets very well as price action clusters in just one section of the Bollinger bands. The selection of up and down moves on the Comex Silver chart is somewhat subjective because we ignore the way prices stayed above the upper band for an extended period in February.

If we treat this basic analysis for what it is and do not try to extend it further we do find it provides a useful means of comparing trading volatility of a group of stocks over an extended period. The standard of comparison must remain consistent for results to be comparable. These rankings are more useful when we include the way volatility changes. Historical volatility does not foreshadow the distant future, but it is helpful in making short-term trading calculations.

WHAT STANDARDS?

Standard deviation provides many challenges. Widely spaced bands tempt the trader with the promise of substantial moves. Narrow bands appear to limit opportunity, although they do reduce the risk of large adverse movements. These broad understandings do apply to stocks where the Bollinger bands are relatively stable. Traders are always attracted to instability because this often precedes major changes in market direction. If traders get the direction right they stand to make a great deal of money.

Changes in volatility, as measured by the Bollinger bands, help identify these trading conditions. In particular we look for two circumstances, each at opposite ends of the spectrum. The first is an unusual widening of the volatility spread. The second is an unusual narrowing of the Bollinger bands. It seems contradictory, such opposite conditions signal trading opportunities, but each delivers a message about out of the ordinary price movements.

Indicators such as Average True Range, Detrended Price Oscillators, Multiple Moving Averages and others included in Ezy Chart, Metastock, SuperCharts and other charting software are also useful. They all attempt to identify unusual changes in price activity. An advantage of Bollinger bands is the way potential changes are assessed against previous volatility to give a guide to price targets and the probability of those targets being achieved.

Volatility is a dynamic process and we attempt to define it with a series of snapshots. These values are plotted as the Bollinger bands. We duplicate the process with an applied example. Take a coin and spin it on its edge. This dynamic process illustrates the key moments of out-of-character behaviour preceding major change and we capture the process by extracting just a few moments of suspended animation.

The first sample point is at the moment the coin is spun. For a very brief time the coin spins almost exactly on its axis without any wobble. We know from experience the coin will become unstable. The wobble around its axis gets wider and wider. The narrow action around the central axis suggests a change in behaviour will follow. The coin spends most of its spinning time in a middle range around the axis. In trading terms the same features emerge when the Bollinger bands compress as shown in Figure 9.5.

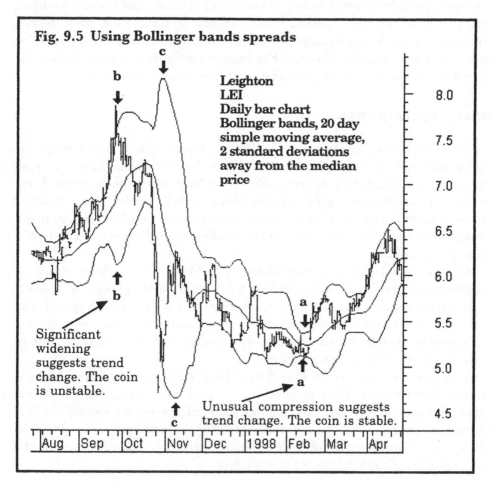

Fig. 9.5 Using Bollinger bands spreads

Leighton
LEI
Daily bar chart
Bollinger bands, 20 day
simple moving average,
2 standard deviations
away from the median
price

Significant
widening
suggests trend
change. The coin
is unstable.

Unusual compression suggests
trend change. The coin is stable.

The narrowing of the bands – the unusual contraction of volatility – precedes a move closer to the average range of volatility than has existed in previous months. At point a-a the spread is two, compared to an average over the previous six weeks of seven. This coin is very stable. Leighton is recovering from a price decline and the quite sudden narrowing of the bands is significantly out of character. When we identify this condition the trader puts this stock on a watch alert.

A contraction of volatility also happens when stocks die. With no trades, no volume, and nobody interested these stocks masquerade as trading candidates because they return a low value on Bollinger band spreads. Despite their low values, they are excluded because the contraction is not out of character. As stocks die the bands narrow at a steady rate, and volume declines. When we apply the Metastock search formula shown below, these returns are excluded after a chart inspection.

After the initial acceleration the spinning coin seems to spend a long time apparently balanced on its edge. The axis does wobble a little but not enough to affect the stability of the coin. Then as the initial acceleration push slows, the axis begins to gyrate noticeably, and then wildly just before the coin loses its balance, clattering to the table top. The change from relative stability to obvious instability is fairly rapid. Sampling, and measuring the width of the wobble, we notice big changes.

In trading terms this is duplicated when the Bollinger bands move apart quickly in a way inconsistent with the previous spread. Some stocks do have significant volatility as a normal trading condition. Any search based on Bollinger band spreads throws them up. We throw them back. A quick check on the chart excludes them because the spreads are consistent with their normal behaviour.

We look for substantial spreads developing quickly and which are inconsistent with the previous weeks or months. The second point, b-b on the Leighton chart in Figure 9.5 shows how rapidly this condition develops.

The spread widens to 16 within a matter of days. As the price collapse accelerates the spread increases dramatically at c-c to 35. When this coin clatters to a stop traders may have lost up to 40% from the high to the low.

Traders who shorted this stock used the changes in volatility to profit grandly.

Two extreme volatility conditions suggest better-than-average trading conditions. A Metastock Explorer search returns the spread values. This formula gives a value to the difference between the upper and lower Bollinger bands. The formula is:

Column A BbandTop(C,20,S,2)

Column B BbandBot(C,20,S,2)

Column C BbandTop(C,20,S,2)-BBandBot(C,20,S,2)

Ezy Chart users must search the charts for these answers, but their task is speeded up by the live charts function which limits the search to parent stocks with attached warrants.

When the Metastock search is completed results are sorted as shown in Figure 9.6. These results are made much more effective if the Metastock exploration is limited to just those parent stocks with warrants attached to them. If this is not possible you will have to manually find and extract the results from the entire data list.

Fig. 9.6 Bollinger band spreads
Selected continuous futures contracts, August 98

CONTRACT	BB Top	BB Bottom	Spread
DOW JONES Nyse	94965	84025	10940
NICKEL	4764	4031	733
SPI Sfe	2884	2542	342
GOLD Comex	2980	2839	141
ZINC	1118	1045	73
SILVER Comex	576	517	59
COPPER Comex	80	72	8
LT CRUDE Comex	14	13	1

It is the change in parent volatility that makes the warrant attractive. The most desirable results – very large, or very small, spreads – are verified by examining the daily bar chart for each selection. This puts the results into context. We need a good stick to act as a lever and these searches find that stick.

STOP LOSS AND DEVIATION

Risk and reward increase proportionally as the standard deviation bands move apart. In opening a derivative trade we use the standard deviation concept to set daily stop loss conditions. We use the probability inherent in the Bollinger band calculations to define and control the potential loss.

Our knowledge of leverage tells us that for a small move in the parent stock we expect a larger move in the derivative instrument. Good money management tells us we should not put at risk more than 2% of our total trading equity.[1]

---

[1] See *Share Trading* for a full discussion of the way this rule is constructed and applied.

Experienced traders are comfortable with adjusting position size so the actual dollar loss on a single trade does not eat up more than 2% of the total capital allocated to all their trading activities.

Derivatives trading introduces a difficult problem because of leverage. An acceptably small loss in the parent stock is magnified in the warrant, or option. Because the derivative is a shadow of the parent, it is difficult to apply some of the more familiar stop loss techniques to a chart of derivative price action.[2] The countback line used as an equity trailing stop loss is not particularly effective on a warrant chart even though it gives excellent signals on the chart of the parent stock.

Ideally, the trader allocates only 2% of his trading capital to each warrant trade on the grounds that should the absolute worst happen – the warrant expires worthless – he stands to lose only a small amount. For traders with limited capital, and for traders who have been mauled by the bear, this may impose untradable conditions. If you only have $21,000 then a warrant trade at around $420 is too small to trade. Even position size of $2,000 makes for very difficult trading.

The best solution depends on trading discipline and a redefinition of probable loss. The premium trader's intention is to trade changes in the value of the warrant price. He does not intend to let the warrant expire worthless so an exit is made before total loss occurs. This exit level determines the amount at risk and if this is confined to less than 2% of trading equity then the derivatives are traded with the same level of risk control as the parent stock.

This does not overcome the problem of rapid and substantial declines in warrant prices. Here leverage and volatility do work against us. We handle this by paying much more attention to volume, but we can define our risk efficiently by using volatility to tip the balance of probability in our favour.

We consider volume in the next chapter so we remain with volatility here.

The usual way of displaying Bollinger bands is to set them two standard deviations away from the median price. This captures 95% of the price moves. A trading band set one standard deviation away captures 67% of the price move. When we use the first as a price target and the second as a stop loss we establish reliable stop loss conditions on the chart of derivative price action.

This is clearly shown in Figure 9.7 for LEIwza. The initial stop loss calculation is designed to protect the trader if he is wrong in his analysis. Using the value of the one standard deviation Bollinger band as a stop loss point the trader applies the usual financial calculations to determine position size.

In summary, these calculations give the following results for LEIwza. With the warrant entry at $0.62 and the lower Bollinger band acting at a stop loss at $0.58 the maximum position size is 50,000 warrants for $31,000. This assumes the trader

---

[2] See *Trading Tactics* for examples of this problem.

has $100,000 in trading capital and pays no brokerage. With any entry at $0.62 the warrant price can drop to $0.58 before money management rules demand an exit.[3] Under ideal circumstances the stop loss exit conditions identified in an analysis of the parent stock would match the Bollinger band exit signal in the warrant. Ideal conditions do not always apply in the market.

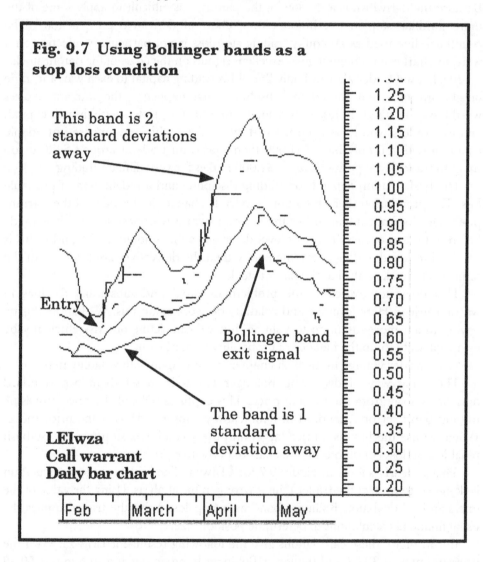

Fig. 9.7 Using Bollinger bands as a stop loss condition

This band is 2 standard deviations away

Entry

Bollinger band exit signal

The band is 1 standard deviation away

**LEIwza
Call warrant
Daily bar chart**

1.25
1.20
1.15
1.10
1.05
1.00
0.95
0.90
0.85
0.80
0.75
0.70
0.65
0.60
0.55
0.50
0.45
0.40
0.35
0.30
0.25
0.20

Feb   March   April   May

---

[3] These calculations are discussed in detail in *Trading Tactics*. spreadsheet examples are included.

As the trade progresses the lower Bollinger band set one standard deviation below the median price continues to act as a stop loss condition. This should remain as a fallback exit condition until other exit conditions are met. These include exit signals generated by the parent stock, or the achievement of pre-set defined financial objectives such as a 20%, 30% or 40% return.

PLOTTING DEVIATION

This combination of one and two standard deviation Bollinger bands on the same screen display is not always a pre-set indicator display. These stop loss conditions are easily plotted with some charting software. Ezy Chart users select Bollinger bands using the display as a stop loss tool. Metastock users must build the indicator in several steps.

To create the Bollinger band stop loss display in Figure 9.7 they start by plotting a standard Bollinger band on any bar chart. For longside trades, click the bottom Bollinger band so the properties box is displayed. Select Colour/Style and change the colour to match the chart background. This leaves the median price and the upper two standard deviation Bollinger band visible.

Select Bollinger bands again from the Indicator menu and drag it on to the display. The property box is automatically displayed. Change the deviations to one and click OK. From the new display, select the upper Bollinger band plotted one standard deviation above the median line. Change its colour to match the chart background.

Now the screen display shows a median price with a Bollinger band one standard deviation below and two standard deviations above. Use the Save As command to save a template for longside warrant trade stop loss calculations. Reverse the procedure to create a template for shortside stop loss calculations.

This Bollinger band stop loss is used in trades designed to take advantage of volatility, leverage, and volume. An analysis of the parent stock triggers the trade, but it is the combination of these purely derivative characteristics which single out this particular warrant as the best trading candidate.

In making the trade we obviously believe prices will range within two standard deviations and we plot this band to define exit targets. In some warrants with extreme volatility there may be sufficient in a single price move over a day to execute a quite profitable trade. In many warrants the trade remains open for several days, or weeks, and the challenge is to manage open profits and protect them.

Bollinger bands provide a partial solution to this challenge. Exit conditions for aggressive traders are when prices meet or exceed the levels plotted by the most distant band. More conservative traders sell when prices fall back to the median level. This does destroy more of open profits. The method we choose to protect open profits depends on how we have structured the trade. Our real concern is limiting a loss when the trade is first opened. Bollinger bands are used to augment other styles of stop loss calculations.

Derivatives trading from the long side places the one standard deviation band below the median line. Traders going short place it above the median line. A higher close destroys their short positions.

FINDING BETTER LEVERS

These broad approaches, and others like them, allow us to identify and attach a ranking value to the level of volatility. Whether we go for more or less volatility depends on our trading needs.

Leverage gives us a principle to apply to enlarge our profits. Volatility helps find, then select a bigger stick to get the profits rolling. In theory derivatives offer considerable leverage but that power must be harnessed to the reality of the market. Building spreadsheet castles showing theoretical leveraged results does not guarantee trading results. By matching the potential volatility on the parent stocks with the calculated results of leverage the trader narrows down the list of trading candidates. Just precisely which candidates are traded depends on two additional factors: volume and time.

CHAPTER 10

TURN UP THE VOLUME

A long stick makes for a better lever, but a long, strong stick is better still. Volume provides the strength. Volatility and leverage beckon the novice trader towards a trap set with volume. Volume is the key essential liquidity necessary for trading. Unless there is a buyer, we cannot be a seller. If buyers and sellers are widely separated in their opinion of the best price, it is difficult to trade at our preferred price. Trading is easier in liquid markets where consistently high volume is traded each day. Volume is the third member of the trading quartet, it follows leverage and volatility, and comes before time.

These volume observations are hardly new, but when we trade derivatives volume is a much more significant factor because we do not have time to wait for buyers to come into the market. The way we factor volume into our derivatives trading equation decides if the volatility and leverage are a hazard or an advantage.

For a moment we revisit volume and its impact on the equity market. As discussed in *Trading Tactics*, in many ways it is difficult to move beyond very broad statements about volume. Volume is required to propel equities into new trends, short or long term. It is the fuel driving the market, and in trading larger stocks, volume clues confirm the strength, the momentum and the sustainability of the trend.

STANDARD VOLUME

Our understanding of volume starts in the equity market. Unfortunately, many of these lessons do not apply to the derivative markets. Many traders concentrate on well-known equities including the major banks, transport companies and retailers.

In these equities our primary concern is the message that volume delivers to us. Martin Pring in *On Momentum* devotes many pages to volume analysis in liquid and deep markets. Our fascination with price and volume indicators is most fruitful in these market conditions. They are deep markets because every day there are many buyers and sellers participating. They are liquid because many trades take place often involving substantial numbers of shares.

In these deep markets we are less concerned about the volume message of our trading. Our orders are swamped in the general order flow. We have little impact on the market, irrespective of where we buy or sell during the day. Traders coming from these markets into less liquid warrant markets must adjust their trading techniques because their orders do impact on the market.

Traders active in mid-cap and speculative stocks are aware of this phenomenon. These markets often have erratic volume, and low liquidity. With only a few buyers we have the opportunity to set the high, or the low for the day in a significant way. In some cases our trade may be the only one for the day, and the mark on the price chart is due to our activity alone.

If our order is beyond the normal size traded, then we have the opportunity, or the misfortune, to bully the market or push it around setting new price benchmarks for the day. Other participants see the size of our order, and use this as a reference point for their own trading activity, perhaps certain our order will act as a backstop. The tactics of this are explored in more detail in *Trading Tactics*.

DROUGHT AND FLOOD

The dynamics of this end of the equity market are most relevant to warrants. The speculative equity market is characterised by two volume approaches. The first is a general scarcity, and the second is the drought and flooding rains variety. Superficially they resemble volume patterns found in warrant trades, but in reality the causes are quite different. The differences, and the trading tactics they engender, are more noticeable if we first understand how the same patterns develop in the equity market.

In mid-cap and speculative stocks volume tends to be consistently lower than in the top 100 stocks. Hardly a startling observation, but unless we acknowledge it we cannot trade this end of the market effectively.

Experienced traders buy trading parcels about the same size as the average order size. Although they may build a much larger position over time, each individual order tends to be around the same size. They pay an increased cost in brokerage, but avoid an increased cost in the market because their true intentions are not fully revealed in a single order.

This market cunning is also designed to make it easier to sell. Not withstanding our plan to sell into a developing trend, or near its top where there are more buyers than usual, we are aware large orders are more difficult to fill. Average size orders for each individual stock are more easily executed and this puts profits into our pockets.

The speculative end of the equity market exhibits a second volume characteristic – the drought and flooding rains variety. For months on end the stock does nothing, then suddenly races upwards. These stocks are propelled by dramatic news, drilling results, a cure for the common cold or yet another potential buyer for that great Australian stock runner, the Orbital engine. In chasing these returns some traders take a cheap early entry and sit patiently for months knowing the potential returns are so large that the wait will be well recompensed. The long drought of trading orders finishes with a flood, pushing the price higher.

When the flood arrives, others, not so patient, jump on board as quickly as possible. Some of the riders do very well using the rally trading techniques discussed in Part I. Many of them ride the runaway train to a standstill. Price trails off in an absolute volume drought. The Jubilee Gold story in Figure 10.1 displays this drought and flood effect. As prices fall, traders desert the market until another trickle of news unleashes a new flood of volume.

TRADING THE DIFFERENCE

Equity traders shifting to warrants carry their understanding of volume in their segment of the equity market. And these experiences do not work in the warrant market. There is a different relationship between volume and price and it allows us to combine leverage and volatility into a better warrant trade. Traders moving from speculative stocks jump to hasty trading conclusions, and fall into the warrant time trap.

The experienced equity trader forgets that in the world of derivatives the future is always known. Derivative instruments are entirely different from equities. Options, warrants, futures – all have known exercise prices on the conclusion of the contract period. With equities there is always tomorrow. With derivatives tomorrow is the apocalypse. The trader does not have the luxury of time to sit out the drought in anticipation of a flood of orders to lift price. In a single warrant trade, time, volume, volatility and leverage all come together in a confusion of influences. Here we consider volume before turning to time.

Traders moving from high volume markets into warrant trading cannot assume easy order execution or complete order fills. Volume behaviour is distorted when the present meets the future. The key relationships are described in specialised market language.

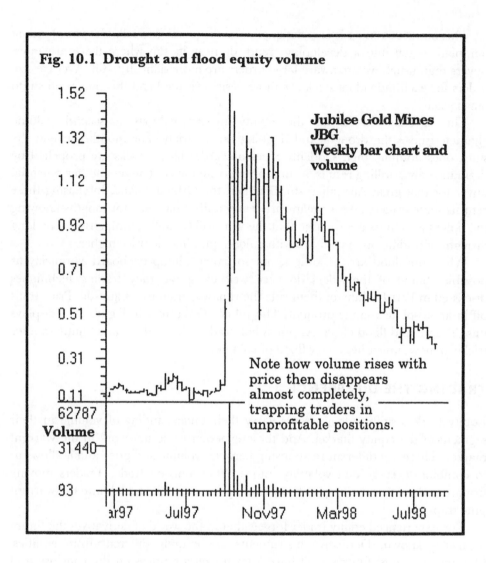

Fig. 10.1 **Drought and flood equity volume**

**Jubilee Gold Mines
JBG
Weekly bar chart and
volume**

Note how volume rises with price then disappears almost completely, trapping traders in unprofitable positions.

AT-THE-MONEY

The derivatives trader works with a known future price and today's market price. This knowledge impacts significantly on the volume relationships in trading. Essentially a warrant has three possible conditions all shown in Figure 10.2. They are:

- ☞ Out-of-the-money
- ☞ At-the-money
- ☞ In-the-money.

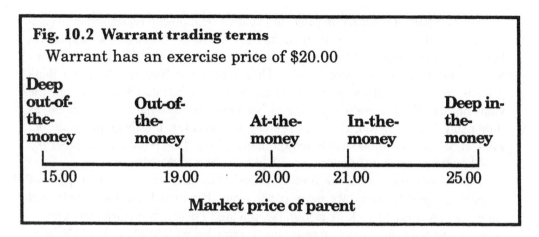

Fig. 10.2 Warrant trading terms
Warrant has an exercise price of $20.00

Deep out-of-the-money	**Out-of-the-money**	**At-the-money**	**In-the-money**	**Deep in-the-money**
15.00	19.00	20.00	21.00	25.00

Market price of parent

We extend the boundaries further at each end by talking of warrants deep-out-of-the-money and deep-in-the-money.

These terms provide the key to avoiding the time trap set by volatility and baited with leverage. This trap is complex, so we make some assumptions in these examples to separate the other mainsprings, time and intrinsic value. Dismantling this trap takes care.

First we assume we are talking about a call warrant priced at $0.50 when the parent shares trade at the warrant exercise price. Later we show how the market calculates this. Second, we assume one warrant converts into one share. In fact conversion ratios could include 1:2, 1:3 and 1:4 but we are less interested in this impact on warrant pricing. Let others make these calculations because we are interested in trading where the volume is highest. What turns the volume up is of less importance than the obvious loudness or silence.

Starting in the middle of Figure 10.2, a warrant is trading at-the-money when its exercise price matches the price of the parent equity. If the mythical NABwrt is exercisable at $20.00 and National Australia Bank is trading at $20.00 then this call warrant is at-the-money.

For just $0.50 some of the conversion trader crowd will buy NABwrt, and then later turn it into an equivalent number of the parent shares when the stock price increases or when additional cash is available. Ignoring brokerage, this is a break-even transaction until National Australia Bank reaches $20.50. Everybody who bought the NABwrt at $0.50 could also convert them into National Australia Bank shares. Many other traders are suddenly interested.

This is rain at the end of a drought, but the clouds are seeded by the relationship between the warrant exercise price and the market price of the parent stock. This is not rain created by a new oil strike or drill result.

The first part of the warrant price and volume relationship is established. When warrants trade at-the-money there is increased interest because they appear to become a sure thing. Current warrant-holders are reluctant to sell because they lose the right to buy the parent stock. They believe the National Australia Bank price is going up, and for every few cents National Australia Bank ticks up, the value of their NABwrt increases. Should National Australia Bank go to $25.00, as they really believe it will, they can exercise the warrant, buy National Australia Bank at $20.00 and immediately sell on market for a 22% return. Remember the actual purchase price is the exercise price plus the cost of the warrant.

This is not our premium trading crowd, but they do provide a pool of deepening liquidity where we more easily swim. Potential buyers see confirmed value so they rush to lock in favourable pricing. Theory does turn into market practice and typically the actual order line is crowded with interest. The ANZwbp real-time screen extract in Figure 10.3 hows the real trading frenzy as the warrant hovers at-the-money. The parent stock, ANZ, is trading at $9.90 and rising. The warrant has an exercise price of $10,000. Buy orders are on the left where the top bid is for 50,000 warrants at 65¢. The seller is asking for 66¢ and has 10,000 to sell.

Fig. 10.3 Trading depth and liquidity when warrant is at-the-money

Market Depth For ANZWBP

Qty	Bid	Ask	Qty
50000	65	66	10000
7000	63	69	10000
14000	60	69	34000
34000	59	70	10000
10000	58	70	50000
27000	57	70	30000
27000	56	70	32000
10000	38	71	18000
30000	38	72	22000
10000	29	73	39000
8000	25	74	40000
		88	2000

ANZwbp put warrant, real time screen, Trading System 2.5 by William Noall Ltd. Exercise price $10.00. Current market price $9.90

As we noted earlier, for many people conversion trading is the standard warrant trading approach promoted by warrant issuers and many brokers. Our trading objectives are quite different as we have no interest in converting warrants into equities. However, we need to understand the motivation of other warrant-holders because they make our premium warrant trading approaches possible.

In general summary we note when warrants are trading at-the-money there is increased market interest in them.

OUT-OF-THE-MONEY

Take a look at one extreme: out-of-the-money warrants. Staying with the National Australia Bank example exercisable at $20.00 the fictional NABwrt warrant is out-of-the-money when the National Australia Bank parent price hovers around $10.00. Understandably few people are interested in buying NABwrt even at just three or four cents. It is like buying a lottery ticket because the chances of National Australia Bank increasing to $20.00 look remote.

The practical confirmation of this attitude in real markets is seen by the spread, or difference, between bid and ask. Out-of-the-money warrants tend to have a wide spread in percentage terms as shown in Figure 10.4. This trading screen displays the order stream for the MIMwfb call warrant, exercisable at $1.00, when the market price for MIM was $0.71 Here the bid is $0.065 and the ask $0.092. Not a great deal in dollar terms, but a spread of 41% is significant in trading terms. Out-of-the-money warrants are very difficult to trade and the wide spread reflects a lack of interest.

This is an ugly screen to look at, but guess which style of equity trader is attracted by the gleam of this potential leverage? Moving straight from the speculative end of the bio-tech, Internet and nickel exploration markets, these traders look at prices quoted in cents, glance upwards at the price chart to find previous highs in the $0.50 range, do the leverage calculations, and buy a substantial parcel of NABwrt at $0.04 from a very relieved seller. These migrants from speculative equity stocks forget the importance of time. Eventually they do learn about it in a very expensive way.

Why is NABwrt available at just $0.04? It is priced so low because the current price of the parent stock is so far away from the known warrant exercise price it is highly unlikely it will recover before the warrant expiry date arrives. The shadow has no life independent of the parent so people do not see potential real profits until the parent price increases.

Fig. 10.4 Trading depth and liquidity when warrant is out-of-the-money

Market Depth For MIMWFB

Qty	Bid	Ask	Qty
20000	6.5	9.2	10000
10000	2	9.5	20000
		12	40000
		12	60000
		13	30000
		13	30000
		13.5	35000
		14.5	20000
		14.5	20000
		14.5	76000
		15	35000
		15	39800
		15	30000
		16	130000
		17	100000

MIMwfb call warrant, real time screen, Trading System 2.5 by William Noall Ltd. Exercise price $1.00. Current market price $0.71.

Speculative equity migrants mistake this volume pattern for the drought and flooding rains characteristics they are accustomed to in their own markets. And yes, there are flooding rains and sometimes warrant prices do run up to $0.50 or more. But, in the same way as many farmers waiting for rain have been ruined by El Nino-induced drought, many warrant traders are killed by the calendar. As options trader Bill McMaster repeats "When you've got options, time goes twice as fast as time."

Some warrant traders believe they can live with this low volume market, surviving on hope. When the flood comes they are well positioned to take advantage of it. Like speculative traders in the equity market they feel the potentially larger return justifies the risk.

These are not our tactics for trading warrant premiums, but it is useful to understand the motivation of this group of speculative traders. After the warrant conversion crowd, they provide a second element in the volume equation.

IN-THE-MONEY

As a call warrant moves into-the-money we would expect volume to increase. After all, if NABwrt is exercisable at $20.00 and the current price National Australia Bank parent price reaches $25.00 as the conversion crowd expected, then the warrant is good value because it comes with an open guaranteed profit. This lure has a fish attached. It remains good value as long as the share price trades above the warrant exercise price.

When it was at-the-money the warrant was also good value and traders engaged in a bidding war to get it. As the warrant moves into-the-money it has guaranteed value and more traders are interested because it is seen as a low risk trade.

In a formal sense, once a warrant passes at-the-money and moves into-the-money, the relationship between price changes in the parent stock and the warrant approaches one for one. This is true if the warrant converts on a one to one ratio. It is still true at different conversion ratios, but warrant prices move in the ratio lockstep. The leverage declines, although the warrant percentage returns remain better than with the parent.

In some ways this warrant becomes less appealing. Price does accelerate rapidly as the warrant moves to at-the-money because there are many buyers and sellers. Then the rate of acceleration slows as the warrant moves into-the-money. We see the practical impact of this theory clearly with the ANZwsp put warrant in Figure 10.5 where buyers out-number sellers. Volume declines, sometimes dramatically. This counter-intuitive outcome annihilates the blue chip trader who has transferred from highly liquid equity trading. He is accustomed to liquid trading at all levels. In this market volume does drive price initially, but it falters just when logic suggests it should increase. Larger orders are difficult to sell, and even on conversion into parent shares, the profit increases only marginally.

Fig. 10.5 Trading depth and liquidity when warrant is in-the-money

Qty	Bid	Ask	Qty
30000	38	45	10000
20000	37		
5000	33		
10000	15		
10000	10		
10000	8		

Market Depth For ANZWSP

ANZwsp put warrant, real time screen, Trading System 2.5 by William Noall Ltd. Exercise price $9.50. Current market price $9.19.

INTRINSIC ARITHMETIC

A moment with simple arithmetic suggests the reason. We construct a theoretical example using Australia New Zealand bank. Remember we look at only one aspect of pricing so we ignore the impact of time. With Australia New Zealand bank trading at $12.00 the mythical call warrant, ANZwrt exercisable at $10.00, is in-the-money. The warrant price is at the very least $2.00 – its intrinsic value. The intrinsic value is the parent share market price less the warrant exercise price and we look at this in more detail in the next chapter. For now we add the warrant premium price to the exercise price and the conversion price is $12.00. Just where do traders drag these warrant price calculations from?

We took ours from the market because the warrant price is closely linked to the parent price in a logical way based on greed. Imagine yourself the proud owner of the ANZwrt in-the-money warrant. The very least you will sell it for is a price equal to what you would get if you converted it to parent shares. That's $12.00 with absolutely no extra for profit or brokerage. The market is usually efficient in matching the prices in these two markets – the parent and the shadow. There is a bit of give and take for the comparative impacts of brokerage, and for some additional factors discussed in the next chapter.

With Australia New Zealand bank at $12.00 the conversion no longer looks extremely enticing if we have to pay $2.00 for the warrant. Conversion may become attractive if we hold the warrant and Australia New Zealand bank continues to rise, but potential conversion returns are reduced. From a trading perspective, buying and converting the warrant becomes slightly less desirable because the parent share has to perform extraordinarily well just to deliver quite ordinary returns.

This is the counter-intuitive impact on volume. An apparently good thing makes buyers wary and less inclined to bid up. The conversion value of the warrant remains almost static as the parent moves deep-into-the-money. The leveraged return available from changes in the warrant price is reduced. This is not good trading territory for premium traders. Sellers also withdraw from the market, further reducing volume.

Our theoretical Australia New Zealand bank model is also a practical one. The real ANZwsp warrant shown in Figure 10.5 is typical of the order lines in this situation. This screen shot is taken on a day when Australia New Zealand bank was moving much lower, propelling the put warrant deeper into-the-money.

The sellers demand even higher prices for the warrant in compensation for the foregone profit available from exercising the warrant. These people are already sitting on open profits. Why should they sell unless a very much better offer comes along? The only better offer available is a higher warrant price so the spread stretches from $0.38 to $0.45 or 18%. This duplicates the widening spreads found with out-of-the-money warrants. The general effect is a decline in volume traded as the warrant moves into-the-money.

TRADING TACTICS

The relationship between price and volume changes in derivatives markets to reflect the known present value of the parent compared to the known future value of the warrant. By constructing a typical diagram of these relationships, as shown in Figure 10.6, the warrant trader selects the most effective areas to apply a combination of leverage and volatility. These are the trading zone areas on both diagrams. Warrants are purchased as they move towards at-the-money and sold when they move into-the-money. In one swoop, the trader captures excellent leverage, increased volatility and the surge in volume.

The observations about warrant volume apply equally to bull and bear markets. The key features of Figure 10.6 are the trading zones of increased volume activity that develops as warrants approach at-the-money and move into-the-money. In practice, the trading zone is not necessarily evenly spaced around the middle

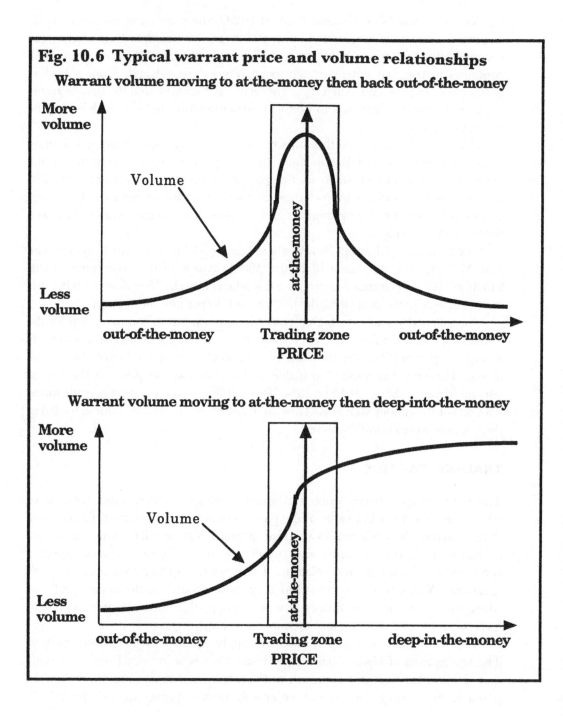

Fig. 10.6 Typical warrant price and volume relationships

at-the-money level. Traders aware of the way trading volume clumps in this area have an early trading edge. Often the band is just a few cents wide, but still offers very rapid returns in the 20% to 50% range for those who anticipate the volume increase and sell into it before it shrinks away.

Prices move more rapidly up and down around the at-the-money level. The frequency of volatility improves. They are more sensitive to parent price moves, sometimes providing multiple trading opportunities over days or weeks. In a derivatives market this is the style of volatility most easily traded because the increased volume allows us to take advantage of it. In this high volume zone the dramatic impact of leverage is reduced. This zone does not include spectacular moves from $0.04 to $0.50. Leverage is still present, but on a reduced scale.

We started with a mythical NABwrt. The premium price move from $0.50 to $1.00 still offers 100% return, which is much greater than the corresponding 22% return from the same price move − $ 20.50 to $25.00 − with the parent stock. Traders in this zone reap the same style of leverage benefits offered by general warrant trading, but they do so with an increased probability of successfully completing the trade.

By trading where volume is highest we improve our chances of being able to fully execute a trade. Warrants are available for purchase, and there are buyers willing to take them off our hands at slightly higher prices. As premium traders we aim to take advantage of the crowd's agenda, often to exercise the warrant, to pursue our own, which is to profit from the volatility of the warrant premium or price.

In later chapters we combine this zone trading approach with other tactics to take effective short positions with the bear.

HOW MUCH TIME?

Like Dorothy, equity traders know this new world is not Kansas. The deceptive allure of leverage is harnessed with a better understanding of volatility and volume, but one further potential pitfall lurks between us and the yellow brick road. Some options traders attempt to build a road-side franchise store because the pitfall comes in the shape of a calendar and a use-by date. Traders accustomed to the options market mistakenly believe their understanding of time is the only valid one and that it gives them an advantage in the warrant market.

These last chapters have shown how we select a long, strong stick to use as a good lever. If this stick is being eaten away by white ants even the best looking lever can snap. In our markets these white ants are called time decay.

CHAPTER 11

BEAR VALUE

The previous chapters used observations about market behaviour to develop a range of trading strategies. These observations tell us when the crowd moves, when it is most active, and when it is least likely to move. Equipped with these alone we stand a better chance of survival in derivatives markets than those who come from equity markets and attempt to apply lessons from that trading experience.

The warrant trading equation includes leverage, volatility, volume and time. The last element in this equation is more formally described, and explained, in the language of options trading. This introduces intrinsic value, time value and time decay to our trading vocabulary. Understanding these concepts and relationships provides a more formal proof to support the patterns of price and volume action we observe on the charts. It also suggests a range of quite specific trading strategies.

Just as the equity trader is required to adjust to the warrant market, so too is the options trader. They cannot build a franchise store beside the yellow brick road because a direct transfer of options concepts and skills to the warrant market spring-loads a number of traps. Chief amongst these is the modified behaviour of time decay.

We do not intend to explore the depths or intricacies of options trading. We are interested in a working knowledge. We look for a general understanding of the impact these elements have in our chosen warrant market. This helps decide where we stand to trade.

Here the reader has a choice. You can rely largely on the consistent, repeated patterns of price and volume activity to develop successful warrant trading strategies. If this is your choice it is recommended you read the first section below and seriously contemplate the financial impact of Figure 11.1. The following chapters examine the way these observations come together in several trades from the short side using warrants.

The second choice is to develop a broad understanding of the well-developed options theories relating to time and intrinsic value. You may well decide not to trade any of these specific approaches, but the explanations do validate the observations made in the previous chapters. The bulk of this chapter deals with an introduction to this theory so we have a working knowledge of it.

It is a complex theory, with many levels and subtleties. It is well researched and written about extensively. Readers who do want to explore specific ideas further should initially turn to Temby and Eng. Others, including McMillian and Fontanills pursue the issues at even more depth. Rather than mention this list of authors again and again, like police Captain Renault in the classic film, *Casablanca*, we regularly advise readers to "Round up the usual suspects," where appropriate. A list of relevant reading from this group of usual suspects, or rather authors, is contained in the annex at the end of the chapter.

A BRIEF INTRODUCTION TO TIME

It is difficult to fully discuss time without starting with intrinsic value, but for the reader in a hurry we will try. Every derivative has a use-by date. On the date of expiry the instrument ceases to exist. All potential gains, or losses, are realised without a hope of any future change. The impact is sudden, sometimes profitable, but more often, unprofitable. The majority of warrants and options expire essentially worthless because they are out-of-the-money.

There is always tomorrow, unless you are trading derivatives. The novice shrugs his shoulders confident he can live with this. The more experienced trader counts up the dollars it has cost him to learn there is no derivative tomorrow. This is one area of trading where sometimes the entire universe appears to conspire against us for an extended period.

It happens like this. Every warrant is a cocktail of analysis and hope. We expect prices to move in our favour, and when leverage and volatility drive warrant prices rapidly beyond our stop loss point we revert to reactions appropriate to the equity markets. We give it time to recover. Stupidly we voluntarily surrender to the warrant the most powerful weapon this market has to use against us.

As the time of expiry moves closer there is less hope the parent will move strongly enough to propel this warrant towards the exercise price. Less hope means less people buying and a gradual trickle of sellers taking larger than expected losses. In the absence of positive movements in the parent stock, the warrant price drifts slowly downwards. Then something dreadful happens – time accelerates and losses explode.

The closer the time to expiry the less likely this parent stock will move enough to push an out-of-the-money warrant into-the-money. Like an alarm ringing through the fog of sleep, traders wake up and rush to abandon the sinking ship. But they are trapped because leverage and volatility now work against them. Often measured in cents, this warrant price is so low that an exit might not even cover brokerage. Who wants the embarrassment of closing a trade and then having to find extra money to pay the brokerage? Better to let it fade into nothingness.

Later we talk of the accelerating impact of time decay. The Savage Resources SVRwfa warrant in Figure 11.1 shows the reality of the theoretical curve. Think of it as a guillotine blade because there is no stopping it when it starts to fall and it cuts the trade with absolute finality.

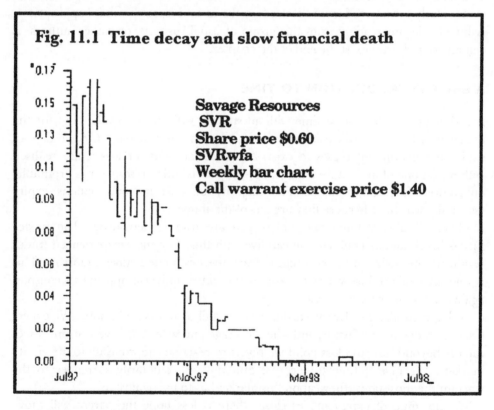

Fig. 11.1 Time decay and slow financial death

Savage Resources
SVR
Share price $0.60
SVRwfa
Weekly bar chart
Call warrant exercise price $1.40

On reflection, perhaps Figure 11.1 is a good reason for reading further rather than skipping to the next chapter. To understand time fully we return to intrinsic value, expanding on our brief encounter in the last chapter.

WE VALUE YOUR TIME

The core of our trading approach uses warrant premiums to leverage returns. We want a better return for exposure to the market over the same time frame and for the same price move in the parent stock. If National Australia Bank shares increase 3% in six weeks we would prefer a National Australia Bank warrant that increases 12% in six weeks. We have suggested if we plant ourselves at the point where volatility, volume and leverage converge then we can gather low risk returns.

Not everybody who trades warrants uses them in this way and options traders hunting in this market use their collection of weapons. A broad understanding of their reasoning allows us to position ourselves to take the best trades to meet our objectives. When others are enthusiastic about a particular stock, or warrant, it is very helpful if we already have some to sell to them. Making money does not mean we all have to be doing the same thing at the same time, nor trading for the same reasons.

In the introduction to this chapter we mentioned the following three aspects of derivative time value:

1. Intrinsic value

2. Time value

3. Time decay.

As a warrant is rather like a very long-dated option, there are some similarities in determining the price of a warrant, and trading opportunities. The most significant of these is the way option traders combine the price of the parent stock, the exercise price of the warrant and the time remaining before the expiry date. Warrant traders also consider the way the conversion ratio modifies the intrinsic value calculation. Options pricing detailed by Temby in Chapter 13 adds the risk-free interest rate and a particular way of calculating volatility or implied volatility.

For traders well practised and well versed in equity markets, these are initially complex issues discussed by the usual suspects gathered in the chapter annex. Our purpose here is not to explore the complexity, but to grasp enough of it to be able to identify when others use option trading approaches and use these crowd reactions to our advantage.

We already know the most important factor is the price of the parent stock. If this price is far above, or below, the warrant exercise price then other factors become less influential. We are buying, or selling, the future at a predetermined point. We have wagered the price of PaRent Stock will be in an advantageous position at the time of warrant exercise in relation to the exercise price. If we are wrong, and we leave it too long, then it is unprofitable to exercise the warrant because we lose more money. By not exercising we lose, at maximum, only the premium. Experienced traders have cut their losses much earlier.

INTRINSIC VALUE

At the time of expiry the warrant is worth only its intrinsic value. It is easiest to consider the concept of intrinsic value by starting at the end of the process and working backwards.

The fictional PRSccc is a call warrant with an expiry date of June 30 at a price of $5.00. It has a conversion value of 1:1 meaning each warrant is equivalent to one parent share. The diagram in Figure 11.2 provides a snapshot of the possible price combinations on June 30. This style of chart is used to illustrate the intrinsic value of PRSccc at the time of expiry. It plots the price of the warrant against various possible parent stock prices.

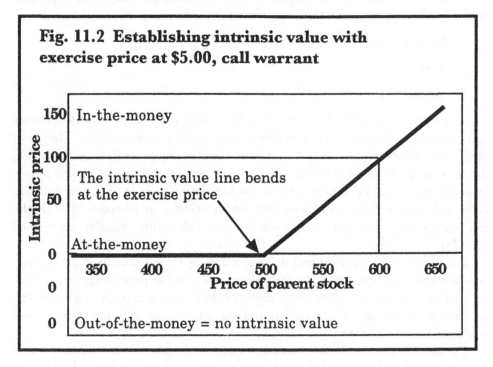

Fig. 11.2 Establishing intrinsic value with exercise price at $5.00, call warrant

When PaRent Stock trades at $4.00 the warrant with an exercise price of $5.00 has no intrinsic value. Why pay $5.00 to exercise the warrant when we could go to the physical market and buy the parent stock at $4.00? In one very important sense, the warrant has no value other than intrinsic value at this price at this point in time. Not surprisingly it is shown as a straight line.

The same applies when the PaRent Stock parent price is at $5.00, although the reasons are less obvious. Ignoring transaction costs, we could exercise the warrant at $5.00 and buy the parent stock at $5.00. It is a break-even proposition. We would do no better or no worse, by going to the physical market and buying PaRent Stock at $5.00. The intrinsic value is still zero.

But the confluence of the exercise price and the parent stock price is an important point because the line plotting intrinsic value always starts, or bends, at this point. This attracts traders with all sorts of motives.

We buy the future at $5.00. As soon as the price of PaRent Stock moves to $5.20 the warrant develops intrinsic value. In crude terms, ignoring the costs of the warrant premium and brokerage, it is worth $0.20 more than the $5.00 exercise price.

On the other end of the scale, when the parent price moves to $5.60 the PRSccc warrant is worth $0.60 just on the basis of comparing the exercise price with the current parent stock price. Although we have constructed a strange looking chart of this relationship, it is nothing more than a graphic representation of simple arithmetic. This charting style comes directly from the options market.

When the call warrant exercise price is subtracted from the stock price a positive answer equals the intrinsic value of the warrant. A negative return, or zero, tells us there is no intrinsic value. In the formal equations used with options, the intrinsic value is equal to the share price minus the exercise price. Warrant traders modify this if the conversion value of the warrant is not 1:1.

This simple spreadsheet arithmetic points the way to warrant trading approaches based on the value of an exercised warrant. We expect more people will be interested in the PRSccc warrant as the stock price nears $5.00 − as it approaches at-the-money value. Interest increases again as the warrant moves into-the-money and the intrinsic value increases. Interest drops away as the warrant moves deep-into-the-money because the potential leverage declines. This provides the theory behind the practical volume patterns discussed in Chapter 10.

Traders familiar with options use this information to trade the intrinsic value of the warrant. In a simple illustration using Figure 11.2 we estimate the advantage involved using the projected warrant premium figures on the vertical scale. In practice, these projections are modified by time and time decay but for the moment we ignore these impacts.

When PaRent Stock is at $5.50 the intrinsic value of the warrant is reflected in the warrant price at $0.50. When the parent price is at $6.00 the intrinsic value is $1.00. This represents an increase of 100%, and this increase is tradeable. In contrast, the price move in the parent PaRent Stock from $5.50 to $6.00, returns a comparatively miserable 9%.

This style of theoretical diagram confirms our earlier observations in Chapters 7 and 8 about trading advantages offered by trading with the hook. Like all simple calculations these figures are somewhat misleading. Reality intrudes in the shape of brokerage, liquidity, conversion ratios and because savvy options traders are also aware of these calculations. However, we stay with these theoretical calculations and these idealised price plots because they provide a way of comparing different approaches without including the modifying impact of the other time-related variables.

Intrinsic value attracts more buyers to the market although many of them do not quite understand the nature of the lure that attracts them. The real market impact of this activity is modified by the time value of the warrant. The interaction of this and time decay acts in unexpected ways to reduce the attractiveness of warrants deep in the money. It provides the theoretical explanation for the real market observations in Chapter 10.

LIMITS ON THE UNLIMITED

Our examples use PRScc call warrants, traded from the long side and buying the future. We expect to buy low and sell infinitely higher. When we trade puts and short the market, we sell the future. The problem is this future is limited by our unfamiliarity with bear market falls.

Equity traders are optimists. They have to be because the ASX makes it very easy to trade from the long side – buy low and sell high, buy high and sell higher. As mentioned in Chapter 1, apart from mastering the mechanics of short trading, we also have to feel morally comfortable with making money when others are losing it.

The speed of a full bear market hits with dramatic falls and delivers dramatic, and often rapid, put profits. Surprisingly, many traders see this as a problem. All this gives trading the short side of the market a different character. Volume and liquidity play a different and significant role.

The real world of warrant trading, shown in Figure 11.3, applies this in practice. Both the BHPwpp put warrant and the BHPwpa call warrant have the same exercise price of $14.25 and both expire in December 1998. In all respects they are identical and we anticipate they would move in lockstep in opposite directions. Such theory is the basis of a number of options trading strategies including straddles and some hedges.

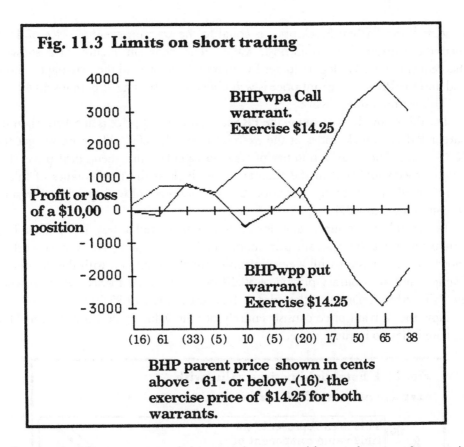

Fig. 11.3 Limits on short trading

4000 —

3000 —

2000 —

1000 —

**BHPwpa Call
warrant.
Exercise $14.25**

**Profit or loss
of a $10,00** 0
position

-1000 —

-2000 —

**BHPwpp put
warrant.
Exercise $14.25**

-3000 —

(16) 61 (33) (5) 10 (5) (20) 17 50 65 38

**BHP parent price shown in cents
above - 61 - or below -(16)- the
exercise price of $14.25 for both
warrants.**

In practice, the put warrant is less reactive, or sensitive, to downward moves in the parent stock. This transforms some low-risk options-style trading approaches into higher risk strategies.

In particular, the put warrant gains value more slowly when the BHP share price falls. When BHP moves in the opposite direction, the put loses value very quickly. In contrast the call warrant is less volatile when BHP prices fall, but more reactive when BHP prices rise. Clearly shorting the market is not an exact mirror image of longside trading. We note these characteristics here because they do modify the following discussion of time value and time decay.

TIME VALUE

Establishing warrant value based on these precise guides to intrinsic value is not always useful in the rough and tumble of trading where prices tend to be approximate rather than conform precisely to theoretical calculations. The theory suggests if the PaRent Stock price is equal to the warrant exercise price of $5.00 then the warrant has no intrinsic value. The chart in Figure 11.2 shows a theoretical reality. We log on to our live market feed, or read the newspaper quotes and find the PRSccc warrant price is well above zero, trading at perhaps $0.40.

This is time value at work.

For this example, we assume the PRSccc call warrant price is at $0.40 when the parent PaRent Stock trades at the exercise price of $5.00. Where do we get this $0.40 from? There are a number of ways to calculate this theoretical price. The usual suspects gathered in the chapter annex look at the mathematics of this in more detail. Most of us just look at the options software-produced results, accepting them as valid.

We calculate the time value for warrants in a similar way to options. In a formal sense it is the warrant price minus its intrinsic value. We want a working knowledge, so we start with a zero intrinsic value. We remain with the theoretical example and an arbitrary pricing of $0.40 for the fictional PRSccc warrant when the PaRent Stock parent stock trades at the exercise price of $5.00.

Now the warrant price consists entirely of time value as shown in Figure 11.4, because it has no intrinsic value.

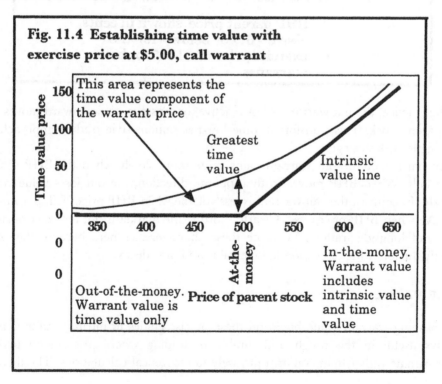

Fig. 11.4 Establishing time value with exercise price at $5.00, call warrant

This matches with reality because warrants do not trade at zero in the real market, when the parent stock trades at the exercise price. This time value is the truly speculative component of warrant trading.

Unlike the intrinsic value, the time value line is plotted as a curve, stretching ahead and behind this single reference point. The driving forces in setting the warrant price on either side of this line are hope and greed. Let's start with hope, as do most warrant traders.

We are buying the future of PaRent Stock at $5.00 and at a current market price of $3.00 the future looks bleak. The parent stock has to perform pretty well, increasing by 66%, to reach the exercise price target of $5.00. Just like everybody else, when I buy the future I do not want to pay a great deal when the current price is deeply out-of-the-money. At perhaps $0.02 or $0.03 it is a nice speculative position, but it would be unwise to make this position a major part of our portfolio.

We all watch the PaRent Stock price increase. At a market price of $4.50 the element of hope acquires a great deal more certainty than when the parent price was at $3.00. A mere 11% price increase takes the PaRent Stock share price to the exercise price. Time holds out the promise of profits. Buyers pay more for a more certain future. Twenty cents is not an unreasonable asking price.

The spreadsheet cowboys come up with two figures and we note them in passing. For speculative warrant premium traders who paid $0.03 the new $0.20 premium offers a seductive 566% return. We return to this crowd of hopefuls later. The second set of figures looks nearly as good, showing a potential 100% return for warrants purchased at $0.20 and sold later at $0.40. This crowd trades differently with lower risk.

The curved line of hope reflects the increasing probability that the exercise price of the warrant will match the current price of the parent stock. The maximum point at which hope is fully confirmed is when exercise price and stock price are equal. Here the pricing of the warrant reflects only the time value as there is no intrinsic value. Remember the diagram in Figure 11.2. The profit line bends when the parent price is at least $0.01 beyond the exercise price – until then there is no intrinsic profit.

We might expect hope to grow as prices move beyond the exercise price, but instead greed starts to take over. If we wager on a proven certainty we turn to different ways to make money. Hope becomes less significant because we have profits in our pocket. Instead, we start crunching the hard numbers – warrant price plus the parent stock price. We try to lock in the best profits.

Just how much more can the parent stock perform? Moving towards the extremes of the possible prices of PaRent Stock we find the warrant price trades for its intrinsic value – market share price minus exercise price – with very little added time premium. The further the parent price moves above the exercise price the more difficult it is to justify an additional time premium on top of the intrinsic value of the warrant. At this stage of the trade profits flow mainly from changes in intrinsic value.

At $6.00 the intrinsic value of PRSccc is $1.00. To make money on the warrant the parent price must move beyond $6.00. If we add just a few cents for time value to this calculation, the warrant is less attractive. Now time might undermine our profits. Warrant buyers will not bid greatly above the intrinsic value.

Again, those who want to explore the complex mathematics of these pricing curves should turn to the usual suspects gathered at the end of the chapter. For our purposes we note that from a time value perspective the greatest value is added as the stock price approaches the warrant exercise price and it diminishes as the stock prices moves beyond the exercise price.

The theory confirms our market observations where trading volume decreases as warrants move deep-into-the-money. It explains the increase in market depth and liquidity when warrants move towards at-the-money. Time adds a little leverage to the volatility.

TIME DECAY

Einstein constructed the general theory of relatively with some difficulty. Had he traded warrants or options he would have found the answers more quickly and in a much more concrete fashion. As all traders discover, time accelerates dramatically as the date of expiry approaches.

The market reality is much harsher than the option theory suggests. The usual options time decay formula confirms the rate of time decay is not linear. If it were it could be shown as a straight line like the plot of intrinsic value. Instead time value decays rapidly in the last weeks before the expiry date. Most options software calculates this by taking the square root of the time remaining and McMillian goes through the calculations in detail. Our interest is in the results.

The typical theoretical time decay result for options, when charted, is shown in Figure 11.5. Results of options analysis produced by most options software assume this theoretical curve. The theory lulls the warrant trader into believing an exit with dignity is possible around the mid-points of the curve before the price collapse accelerates out of control. This is cold comfort for options traders entering the warrant market. The theoretical curve springs a nasty trap.

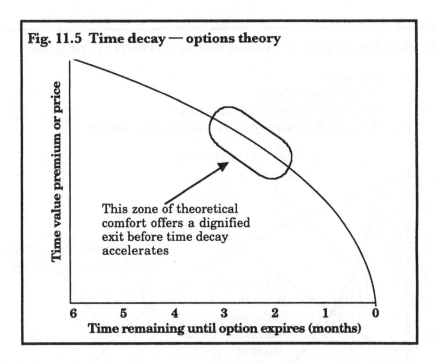

Fig. 11.5 Time decay — options theory

Time value premium or price (vertical axis)

This zone of theoretical comfort offers a dignified exit before time decay accelerates

6   5   4   3   2   1   0
Time remaining until option expires (months)

Market reality suggests warrant time decay is most corrosive in this period. Prices collapse most rapidly in this area. The real curve is inverted as Figure 11.6 confirms. This difference traps options and equity traders in losing warrant positions.

Options trading is a well-practised art with fairly well-defined circumstances for identifying the impact of time decay. The option trader, or his software, plots the typical curve with confidence and a high degree of certainty. Trades are taken up to the cusp of time decay with a level of accuracy not possible in warrant markets. This may reflect the dominance of options markets by Registered Trader market-makers who, in making the market, have a professional approach to these theoretical option pricing calculations.

The real world of warrants is not as orderly and is more problematic. The impact of time decay is often accelerated abnormally. It also seems to be more variable, accelerating much earlier than anticipated by options pricing models or sometimes even much later. This makes the transfer of options time value trading approaches to the warrant market particularly hazardous. They do not have a franchise on the yellow brick road.

It is an observation without a verifiable explanation. Possibly it reflects the absence of market-makers which leaves warrant pricing at the mercy of real market forces. Warrants are traded on the SEATS, just like equities. Buyers are matched

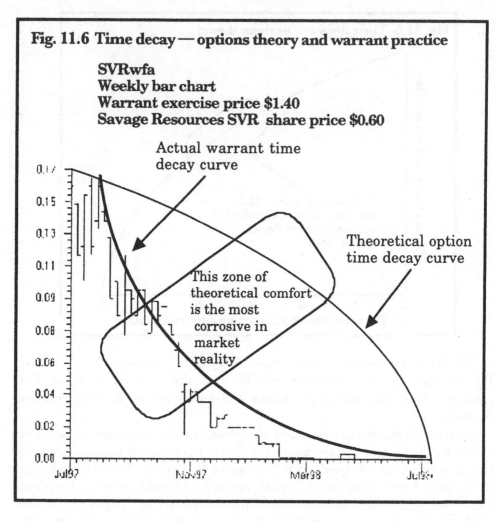

Fig. 11.6 Time decay — options theory and warrant practice

SVRwfa
Weekly bar chart
Warrant exercise price $1.40
Savage Resources SVR share price $0.60

Actual warrant time decay curve

Theoretical option time decay curve

This zone of theoretical comfort is the most corrosive in market reality

with sellers, not with middlemen. This transparency exposes the market as less than efficient, and this signals caution in applying option modelling results from options software to warrants.

A LONG WAY TO SHORT

All of this seems to be a long detour from short trading but when we use derivatives to enhance our returns, or to trade in falling markets by going short, we need to identify how some in the crowd assess the price action and apply all four elements of the warrant trading equation – leverage, volatility, volume and time – to decide price.

In summary there are three types of basic trading opportunities produced by the four elements in the trading equation. They are shown in Figure 11.7.

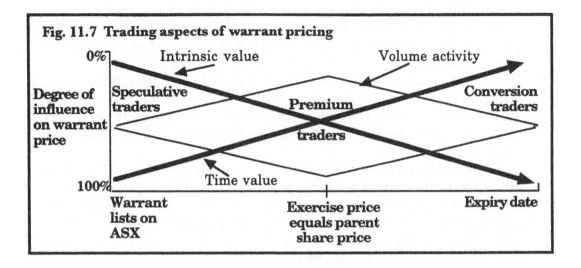

Fig. 11.7 Trading aspects of warrant pricing

The first are conservative trades based on increases in intrinsic value, often with the intention of converting the warrant into shares. In market terms this assures the trader of a lockstep increase in the warrant price as the parent stock moves beyond the exercise price from $6.00 to $6.50. This crowd from the equity market is encouraged to take this view by magazine writers and common warrant publicity. The warrant price consists only of time value until the parent price equals the warrant exercise price.

The second style is speculative trading based on time value, moving from the parent price of $4.50 to the maximum time value premium at the exercise price of $5.00 as shown in Figure 11.4. This makes possible trading time value from, perhaps, $0.10 to $0.40. This trading solution speculates on time, not on a new gold discovery or a cure for cancer. Many in this crowd have traded speculative equities for leverage and they hope to transfer the skills to the warrant market.

The third style captures our attention. It brings together the optimum conditions of time, intrinsic value and volume. The active premium trader takes a leveraged return from the purchase price of, perhaps, $0.05 and a sale price of $0.10. This is the crowd of premium traders and we stand in the middle of it.

The most consistent derivative trading opportunities are a complete package containing leverage, volatility and volume. Other opportunities exist where only one or two of these factors are present, but they have reduced profitability in the general warrant market. Individual components, such as leverage, are used successfully in clearly-defined market events. Although this application has been shown in a bear trading context, obviously it also applies to a bullish market, or bullish stocks, when events which are reasonably anticipated push up prices.

Warrants and options are the most accessible derivative trading instruments for private traders to use in shorting the market. Both define and confine risk in a more user-friendly manner than futures and commodities contracts.

Warrant trading in particular is the focus of Part III of this book. Readers who would like to explore the short trading strategies applicable to commodity markets will find these covered particularly well in *Schwager on Futures* and *The Art of Short Trading* by Kathryn Staley. Chris Tate gives a basic introduction in *Understanding Futures Trading in Australia.*

For our wider exploration of trading approaches the significance of this brief overview of the formal option concepts is in the way these conditions attract other traders to the market. We cannot trade when there is no-one to trade with. We cannot use the power of raw leverage and volatility if no-one else wants to play the game. This is not Kansas and just like equity traders, option traders do not have a franchise of the trading techniques for this market.

By developing an understanding of where the crowd is likely to assemble we position ourselves in warrant trades to reap the benefits of their enthusiasm and willingness to buy our warrants. The next part shows how these diverse understandings are matched with a tool-box of indicators to construct profitable short trades in the bear market.

Annex to Chapter 11

THE USUAL SUSPECTS

IT IS NOT our purpose or intention to consider detailed options trading strategies built around volatility, intrinsic value and time. These sometimes complex strategies are better explained by the recognised experts. Our concern is to use derivatives to survive. Achieve this in a bear market and then you have the luxury of looking at more sophisticated approaches.

When you are ready to move beyond survival these books provide a starting point.

    ↪   *Understanding Options Trading in Australia* Christopher Tate

    ↪   *Options: Perception and Deception* Charles Cottle

Readers hungry for greater detail can find it in this collection.

- ☞ *Trading Stock Options and Warrants*, Chris Temby

- ☞ *The Elements of Successful Trading*, Robert Rotella

- ☞ *Options: Trading Strategies that Work*, William Eng (Australian edition edited by Daryl Guppy)

- ☞ *Technical Analysis for Trading Index Warrants*, Chris Temby.

Equipped with this level of understanding it is useful to consider the variety of trading strategies available. These books will help.

- ☞ *Trading Rules* William Eng & Daryl Guppy

- ☞ *The Options Course* George Fontanills

- ☞ *The Secret of Writing Options* Louise Bedford

- ☞ *Options as a Strategic Investment* Lawrence McMillian

- ☞ *Trade Like a Bookie Course* David Caplan

- ☞ *Day Trading Stock Index Futures* Gary Smith

- ☞ *Trading in Global Currency Markets* Cornelius Luca.

Readers who wish to explore at greater levels of complexity will find these books helpful.

- ☞ *Buying and Selling Volatility* Kevin Connolly

- ☞ *Option Volatility and Pricing* Sheldon Natenberg.

PART III

SHORT BEARS

CHAPTER 12

HUNTING WITH THE BEAR

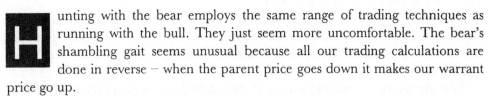unting with the bear employs the same range of trading techniques as running with the bull. They just seem more uncomfortable. The bear's shambling gait seems unusual because all our trading calculations are done in reverse – when the parent price goes down it makes our warrant price go up.

This discomfort increases again because our parent stock analysis is only the basis for action taken in another market. Because the shadow – the derivative – has no substance, we do not apply the standard tools of technical analysis to a warrant chart. The gross and extreme reactions of warrant price are caused by the leveraged relationship between the shadow and the parent. We trade the shadow, but entry and exit signals usually come from our analysis of the parent.

In this chapter we bring together the theory from Part II in a practical way applying both multiple moving average and count back line techniques to manage a warrant premium trade. Rather than repeat old material in full we provide a brief summary of each of these indicators. Readers unfamiliar with these trading tools should consult *Share Trading* and *Trading Tactics* for full development and construction details.

The search for suitable trading candidates starts amongst the parent stocks and we look for stocks with behaviour consistent with our view of the market. If we believe the market is making a small rally, we look for rising stocks, and the reverse in falling markets. To hunt with the bear we must be convinced the market, or market segment, is in a sustained downtrend, or about to collapse into one. This means many trade entries, as with the following examples, are not made at the very beginning of the downtrend. The trader surrenders some profit in return for increased certainty the new trend is sound. Short trading carries extra penalties for getting the trend wrong. As shown in Figure 11.3 in the previous chapter, short trades are slow to move when parent prices first drop, but fast to record a loss as soon as parent prices edge up.

In unusual circumstances we might form a bearish view about an individual stock. If so, the analysis steps are the same. We look for stocks already moving in the expected direction, or which look particularly unstable.

ON THE WALL

Hunting with the bear provides two major trading opportunities. The first is a long-term slide in prices we associate with a bear market. We start our example with the identification, assessment and analysis processes followed on a single day in early August 1998, to select the best candidate from amongst the range of 23 available companies with put warrants.

The second style of trading opportunity is found in a sharp, rapid decline in an otherwise strong market. The market stumble in October 1997 is a good example of this trading situation. These were discussed in Chapter 8 so we mention them again only in passing.

Because we use put warrants to short the market our hunting ground is already defined. They are available over about 23 parent stocks, the All Ordinaries index and the Gold index. This figure changes depending on market conditions. We expect the number of available puts to expand greatly in a prolonged bear market.

Group these parent stocks into a single search file. Ezy Chart users do this quickly with the live chart function to save a standard bar chart display of each parent stock. Metastock users turn to the SmartChart function, although this is not quite as versatile as the Ezy Chart equivalent. No matter which style of trading opportunity we end up selecting, time, intrinsic, or premium value, the search starts with this select group.

Short trading leaves little room for subtleties. A bar chart either shows price action falling, or it does not. The direction of price should be clear when the chart is pinned to the wall on the opposite side of the room. We trade with the obvious trend. Using a short trade we rarely take a position in anticipation of price developments. Instead, we look for proof the price decline has started. We need a strong signal because when we come to trade the warrant premium, time is not on our side.

Discard charts with questionable trends. Inspect the others closely. Look for strong action in a downward direction, as shown with retailing giant Coles Myer in Figure 12.1. The direction of price action on this chart is clear from the other side of the room.

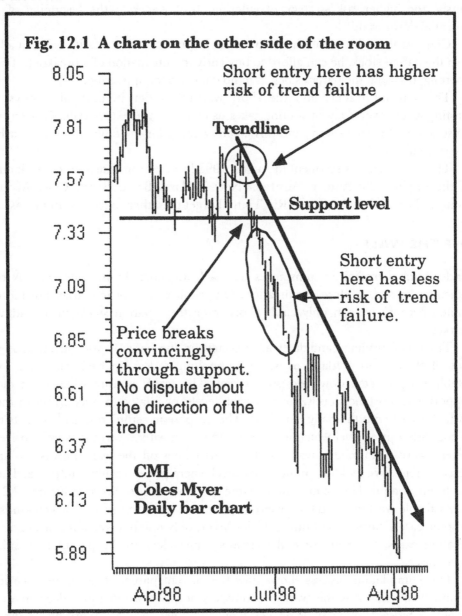

Fig. 12.1 A chart on the other side of the room

Short entry here has higher risk of trend failure

Trendline

Support level

Short entry here has less risk of trend failure.

Price breaks convincingly through support. No dispute about the direction of the trend

CML Coles Myer Daily bar chart

Two types of evidence support this long-distance analysis. First is the strong break below the support level. Second is the unequivocal placement of the trend line.

There is little room for argument here about the existence of a strong down trend. Remember our objective is to enter established down trends, rather than to pursue the higher risk strategy of entering short trades at the beginning of a potential down trend.

Contrast this with a bullish equity trade. Because a bullish trader will actually own the parent stock, he can afford to buy early in anticipation of a breakout. If he is wrong, his asset, the parent stock, is in no danger of disappearing.

The warrant trader, and the short warrant trader in particular, buys a wasting asset. Every day of waiting takes us closer to the expiry date. Our entry must be timed more exactly, and this means waiting for the down trend to clearly assert itself.

This same visual assessment in August 1998 leaves seven charts on the wall out of the original 23: Amcor, Australia New Zealand Bank, Boral, Coles Myer, Santos, Normandy Mining and Rio Tinto. Forget the other sixteen doubtful cases.

OFF THE WALL

Under normal trading circumstances we reach immediately into our tool-box of indicators to start a close examination. Our choices in a bear market are more limited because we can only easily short trade these parent stocks in a shadow market.

The initial trading candidates are selected on the basis of price action alone. Not all of them are tradable as warrant premium trades. For each candidate we establish a projected downside price target. The target is usually based on old support and resistance levels, consolidation levels, or related to price spikes in the past. We start with the daily bar chart. The purpose in setting downside targets is to establish a price level which we later try to match with a warrant exercise price. Where there is no match available, the chart comes off the wall. This is not an exact exercise. We look for an indicative level where prices are likely to pause. The results are compiled in column three on the spreadsheet grid shown in Figure 12.2.

Available warrants and their exercise prices are listed in the next two columns. In some cases, Normandy Mining, Coles Myer, only one put warrant is available. In other cases, there are several warrants, some close to the parent downside target price.

This compilation process shows how the current parent stock share price in column two relates to the warrant exercise price. We avoid those deep in the money – those already showing good profits – like Amcor. Warrants trading deep-in-the-money trade at intrinsic value only so leverage is reduced with thin and erratic volumes. They are not good premium trading candidates.

Fig. 12.2 Calculating target and exercise price for put warrants

Code	Current stock price	Stock Target price	Warrant code	Warrant exercise price	Comment
amc	$6.88	$6.32	amcwdp	$7.60	deep in money
anz	$10.45	$9.62	anzwsp	$9.50	near the money
			anzwfp	$9.50	near the money
			anzwbp	$10.00	in the money
			anzwxp	$10.00	in the money
bor	$2.88	$2.71	borwsp	$3.00	deep in money
cml	$6.02	$5.25	cmlwxp	$7.50	deep in money
ndy	$1.25	$1.10	ndywdp	$1.50	deep in money
rio	$18.30	$17.37	riowmp	$20.00	deep in money
sto	$4.27	$3.60	stowbp	$5.75	deep in money

This list does not include any out-of-the-money opportunities. Had it done so, these would have provided a more speculative opportunity with high time value and low intrinsic value. These warrants are very speculative because price must fall even further than our projections. Additionally as suggested by Figure 12.3 it does take additional time for a put warrant to react to the fall in the parent stock. Out-of-the-money puts have a reduced speculative component when compared with their call counterparts.

Attractive premium trading put warrant candidates on this list are clustered where the exercise price is near the current parent price. We expect to trade a high time value as well as picking up the fastest increases in intrinsic value. Additionally we anticipate better volume and more liquidity.

In some cases analysis of the daily chart showing twelve months of data is not useful because no other downside target reference points are available. Prices are so low there is no reliable guide to historical lows on the chart display. The daily bar charts of Coles Myer, Rio Tinto and Normandy Mining have this problem in August 1998. We reach more accurate targets for these stocks by building a point and figure chart. This style of charting removes the strict march of time in favour of plotting the direction and extent of price moves.

Up-moves are displayed as an X and downmoves as an O. The scale, or box size, is decided by the user based on the usual bid size for the stock. The reversal is usually three boxes and is designed to filter out insignificant price activity. The result is a compressed view of price concentrating on the direction. This displays more information on a single chart or screen. The particular strength of point and figure charting is its ability to expose the structure of the market based on support and resistance levels.[1]

A point and figure chart shows several downside targets for Coles Myer in Figure 12.3.

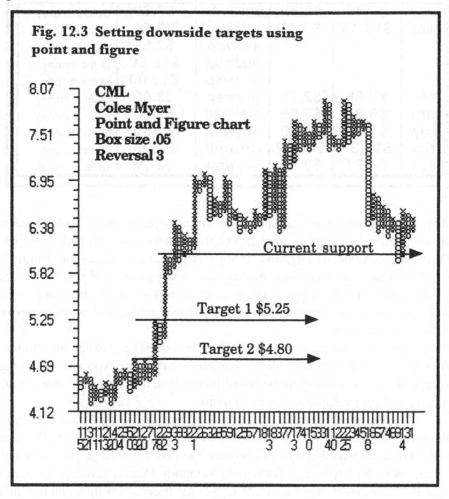

Fig. 12.3 Setting downside targets using point and figure

---

[1] See *Share Trading* for a complete explanation of point and figure techniques.

The displayed data starts in October 1995. Which target is appropriate depends upon our opinion of the severity of the Coles Myer market collapse. In a severe fall we aim for target two at $4.80. In the initial stages of a down market we aim for the first target at $5.25. The same process is used with all potential trading candidates, but often the daily bar chart will provide enough information. The objective is to decide which charts come off the wall and into the rubbish bin.

CONFIRMATION BY EXAMINATION

The Coles Myer bar chart in Figure 12.1 is a natural selection of an established down trend. Many charts are not because the initial selection is based on the collapse of an uptrend. When a straight edge upward sloping trend line is broken the short side trader looks at it eagerly. Hope is a wonderful emotion, even for short traders, and many survive on it and coffee. Hope distorts our view of price activity because when a chart is pinned on the wall we still see a falling trend even though prices may have closed higher for the last six days.

Trading the short side carries increased risk created by time decay, decreased volatility, lower leverage and market unfamiliarity with the instrument. Traders cannot afford to let hope get in the way of reality so as a final check on market strength we use the multiple moving average (MMA) indicator. The construction and use of this indicator is explained briefly in Chapter 5 and covered more fully in *Trading Tactics*.

We look for a clear downside break of an existing uptrend for short side trades designed for extended time frames. The validity of the straight edge trend line break is confirmed by the MMA. With longside trading we often move on the trend line break in anticipation of confirmation from the MMA. This is a less successful strategy with bear trading because time works against us with a vengeance. Trading from the short side is not a natural choice for many traders, so volume is often scarce. The Woolworths chart in Figure 12.4 shows the error of an early shortside entry based on a straight edge trend break alone.

Here the trend break shown by the straight edge trendline is quite valid, but the stock continues upwards, using the trend line as a resistance level rather than a support level. A short trade taken on the straight edge trend line break signal alone is uncomfortable for many weeks because the trader is unsure of the strength of the rally. Applying the MMA test reveals this trend line break is not solid. It is an early warning signal, but it fails the across-the-room test.

The MMA is more often used in a bull market as an advance signal of a trend change, or of increased market volatility, but it is also used to confirm the strength of a trend. Sustained activity of the short-term group of averages below the long-term group confirms a strong down trend. Traders know short-term rallies

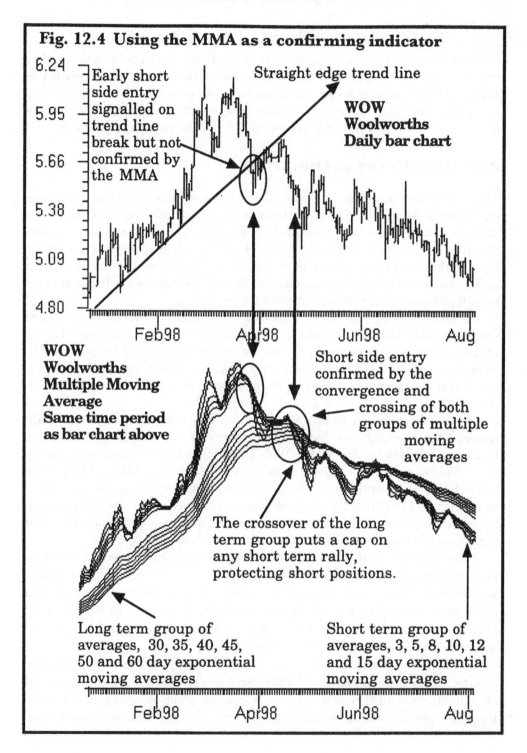

Fig. 12.4 Using the MMA as a confirming indicator

Early short side entry signalled on trend line break but not confirmed by the MMA

Straight edge trend line

WOW Woolworths Daily bar chart

WOW Woolworths Multiple Moving Average Same time period as bar chart above

Short side entry confirmed by the convergence and crossing of both groups of multiple moving averages

The crossover of the long term group puts a cap on any short term rally, protecting short positions.

Long term group of averages, 30, 35, 40, 45, 50 and 60 day exponential moving averages

Short term group of averages, 3, 5, 8, 10, 12 and 15 day exponential moving averages are capped by the width and strength of the long-term group of averages. Warrant put positions are taken with confidence. The short-term group will fluctuate, but while the long-term group remains in a steady band heading down it suggests long-term resistance.

When the short- and long-term groups of averages show a developing down trend the trader selects a trading strategy based on a longer term exposure to the market. Australia New Zealand Bank shown in Figure 12.5 signals a trade lasting perhaps for weeks, or even a month or two. The distance between the two groups of averages, and the way each group has spread out, suggest a well established down trend. This is not a three to five day trade opportunity.

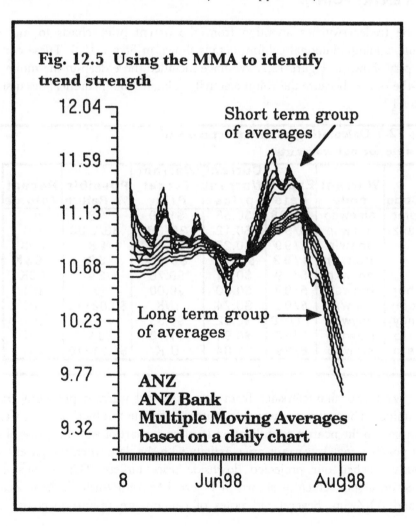

Fig. 12.5 Using the MMA to identify trend strength

Short term group of averages

Long term group of averages

ANZ
ANZ Bank
Multiple Moving Averages
based on a daily chart

Although our preferred premium trading is at the points of highest liquidity, this potentially long-term Australia New Zealand bank trade offers a high degree of safety. Where the long-term group of averages is well separated we trade with increased confidence of price bouncing down from this area. The Australia New Zealand bank market is in a terminal down trend driven by a powerful trend change.

Once our analysis of the parent stock is confirmed we are in a better position to assess the best warrant trade available. More charts are torn off the wall until only one or two remain.

GREEK ENTRY POINTS

Now the trader switches attention from the parent price charts to individual warrants, adding additional column details shown in Figure 12.6. These continue the display shown in Figure 12.2. We have included those deep-in-the-money and out-of-the money because the volume activity validates the theoretical discussion in Chapter 10.

Fig. 12.6 Calculating potential return and volume for put warrants

Code	Warrant code	Expiry date	Current Warrant price	Warrant Target Price	Possible % Return	Recent Volume
amc	amcwdp	10/98	$0.55	$1.09	98	nil
anz	anzwsp	9/98	$0.12	22/36	.83/2.00	nil
	anzwfp	1/99	$0.25	$0.32	28	20K
	anzwbp	**4/99**	**$0.41**	**$0.65**	**58**	**105K**
	anzwxp	8/99	$0.61	$0.76	24	60K
bor	borwsp	5/99	$0.00	$0.00	0	nil
cml	cmlwxp	8/99	$0.74	U/K	$0.82=10	nil
ndy	ndywdp	11/98	$0.22	$0.33	5	nil
rio	riowmp	9/98	$0.94	$1.73	84	3K
sto	stowbp	6/99	$1.64	U/K	$1.81=10	nil

We want two characteristics from our preferred warrant premium· trading opportunities. The first is a reasonable return. Calculate this by projecting warrant price targets to the nearest consolidation level on a chart of warrant price history. Where possible, match warrant price activity with the date when the parent stock previously reached our projected downside price targets. This is most easily achieved on a split screen as shown in Figure 12.7 with Australia New Zealand bank and ANZwbp. Several old notes of caution are re-introduced by these screens.

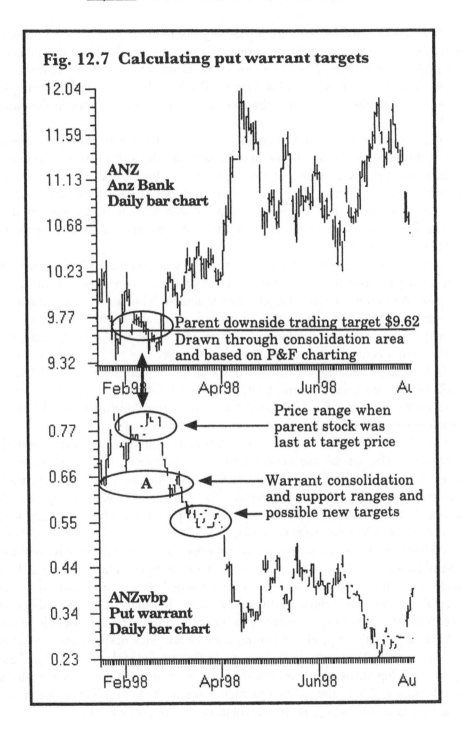

Fig. 12.7 Calculating put warrant targets

ANZ
Anz Bank
Daily bar chart

Parent downside trading target $9.62
Drawn through consolidation area
and based on P&F charting

Price range when
parent stock was
last at target price

Warrant consolidation
and support ranges and
possible new targets

A

ANZwbp
Put warrant
Daily bar chart

The first is issued by the parent. Although in many important ways the price activity of the warrant mirrors the parent, it is not an exact fit. The exact nature of this relationship is defined by the options term Delta. This is just one of the Greek terms used in the Black-Scholes Option Pricing Model equation. Delta is a measure of how the option price changes for a 1 point price change in the parent stock.

The second is the almost invisible impact of time decay. Options software factors this into calculations as another Greek term, Theta. It measures the change in the option price with respect to a change in time. Quite literally these terms, and the other options Greeks, do make options trading "All Greek" to many people and we avoid them for the same reason. Those who want to explore these relationships in more detail can start with the list of usual suspects gathered at the end of the last chapter.

Our purpose here is not to place a precise number on these Greek values, but to recognise this is why today's warrant price projection is not quite as high as in the past. We aim for a lower target, around area A. This is due to the impact of time decay, Theta, but observation provides a more accessible, if less rigorously defined, answer. The consolidation levels of warrant activity quickly establish a market-driven guide to probable future warrant value.

In February 1998 when Australia New Zealand bank traded around $9.62 the ANZwbp warrant traded around $0.82. We make these assessments in August, 20 weeks closer to expiry, so we expect the warrant to trade slightly lower. We select the lower edges of the consolidation areas as two possible targets.

Complete the same calculations for each trading candidate and add them to the spreadsheet. The possible theoretical returns based on an entry at current warrant prices, is shown in column six, Figure 12.6. But without volume we cannot trade. The last spreadsheet column hammers the calculations with reality. So the projected 98% return from Amcor is shown as pure theory because there is no recent volume. These warrants we avoid.

With others we cannot project a warrant price target because there is no history of warrant activity. Perhaps the warrant has recently listed. This is shown as U/K on the spreadsheet. We do expect to be rewarded in any trade, so we set an acceptable percentage return for these unknowns. We make a decision about the probability of warrant prices reaching the target necessary for a reasonable return, perhaps 10%. With oil producer Santos, the warrant price needs to move to $1.81 for a 10% return. Without price history it is difficult to judge the probability of this. Options pricing theory and models do provide an answer but it is not always directly transferable to the warrant market. Sometimes, as with Santos, a practical decision is made for us because recent volume is low or non-existent.

The best premium trading opportunities come from matching volume with return. In this elimination search the choice is narrowed down to the Australia New Zealand bank warrant series. The final decision depends on the opening trading activity shown in Figure 12.8.

As a final selection criterion, all other things being equal, a warrant with some months to run – far dated – is preferred to a warrant expiring this month – near dated. Quite simply, should we make an error, the long-dated warrant hands us extra time to exit with dignity.

Fig. 12.8 Depth of market on the open of trade

BID AND ASK TRADING SCREEN

		BID	ASK	LAST	
ANZWBP	AN	46.5	48	47	3
ANZWXP	AN	64	67	66	2
RIO	RI	1821	1829	1825	1

DEPTH OF MARKET SCREEN FOR ANZwbp

Qty	Bid	Ask	Qty	
20000	46.5	48	20000	
45000	45.5	49	30000	
12000	43.5	49	15000	
28000	43	50	20000	
12000	42.5	50	20000	
10000	42	51	10000	
27000	41.5	52	33000	
10000	38	53	20000	
30000	38	53	10000	
30000	37.5	53	16000	
10000	29	54	14000	

Screen shot from William Noalls Ltd Trading System 2.5, ANZwbp put warrant order line.

REAL TIME ENTRY POINTS

Prior to the open of the ASX market, buyers and sellers jockey for position. With three possible choices from Figure 12.6, ANZwfp, ANZwbp and ANZwxp, we take the one showing the best opportunity on the day. The asking price may well be above yesterday's close so we must know how much we can afford to pay because this affects our profit. The target exit price remains the same. We suspect we know where this price run is going to stop, so all that changes is how far we have to chase price to get an entry.

With ANZwbp the theoretical entry is $0.41 with an exit at $0.65 for 58%. The order lines just on the open of trading, Figure 12.8, show we have to pay $0.48, reducing the return to 35%. Aggressive traders take this entry, while more conservative traders wait for a pull-back. When trade opens the next day at $0.43 they are rewarded. The potential return is a more acceptable 51% so the trade is taken.

The alternative trade, ANZwxp, opens at $0.67 well above the $0.61 level where the initial calculations were made. This price is taken from the bid and ask trading screen in Figure 12.8. Although this still suggests a 13% profit, this trade is less comfortable because the order line shows limited strength. Although not shown on this live trading screen extract, the final candidate, ANZwfp, cuts into projected profits even further.

The structure of the order line on the day is a factor in final selection. In a short-term trade we want buying pressure. In a longer-term trade we may decide to take advantage of selling pressure, shown in Figure 12.9, to get even better entry prices. The ANZwbp order line is closest to the middle example in Figure 12.9, so we wait for our target price. Exactly how we factor volume on the day into our trading decision depends on the type of trade and the strength of the trend shown in our initial analysis of the parent stock.

The way the orders line up has an influence on the way we treat short side trades. Some intended trades become impossible because the order line does not support the technique. We choose from three trading techniques.

Board Shorts

Surfers, and those with ugly knees, favour long shorts. In market terms these are long-term shortside trades designed to get into an established trend and to stay with it for an extended period, perhaps weeks or in a severe bear market, a month or two. The entry is not concerned with good trading volume because the intention is to trade the intrinsic value with an option of exercising the warrant to take full advantage of the short position. This technique is also used by speculative traders taking very early cheap positions in out-of-the-money warrants with the intention of trading time value.

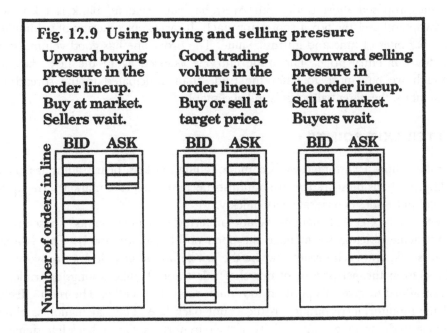

Fig. 12.9 Using buying and selling pressure

Upward buying pressure in the order lineup. Buy at market. Sellers wait.

Good trading volume in the order lineup. Buy or sell at target price.

Downward selling pressure in the order lineup. Sell at market. Buyers wait.

School Shorts

Schoolboys are forced into mid-length uniform shorts by conservative school councils. In our market they are the mid-term short trades, usually taken in anticipation of the specific impact of an outside factor on the market. Shortside trades taken in October are the best example. These are often based around specific market events. The time horizon is limited to just a few weeks. The trader anticipates a particular impact, and if it doesn't occur, the trade is exited. These trades depend on just a few external conditions and are closely managed. Volume on the entry is not important, but the objective is to sell into heavy volume and high liquidity.

Boxer Shorts

These are the briefest shortside trades of all, perhaps three to five days in our market. They are not an exclusive bear market tactic. We frequently use these in bull markets to short speculative rallies. We do not expect the retreat to begin a bear trend. Not quite day trades, they work best with good volume on each side of the trade. Traders jump ahead of good bid volume, buying at market. The objective is to ride the momentum so they try to sell before buying volume drops off.

These techniques were examined in Chapter 2 and they were used to trade rallies in a downtrend.

Our proposed short trade with Australia New Zealand bank is taken with ANZwbp and uses the boxer shorts approach. It meets our criterion of volume and offers big bites of time and intrinsic value. The order line has good volume so we wait for our entry price. The trade entry is assessed again the next day, and although we pay more to enter the trade than anticipated in the spreadsheet calculations, the potential profit is still acceptable.

BETTER EXIT POINTS

No matter how accustomed we become to falling markets, bear trading is nervous trading. Perhaps most traders are optimists because when the market turns up the value of put trades deteriorate very quickly.

The spreadsheet calculations include preferred target exit points. These are not always achievable, so we manage the open position more closely. This is a sick parent stock, and each breath may be the last before an unwelcome recovery – or at least from the perspective of our shortside trade. Unlike a longside trade, we cannot afford to give this position too much room to breathe. The most effective tool for monitoring respiration is the count back line. This calculation is closely matched to the trading range activity of the parent stock. Count back line signals in the parent stock override the theoretical stock price targets we established with hope because they give early warning of a trend change.

Board short and boxer short style trades in particular make use of the count back line to manage open put positions. The parent stock is closely monitored, and when an exit signal is given, the warrant position is immediately closed at the current market price.

Many longside traders are accustomed to using the count back line in a down trend to establish the pivot point low. As each new low in the current trend is made, the count back line is calculated by counting back three significant and higher bars. Ezy Chart users automate this calculation using the break-out line tool, count back method. Metastock users plot the calculations by hand as explained fully in *Share Trading*.

The advantage of the count back line in a shortside trade is the early trend break signal. Because a short trade deteriorates very quickly the trader acts on the count back line signal without waiting for confirmation from a straight edge trend line, or multiple moving averages. We are slow to get in, but fast to get out. We are protecting an open profit.

In contrast, the longside trader can afford to wait for full trend confirmation before making an entry. He has nothing at risk from the trend change until he actually buys stock.

In managing an open put trade the trader calculates the count back line from each new low in the parent stock downtrend. The results of this technique are shown on the News Corporation bar chart in Figure 12.10.

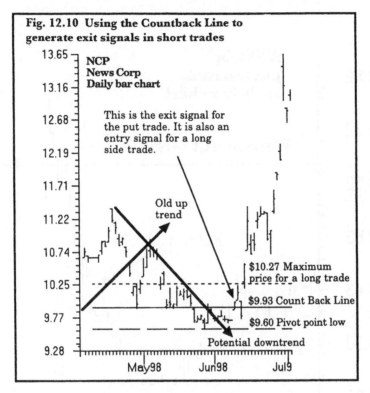

Fig. 12.10 Using the Countback Line to generate exit signals in short trades

NCP
News Corp
Daily bar chart

This is the exit signal for the put trade. It is also an entry signal for a long side trade.

Old up trend

$10.27 Maximum price for a long trade

$9.93 Count Back Line

$9.60 Pivot point low

Potential downtrend

May98   Jun98   Jul9

The process is the same as for a familiar longside trade, but the action taken on the count back line signal is different. For shortside traders the first close above the count back line is now an exit signal.

LOVE THE BEAR

Hunting with the bears uses quite straightforward trading tactics to aggressively maximise the impact of leverage and volatility in a falling market as shown in the final result of the ANZwbp trade in Figure 12.11.

This trade was better than planned. We did set a target and traders with sell orders already in line were well rewarded. Others rode a little further, jumping clear as volume began to decline. The dramatic market dip in September pushed ANZwbp towards all time highs and provided an unexpected spike trading opportunity.

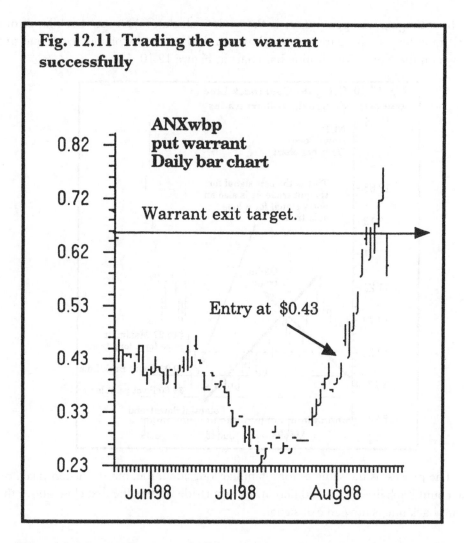

Fig. 12.11 Trading the put warrant successfully

ANXwbp
put warrant
Daily bar chart

Warrant exit target.

Entry at $0.43

Jun98   Jul98   Aug98

When shorting ordinary stock becomes an easier and accepted practice in Australia through a change in ASX rules and broker attitudes, a wider range of trading tactics will become available on the short side for equity traders.

Traders active in other derivative markets, such as commodities and futures, already have a wider arsenal of trading weapons available because of the liquidity in those markets. Our choices as private traders in equity and related markets, are more limited. The limit is primarily defined by the lack of volume. Until the depth of market increases bear traders using warrants must make liquidity a primary consideration in every transaction.

CHAPTER 13

HEDGING THE MARKET

Contributing author Chris Temby.

E quity traders do not always want to sell stock in a falling market and derivatives, particularly options, provide some hedging alternatives. Chris Temby, author of *Trading Stock Options and Warrants* provides this introduction to writing call options against stock already held. Readers who wish to explore these types of strategies in detail will find Temby's book an excellent starting point.

We may own stock which is part of a long-term holding portfolio, and do not wish to sell the stock, even though the market is showing signs of the start of a long-term down trend.

One method to offset the fall in value of the stock in a market down trend is to write call options against that stock. This chapter discusses the general principles involved, and gives numerical examples using Westpac as the held stock. A summary of factors which influence the price of an option is included in the Annex to this chapter. All calculations below use the information from Figure 13.1.

OPTIONS AT WORK

Our primary aim is to examine some ways of generating income through the use of writing call options against held stock. We look at profit strategies, as well as defensive strategies to handle the times the market turns against our analysis. However, before moving to these strategies, we must look at the relationship between the option time premium and the exercise price, as a careful blending of these two parameters is the secret of success.

OPTION TIME PREMIUM VS EXERCISE PRICE

The full set of option prices is printed daily in *The Australian* and the *Financial Review*. The extract shown in Figure 13.1 is from *The Australian* and the column headings are the stock name; expiry month; exercise price; buyer quote: seller quote; last sale price; number of options traded that day; and the total number of options contracts open in that series, shown as open interest.

Fig. 13.1 Westpac call options. Extract from The Australian, Friday, June 5, 1998

Westpac last sale price $10.046

Expiry month	Exercise price	Buyer	Seller	Last sale	Volume '000	Open interest
Jul	7.50	2.55	2.69	2.91		
Jul	8.00	2.05	2.19	2.10		55
Jul	8.50	1.58	1.70	2.02		
Jul	8.75	1.34	1.46	1.86		
Jul	9.00	1.13	1.23	1.42		
Jul	9.25	0.92	1.02	1.09		
Jul	9.50	0.73	0.83	1.27		3
Jul	9.75	0.57	0.65	0.69		52
Jul	10.00	0.42	0.50	0.48	110	521
Jul	10.25	0.30	0.38	0.36	212	184
Jul	10.50	0.21	0.28	0.25	7	5281
Jul	10.75	0.14	0.20	0.17		654
Jul	11.00	0.09	0.13	0.10	10	2037
Jul	11.25	0.06	0.10	0.16		2577
Jul	11.50	0.03	0.07	0.08		1730
Jul	11.75	0.01	0.05	0.14		15

The option time premium is dependent on the exercise price, and has a maximum value when the option is at-the-money. Using the data available from Figure 13.1, the call option time premium can be calculated for several different exercise prices. Figure 13.2 shows the time premium values for the July expiry series. The 9.50 and 9.75 exercise price options have no sales this day so the mid price between the buyer/seller quotes are taken.

Fig. 13.2 Call option time premium *vs* exercise price					
Exercise price ($)	9.50	9.75	10.00	10.25	10.50
Option price (c)	**78**	**61**	**48**	**36**	**25**
Time premium (c)	23	31	43	36	25

The time premium values are listed in Figure 13.2. The time premium for the call option with 9.50 exercise price is calculated as:

Time premium = option price - intrinsic value
$$= 78 - (1005 - 950)$$
$$= 23¢$$

The share price is $10.05, so the call option with exercise price 10.00 is very close to being at-the-money, so will have the largest time premium. The values in Figure 13.2 verify this fact.

RISK/RETURN MATRIX

The next step along the way to implementing a written call option strategy is to construct a risk/return matrix. We use the Black-Scholes Option Pricing Model (BSOPM) for this purpose. However, it is not essential for the reader to use the BSOPM, as once the risk/reward concept is understood, the option values listed in the daily newspapers can be used to determine risks and rewards.

Figure 13.3 lists the call option prices with ten, six and four weeks to expiry, with Westpac prices of $10.00, $10.25 and $10.50, and option exercise prices of 10.00, 10.25, 10.50 and 10.75. The values used in the BSOPM are volatility 27% and risk-free rate 4%.

The option prices move diagonally downwards through the table from left to right, i.e. Westpac at $10.00 and exercise price of 10.00 gives a similar option price to Westpac at 10.25 and exercise price of 10.25, etc.

From the data in Figure 13.3 it is a simple matter to calculate the risk/return for a trade in terms of safety margin vs maximum profit. The maximum profit is the initial value of, say, one option. The safety margin for our written call option is the amount the share price must move, so that at expiry the option value equals its purchase price.

Fig. 13.3 Westpac call option prices in cents

Westpac Price ($)	10.00	10.25	10.50
10 Weeks to Expiry			
10.00 exercise	51	66	82
10.25 exercise	39 *	52	67
10.50 exercise	30	41	53
10.75 exercise	22	31	42
6 Weeks to Expiry			
10.00 exercise	39	54	71
10.25 exercise	28	40 #	55
10.50 exercise	19	29	41
10.75 exercise	13	20	30
4 Weeks to Expiry			
10.00 exercise	31	46	64
10.25 exercise	20	32	47
10.50 exercise	13	21	33
10.75 exercise	7	13	22

For the option priced at 39¢ in Figure 13.3 (and marked with the *), the safety margin is 1025 -1000 + 39 = 64¢. If the share price has risen more than the safety margin at expiry, then on buying back the options to close the trade we start making a loss.

Figure 13.4 lists the safety margin and profit for various exercise price call options, with ten weeks to expiry, and Westpac trading at $10.00 when the option trade is written.

Fig. 13.4 Safety margin and profit for written call options

Option	Safety Margin (c)	Profit per Option ($)
At-the-money 10.00	51	510
1st out-of-the-money	64	390
2nd out-of-the-money	80	300
3rd out-of-the-money	97	220

PROFIT STRATEGIES – RISK/RETURN FOR IST-OUT-OF-THE-MONEY OPTION

As an example of using the data in Figure 13.3, we work through the case where Westpac is trading at $10.00, and write two Westpac call options with exercise price 10.25, and ten weeks to expiry. (This trade assumes we own 2,000 Westpac shares.) The option is priced at 39¢ so the transaction is shown in Figure 13.5. If Westpac never rises above $10.25 during the ten week life of the option there is no likelihood of being exercised (called on to deliver the 2,000 shares at $10.25 each). Further, if Westpac closes below $10.25 at the option expiry date, then the option value is zero and the profit on the transaction is $730.

Fig. 13.5 Risk/return calculation

	Credit $	Debit $
Write 2 options @ 39 c	780	
Brokerage		50
Net credit	**730**	

PROFIT STRATEGIES – ROLLING DOWN

Suppose a successful written call option on the Westpac shares has been made, with the options expiring worthless after the ten week expiry time. Suppose also that Westpac has fallen to $9.65 during that time. The question to ask now is whether the market is likely to continue falling, and so to repeat the trade. If we are confident that Westpac will continue falling, then we could write two more call options.

This time the exercise price is chosen at either 9.75 or 10.00 (the new 1st and 2nd-out-of-the-money options). If the more conservative 10.00 exercise price option is chosen, and there is a series available with, say, six weeks to expiry, then the options would be priced about 25¢, so the two call options could be sold for a net credit of $450.

PAY OFF DIAGRAM

In working out option strategies, it is customary to construct the pay off diagram, which shows the value of the option at expiry for a range of share prices (ignoring any brokerage charges). Figure 13.6 shows the pay off diagram for the first example above where the Westpac 10.25 call option was sold for 39¢.

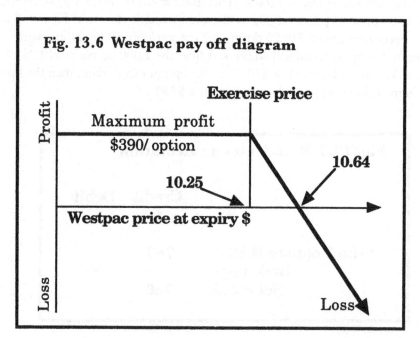

Fig. 13.6 Westpac pay off diagram

If Westpac is below $10.25 at the option expiry, then the maximum profit of $390 per option contract is achieved as the option has expired worthless. The break-even point is $10.64, because if Westpac is $10.64 at expiry the option value is: 10.64 -10.25 = 39¢ and is the price at which the option was written. If Westpac is above $10.64 at option expiry, then the option value will be above 39¢, and represents a loss in buying back the option.

The break-even point is a theoretical value, whereas in practice, if we do not want to be exercised, the written call options should be bought back soon after the share price reaches the exercise price.

DEFENSIVE STRATEGIES – BUY THE OPTION BACK

Figure 13.6 shows the pay off diagram for a single option and ignoring brokerage. In this example, if Westpac closes above the $10.25 exercise price at the option expiry date, it is very likely that the options will be exercised. However, before this time a number of choices are available, and the various possible defensive strategies should have been considered before opening the trade.

The first of these strategies is to buy back the options. Suppose with one week to go to expiry Westpac is trading above the 10.25 exercise price. The option will almost certainly be exercised, even if Westpac is only a few cents above $10.25. Even though we sold the option at 39¢, it may have been bought and sold several times since then, and be held by someone who bought it for a few cents who is planning to exercise if Westpac is above say $10.30 at option expiry.

If our strategy does not allow being exercised, then with Westpac trading above the 10.25 exercise price close to expiry, we must buy back the options and so cancel our liability to exercise.

In our example, we sold two options at 39¢. Suppose near expiry Westpac is trading at $10.30 and the options are priced at, say, 8¢ (i.e. have time premium of 8 - (1030 - 1025) = 3¢). The transaction costs are shown in Figure 13.7.

Fig. 13.7 Buy options back

	Credit $	Debit $
Write 2 options @ 39 c	780	
Brokerage		50
Buy 2 options @ 8 c		160
Brokerage		50
Net profit	**520**	

Buying back the call options gives a profit of $520. In this example we get the best of both worlds, as we make a profit of $520 on the option transaction, and the value of our Westpac shares rises also.

DEFENSIVE STRATEGIES – ROLLING UP

As a second example, suppose four weeks after we sold the two options at 39¢, Westpac rises to $10.25. The option now has six weeks to expiry and is selling at 40¢ (marked # in Figure 13.3). Our options have now become at-the-money, and any further rise in Westpac could result in the options being exercised. We decide to buy back the options and so close out the trade. The transaction costs are shown in Figure 13.8.

Fig. 13.8 Rolling up	Credit $	Debit $
Write 2 options @ 39 c	780	
Brokerage		50
Buy 2 options @ 40 c		800
Brokerage		50
Net loss		**120**

Buying back the call options results in a loss of $120.

We are now free to write fresh call options. With Westpac trading at $10.25 we would choose the series with a exercise price of 10.50. This is an example of "rolling up". In practice it is necessary to assess the market before rolling up. Remember we only write call options against our held stock if our analysis indicates that the stock is in a down trend, or moving sideways. Writing call options is not a profitable strategy if the stock is in an up trend.

The data in Figure 13.3 allows us to experience the trade before it happens, by postulating various stock price moves and calculating the theoretical profit/loss results.

DEFENSIVE STRATEGIES – ALLOW THE OPTIONS TO BE EXERCISED

Suppose that near the option expiry time Westpac is trading above $10.25. We know that in these circumstances the options will be exercised, and we accept that course of action. The transaction costs are shown in Figure 13.9.

The real profit from the trade will be dependent upon the initial purchase price of the Westpac shares.

As mentioned at the start of the chapter, before writing the call options it is necessary to decide whether allowing the options to be exercised is an allowable strategy.

	Credit $	Debit $
Fig. 13.9 Options exercised		
Write 2 options @ 39 c	780	
Brokerage		50
Sell 2000 Westpac @ $10.25	20500	
Brokerage		70
Net credit	**21160**	

SPREADS

"Spreads" is the term applied to having two option trades open on a particular stock at the same time. Spreads are normally used to generate a profit if the share price moves in a particular price range, or to cushion the loss on the trade if the market moves contrary to our expectations. The disadvantage of spreads is that brokerage charges are higher (two option positions instead of one), which for small traders eats into the available profit. Spreads are discussed in Tate's book *Understanding Options Trading in Australia.*

RETURN ON WRITING CALL OPTIONS

In options terminology, the annual percentage return is a measure of the return available to the writer of an option if the option is held to expiry. The definition is:

$$\text{Annual \% return} = 100 \times \frac{\text{time premium}}{\text{stock price}} \times \frac{365}{\text{days to expiry}} \%$$

For the first example above with Westpac at $10.00 and the out-of-the-money 10.25 call option at 39¢, the option price is all time premium. With expiry time of ten weeks, then the result is:

$$\text{Annual \% return} = 100 \times \frac{39}{1000} \times \frac{365}{70} \%$$

The annual percentage return values for options are printed in the *Financial Review* each day. The numbers are somewhat theoretical, as they cannot include brokerage or parcel sizes.

In practice, the gross return on the 2,000 Westpac shares would be the normal dividend, plus any profits made from writing options. Suppose the annual dividend is 41¢ per share, and during a year one option trade is written at 39¢ as described above, with the options expiring worthless. The gross return for the year becomes:

Return = 2000 x 0.41 + 730
= 820 + 730
= $1550

In this example, writing the call options results in effectively doubling the dividend return on the shares for the year.

APPLICATION TO OTHER STOCKS

The examples above are all for two call options on Westpac. The same overall principles apply to other stocks. Further, the options market works in such a way, that for a given risk, a similar return is available across different stocks.

Thus at-the-money call options on a stock priced at $10.00 with five weeks to expiry, will be about twice as expensive as at-the-money call options on a stock priced at $5.00 with the same time to expiry. Variations to this relationship do occur, and are caused by the stocks having different volatilities, or closeness to a dividend payment.

It is permissible to use held stock as collateral to write call options in another stock. Thus if we hold, say, 2,000 Westpac shares valued at $20,000, we can lodge that as collateral to write call options in, say, BHP. However, the Westpac share value is marked down to 70% of the market value, i.e. to $14,000. Thus BHP call options can be written to control up to $14,000 worth of **BHP** shares.

This is just a brief introduction to some of the possibilities available for using options to enhance our survival in a bear market. Although these strategies may appear complex to equity traders at first sight, they are quite straightforward examples of the way options are used to make a profit in a falling market without the need to sell shares from our portfolio. Take another look at the list of usual suspects at the end of Chapter 11 if you wish to explore these types of solutions further.

Annex to Chapter 13

PRICING AN OPTION

THE FACTORS which influence the price of an option are:

1. The stock price
2. The option exercise (or strike) price
3. The time to expiry
4. The risk-free interest rate for the same length of time as the option time to expiry
5. The stock volatility.

The so called "fair price" of an option can be calculated quite accurately using one of the Option Pricing Models. Details of the Black-Scholes Option Pricing Model (BSOPM) can be found in *Trading Stock Options and Warrants*.

INTRINSIC VALUE AND TIME PREMIUM

The price of an option comprises the intrinsic value and the time premium. Suppose Westpac is trading at $10.05 and a call option with exercise price 9.75 is priced at $0.57.

$$\text{Then intrinsic value} \quad = \text{share price - exercise price}$$
$$= 10.05 - 9.75$$
$$= \$0.30$$

And time premium = option price - intrinsic value

= 0.57 - 0.30

= $0.27

A call option which is at-the-money or out-of-the-money has no intrinsic value. The value of the option is solely the time premium.

TIME TO EXPIRY

The time premium is a wasting asset, and falls fairly uniformly as the time to expiry shortens. At the expiry date the time premium is zero. Using data from the published options quotes, the Westpac call option closing prices with exercise price of 10.00 and varying times to expiry can be extracted, and are listed in Figure 13.10. These option prices are for 4/6/98, so the number of weeks to expiry is calculated from this date.

Fig. 13.10 Option price *vs* time to expiry

Expiry Month	June	July	Aug	Oct
Weeks to expiry	3	8	-	21
Option price (c)	30	48	-	73

RISK-FREE INTEREST RATE

The risk-free interest rate is the rate that an investor could earn on money placed in a term deposit for the same length of time as the option has to expiry.

VOLATILITY

Volatility is the term used to describe the daily up and down variation in the stock price over a length of time, and volatility is expressed as a percentage. The option price is quite sensitive to changes in the stock volatility. If the stock price has been reasonably sedate, and then enters a period with larger daily price variations, the volatility increases, and so too does the price of the stock's options.

ABOUT THE AUTHOR

Chris Temby is private investor who has traded options on the Australian Stock Exchange for over 20 years from his home in Adelaide. He is author of *Trading Stock Options and Warrants* and *Technical Analysis for Trading Index Warrants*. In the early 1980s when personal computers became available, he developed his own programs for analysing the stock market and trading options, which were successfully marketed commercially. He holds a Master's Degree in Electronic Engineering and a diploma in Computing Science, both from the University of Adelaide. He is a member of the Australian Technical Analysts Association.

CHAPTER 14

SHORT BEAR EQUITIES

Contributing author Colin Nicholson.

Although large and professional traders use the facility extensively, there remains a common misconception among smaller traders that you cannot short sell shares in the Australian market. One reason is that the Australian Stock Exchange (ASX), for some reason, seems very reluctant to tell anyone about it. In researching this chapter, the writer was unable to obtain any assistance from the Australian Stock Exchange other than the offer to allow him to purchase a copy of the rules.

Some brokers are also reluctant to give information about it. One of the writer's brokers even refuses to execute short sales. However, another of his brokers was more than helpful. Possibly, brokers are reluctant to handle the additional procedures, but more likely, they see themselves as trying to protect investors from themselves. This springs from the logical idea that, if you go long, your potential loss is limited, while your potential profit is unlimited. However, if you go short, your potential loss is unlimited, while your potential profit is limited.

This logical idea is true in theory. In a long trade, the worst that can happen is that you lose 100% of your capital. However there is unlimited profit opportunity, because there is no theoretical limit to how high prices can go. In a short trade, the best that can happen is that price falls to one tick, so you make 100% on your capital (assuming no leverage). However, there is no limit to your potential losses, because there is no theoretical limit to how high prices can go.

Indeed, the history of financial markets is littered with stories of famous "short squeezes", where short sellers found that all of the remaining stock was held by a "corner". Alternatively, the short seller found that they had shorted more stock than was issued. In these situations, there is no practical limit to the price that can be demanded by a holder from short sellers desperate to close their positions. However, as will be shown below, the rules for short selling on the ASX make it very difficult to establish a "corner" and for all practical purposes, such a possibility can be discounted. Nevertheless, short selling has features that make it more risky than trading from the long side.

This chapter is not written to encourage anyone to short sell shares. It is simply to inform readers, who might otherwise not be aware that short selling is a factor in the Australian sharemarket.

WHICH STOCKS MAY BE SOLD SHORT

Not all stocks may be sold short. This is part of the ASX protection against corners. Moreover, the list is changed by the Stock Exchange quite regularly. At August 1997, there were 225 stocks on the "Approved Securities" list. The basic guidelines are:

- The stock must have at least 50 million shares on offer
- The stock must have a capitalisation of at least $100 million
- The ASX must be satisfied with the level of liquidity.

If a stock meets these guidelines, it will most likely be on the list. As the list changes all the time, there is no point listing the stocks here. However, any broker should be able to provide an up-to-date list.

LIMITS ON SHORT SELLING

There are restrictions on how many shares may be sold short. A short sale of an Approved Security may not be made if the sale would have the effect of causing more than 10% of the issued number of shares to be sold short. This, combined with the guidelines described above, is the major way in which the abuses of the past can be avoided.

There is one other important limitation on executing a short sale. That is the ASX requirement that a short sale not be made at a price lower than the price at which the last sale took place. This is designed to prevent short sellers driving the price down. It can make it difficult to do a short sale in a weak market.

PROCEDURES AND REQUIREMENTS FOR SHORT SELLING

Firstly, the short seller must inform the broker in advance that the order is to sell short. The broker then has the responsibility to ensure that the stock is on the Approved Security list and that the number of shares is within the 10% limit.

When the deal is executed, the sale is flagged to the market as a short sale with the parameter "S". It is also shown on the contract note as a short sale.

Secondly, the broker must secure from the short seller a margin of 20% or more of the value of the short sale, which is held in trust until the short sale is covered by repurchasing the shares. The margin may be in the form of cash or listed securities. In the case of securities, they are counted at up to 90% of their market value, the actual discount being at the discretion of the broker. Should the price of the shares sold short rise by 10%, the broker will require additional cash or up to 90% of the value of securities to be lodged to bring the margin back to 20%. Similarly, if the value of the securities lodged as margin falls, additional margin will be required. The broker also has the power to at any time call for margin to the extent of the entire cost of covering the short position. If this call is not met promptly, the broker has the power to cover the position on your behalf.

Thirdly, the broker and the short seller have a responsibility to deliver scrip on the T+3 rules. This is done by borrowing stock, naturally at a cost. This process carries a risk and is costly to monitor and maintain, so additional fees may be charged by the broker. Generally, the short seller is also required to pay the lender any dividends and the lender may also be entitled to any attaching franking credits, which, if the short seller cannot supply, must be settled in cash in addition to the amount of the dividend. The cost of borrowing scrip can, of course, be offset by the income from placing the up to 80% of capital not required as margin on the money market.

Most brokers will also require the short seller to sign a "Risk Disclosure" agreement similar to that required by the Australian Options Market.

It is possible to short sell Australian shares and it happens all the time. The advantage may lie in the fact that markets generally fall much more quickly than they rise. However, the process is more complicated than taking a long position and does involve greater risk.

ABOUT THE AUTHOR

Colin Nicholson, BEc FSIA is a private share trader, President of the Australian Technical Analysts Association and Principal Lecturer for Technical Analysis at the Securities Institute of Australia. Colin acknowledges the assistance of Robert Glenn of ABS White & Co in the preparation of this chapter which originally appeared as an article and is reprinted with permission from the September issue of the Australian Technical Analysts Association Newsletter. Contact the Association at GPO Box 2774, Sydney, NSW, 1043.

PART IV

GRIN AND BEAR IT

CHAPTER 15

THE GOOD, THE BAD AND THE BEAR

T o suggest a link between the behaviour of rats and the behaviour of traders seems quite reasonable to the general public. Traders are more appalled at the suggestion, but examination reveals closer links than most traders are comfortable with. Trading is more than just understanding and mastering the tools and techniques available. As our trading experience grows we realise our success or failure depends equally as much upon ourselves and our discipline as it does upon the tools we select.

Those serious about trading have already selected a market segment they prefer. The choice is based on industry group or market classification, such as the top 100 industrials. Other traders look for stocks performing in particular ways, selecting on the basis of indicator signals and trading conditions.

The better traders make a serious attempt to match trading style with their personality. Those with patience look for longer-term trading opportunities, content to wait until the trend is established. The more aggressive hunt for trend break-outs. Our trading styles are as individual as our personalities and the best guide to the correct selection of style is how well we sleep at night.

Most importantly better traders understand the essential difference between price and value and the way market operations depend upon this and are driven by it. Value is how much we believe the stock is worth. Price is how much we pay to get it. If price and value are the same, there is no trade and no market because there is no risk and therefore, no reward.

We are experienced traders so preparation and selection work is always fully completed. We are in touch with the market, so when the bear bites we know we have to gather more information about this new market. The previous chapters consider a combination of tools and market segments, some of which you may feel comfortable with. The bear market forces some traders to venture into the world of derivatives for the first time. Understanding the language, the terms, and the vast range of trading tactics available in these new market segments takes time. Initially we believe the first task is mastering these mechanics, and if at first we don't succeed, or when we start to lose, we blame inadequate research.

In fact the blame often lies elsewhere, but many traders find it easier to change tools and techniques than to change trading habits. It is these habits that bring us back to the rats.

GREATER FOOLS

We suggested earlier that in a bull market the market pays for your mistakes. This is not just a snappy summary. It goes to the very core of a bull market where so many new people are involved and so many of them believe the market can only go up. In the middle stages the market is overwhelmed by fools. No matter what price we pay for a stock there is usually another fool prepared to pay us even more money for the same stock.

This is sometimes called the Greater Fool theory and real market activity seems to validate it.

Further more, in this strongly trending market, if there is a dip in prices it is usually fleeting. Prices soon rally, so the heart-stopping fear is a temporary thrill on the road to success. In this financial garden of Eden the weeds of bad habits grow easily under the cover of the money tree.

The foot-hold in which weeds thrive are any cracks in risk control measures and stop loss strategies. The stop loss is designed initially to protect traders against an adverse move early in the trade. It plays two roles, and the first is to protect our trading capital. The rule we prefer is the 2% rule which means no single trade puts at risk more than 2% of our total trading capital. As soon as potential loss, based on today's close, equals more than 2% of our total trading capital, the trade is closed – according to the money management theory.

In practice, the bull market encourages us to forego this trading discipline because there is an increased probability of a new price rally. Just as the theory suggests, along comes a greater fool who throws money at the stock, lifting prices above our entry level and turning the loser into a winner. This greater fool infection is not limited to novice players or mums and dads participating in a new float for the first time. It was institutional traders who drove AMP up to $45.00 when it first listed in 1998. It was the mums and dads who found more reasonable value in AMP around $21.00.

As soon as we buy shares it seems stop loss slips into the second role. Now our concern is to protect open profits. Our trade is making money, and if prices start to slide we lose part of our paper profit. Money management theory encourages us to plot a trailing stop loss. This imaginary point is set below the most recent close. If prices close below the point, we exit the trade because it suggests the trend is about to change. Our profits are under attack. Again, in a bull market, a greater fool often comes to our rescue. These fools see price retreats as a bargain-buying opportunity, so they buy extra stock, pushing prices up. The message for novice traders is not even subtle. It is clear: an exit based on the stop loss takes us out of the trade too early so we miss too many profits. They throw this rule out the window.

There are many money management models, ranging from the 2% rule to Ralph Vinces Optimal-F explained at length in _Portfolio Management Formulas_. There are many combinations of trailing stop loss conditions. They include using the count back line, setting the stop on a percentage pull-back, or creating a dollar retracement point. All the techniques have one thing in common. They aim to protect open profits so the trader keeps most of what he has earned.

RATS TO THE BULL

In a bull market stop loss techniques often seem largely irrelevant because the market keeps climbing higher. Traders who follow the rules are sometimes whipsawed in and out of positions. Their stop loss signals an exit, so they close the trade. Then just a few days later, the retreat turns to a rally and prices resume the upward trend for weeks or months. They were shaken out of the trade by just a temporary blip, and as a result, miss out on substantial profits. The temptation is irresistible. Next time their stop loss conditions signal an exit they ignore it, believing the worst outcome is for prices to pause before continuing upwards.

Little do they know the rats are winning. The bull market appears to temporarily suspend the laws of risk control and money management. This suspension attracts many new people to the market because it seems as if traders make money without hard work. The novice is easily enticed and in time many experienced traders succumb to the head-long bull market rush. These rats are simple people, so we understand them with a simple experiment. In this quite non-scientific example, based on similar real experimental research, we build two cages. Into the first go the novice rats. All they have to do is learn to press the lever on the wall connected to a hopper full of food. Whenever a rat presses the lever, food is randomly released. Sometimes no food comes down but this changes after a couple of extra taps on the lever. This is habit forming. This cage we call the bull pen.

The second cage is more complex because it holds brighter-than-average rats. In addition to the same lever on the wall there is also a light. When the light glows and the lever is depressed, food is released. If the light does not glow and the lever is pressed, no food is ever released. This is as simple as learning gets. This cage we call the trading pit.

IN THE BULL PEN

In the bull pen the rats attempt to feed whenever they feel hungry. There is a random connection between tapping the lever and getting food. They soon understand one tap is as good as the next because without knowing the probability of success, there is every chance success is just one tap away.

Rats are foolish folk and our bull pen is replicated in clubs, hotels and casinos around the nation. These rats sit in front of poker machines, tapping at the keys chasing a randomly-distributed reward. Habitual tapping has little to do with intelligence, or lack of it. It has a lot to do with developing habits because these unthinking actions are reinforced by random, and sometimes quite substantial, rewards.

How easy it is to transfer these taps to the market screen. The bull market delivers consistent rewards at random intervals. It does not matter how you tap, quickly, slowly, from the left or the right, at your favourite stock, or at one recommended by a friend, a broker or a magazine. Most times there is a reward.

LIFE IN THE PIT

Pity the rats trapped in the trading pit. This is a much harder universe because they must wait for a signal before hitting the lever. At times hunger overcomes common sense and they wander up to the lever, punching at it randomly. Nothing happens. Within just a few hours they learn it is pointless tapping the lever unless the light is on. This is the good aspect of trading behaviour because it is a learning experience.

This is a long way from Pavlov's dogs. They associated food with the sound of a bell ringing. Pavlov developed habits divorced from learning. He made the dogs salivate just at the sound of the bell because they anticipated food, even if they could not smell it. Ring a bell, and these dogs could just as easily eat the visiting Avon lady as a piece of steak.

Our rats in the trading pit are much more intelligent. They learn the soft glow of light permits them to take action to obtain food with consistent regularity. It is not delivered on a plate. Once one thing happens – when they get the signal – then they must act to obtain a reward. This trading pit has two connected decisions which when followed deliver a certain reward. This behaviour is more than a habit. This experience also develops learned behaviour about what to do, and what not to do. The rats in the trading pit quickly understand it is no use tapping the lever when the light is out because no food is released.

These test results are hardly startling and have been duplicated many times by behavioural scientists, university lecturers, educational faculties, and market participants. For us, the really interesting events take place when we collect all the rats and throw them together in the bull pen.

LIGHTS AND ACTION IN THE BULL PEN

Learning is not the same as discipline and for ordinary traders the difference comes as a financial shock. Collect all the rats from the trading pit and throw them into the bull pen. Add one feature to the bull pen. Now it has a light and when it glows, food is guaranteed. However food is still also distributed randomly so not every food drop is signalled by the light.

Now we have created the situation where if there is light there is food, but where there is food there is not necessarily light. Very confusing for the average rat.

What is interesting is the way the behaviour of the two groups of rats changes. Those from the bull pen continue their moronic tapping. Tap often enough and food will come. Who cares if the light is on or off?

Despite the certainty of reward from their learned behaviour, many trading pit rats soon catch new habits. They are not stupid. The tapping habit is just as profitable as the learned behaviours and the results are hard to distinguish. The light glows regularly, but in the frenzy of tapping the causal link between the light and reward is overwhelmed by the random rush of food deliveries.

Very soon most of the trading pit rats adopt the habits of the original bull pen population. In a bull market it is so easy to replace learning with habits because the bull market distributes random rewards. Traders can make mistakes – tap on the lever whenever they want – because in a buoyant market the inevitable rise in prices will compensate for any error – food is eventually delivered.

The trading skills of money management and stop loss control appear irrelevant when the market is so rewarding. This random distribution of rewards breaks down the discipline we need to trade effectively. Many traders do not realise this. More errors and increasingly sloppy trading habits creep into their trading patterns, but the random and frequent distribution of rewards from a market overflowing with money hides these errors. What is now habit, many traders mistake for learning and skill. Eventually they confuse a bull market with trading brains.

THE BEAR CAGE

Randomised rewards destroy learning and discipline. The trading pit rats rapidly unlearn their responses in favour of continuous tapping in pursuit of random rewards. Collect all these rats again and drop them into a new bear cage. Here, frequent random delivery is replaced by infrequent random delivery. When the light glows, food is always delivered. The only change is the frequency of random food delivery. Now food is always available when the light is on, and very rarely available when the light is off.

The trading pit rats do not revert to their learned behaviours. It is hard to break newly-acquired habits. The bull pen rats keep their habits. Trading life does not get much uglier than this.

A few of the rats, the more stubborn, the skilled professionals and the trading pit superstars did not forget the discipline of the trading pit. In the frenzy of random returns they continued to wait for the light to glow before tapping the lever. Sometimes they were squeezed out by bull pen rats who were still busy tapping away, but most times they were fed.

The bull pen rats have a problem. All they know is a bad habit – pressing the lever all day. Any rat who acquired the habit does the same thing. In the new conditions this rarely results in food. Rats who spend all day at the lever expend a lot of energy, tapping away for little or no reward. They cannot stop because the very randomness of their experience gives them every encouragement to continue. Less skilled traders expend a lot of cash, tapping away at trades for no reward. The next one must be a winner.

Habitual rats tap the lever until they die of exhaustion. Every tap appears to have an equal chance of winning so they have no means or motivation to modify their behaviour. Every punch of the poker machine button appears to have the same chance of success. Every new trade could be a winner. When these players continue, because the prospect of winning is so exciting, then they are gambling. When the thrill is more important than sustenance, these players have serious problems.[1]

The rats from the trading pit who developed discipline in addition to learning, do not alter their behaviour. They lounge comfortably in the corner of the cage, waiting for the light. They concentrate on honing speed. By conserving their energy – or their capital – they are first to the lever when the light glows, confident of success. These traders survive in all market conditions because they have a consistent plan and the discipline to follow it even when other rewards are available from unplanned activity.

---

[1] A full discussion of the way to recognise gambling behaviours in traders is contained in *Trading Tactics*.

HABITUAL WINNERS ARE LOSERS

It is not, after all, such a great leap from rats to market traders. Perhaps it is the raw intensity of emotions let loose in an unfettered trading environment that narrows the gap. When we trade we unlock two of the most powerful of human emotions. Greed and fear. In all of our civilised behaviour, these two emotions are locked up. It is only in the market that they can be respectably let loose.

I have no desire to get in touch with my inner rat, but I do need to understand the way random results develop habitual responses rather than disciplined and learned strategies for survival and success.

Bear markets make us face up to our bad habits because there is no easy escape from the consequences. For many traders changing existing habits, thought patterns and attitudes remains the most significant challenge of better trading. It is difficult for traders from the trading pit, but it is even more difficult for traders from the bull pen.

When random rewards are distributed frequently it is easy to become a habitual winner. The danger is that when we win, we do not know why we have won. The greatest danger of all for continued trading survival is when we know we have ignored our trading plans and have still won. Once developed, the habit of hitting the lever is hard to break. Total financial ruin is the most common cure. As trading survivors we want to avoid this solution so we refresh the memory of our learning. For the novice who is starting to lose money it is an opportunity to begin from scratch.

Now all of the material on developing trading plans, on setting stop loss points and developing the discipline to act on trading signals is revisited with new understanding. This is no longer theory. We have been in the bear market and carry the scars. Good traders know they cannot afford to continue with bad habits that eat away at their trading capital. While not every trade is a winner in a bear market, every trade does limit losses and protect profits in a much more pro-active way. At times it may seem we have to learn to trade again because the probability of loss increases so dramatically.

There are some new techniques to learn, including trading short-term rallies, resisting the temptation to bottom-fish – which is more often really trying to catch falling knives – and making better use of the short side of the market. However, it would be a mistake to consider that mastery of the bear market rests only with learning these new techniques, with collecting a few more indicators and understanding some new form of technical analysis relevant to different market segments.

The first step in survival is recognising, isolating and excising the bad habits developed in the luxury of the bull market. For Bill Lipschutz, a market wizard currency trader, trading survival includes, "The ability and willingness to look into yourself and force a basic character change (which) is pretty rare. You reach down inside and you either come up with the goods, or you don't."

These are hard times, forcing us to separate good practices from bad habits. The first survival step is planning trades in a world where there is a greater probability of loss. For some it is almost learning to trade again.

CHAPTER 16

LEARNING TO TRADE AGAIN

During a recent job interview I conducted, a CEO applicant for the position told me "I don't like losing. I don't lose." It was one of the factors that lost him the job because it marked him as a poor trader. We fool ourselves if we think it is possible to win all of the time, or even most of the time, in the market. The disciplined successful trader appreciates that a loss does not make him a loser while unsuccessful traders would rather lose money than admit they are wrong. Marty Schwartz, interviewed in *Market Wizards* believes he, "became a winning trader when he was able to say, 'To hell with my ego, making money is more important.'"

In the Northern Territory wet season it rains for days and weeks on end, testing the strongest raincoats. In a bear market potential trading losses dominate the market for days and weeks and months on end. Any weaknesses in our attitude to loss and the way we handle trading losses are brutally exposed.

In the hard conditions of a bear market, these lessons are even more important because the trading balance is tipped towards potential loss. If we have prospered in the bull market we may need to learn to trade again in terms of the way we physically manage risk – actually placing a sell order to take a loss. Longside traders in falling markets cut losses very quickly to avoid being hammered. The market pressure is down and it is easier to drown than to swim in the falling tide. Shortside traders using derivatives contend with the stench of time decay and increased volatility on the upside of any parent price move. Winning derivative positions turn into losers with remarkable speed. Losing is now a very real market reality the trader cannot afford to ignore.

Bear markets increase the frequency and potential for severe loss. How we react to losing determines our survival in a bear market to a much greater extent than in a bull market. There is just less room for error.

Traders are in the business of effectively and aggressively managing risk. We seek out risk, because without it there is no reward and this creates a dilemma. On the one hand, if we are terrified by the fear of loss, we cannot trade. On the other hand, if we are absolutely fearless, we cannot trade for long. In the comfort of a bull market we understand the key to our trading survival lies somewhere between these extremes, but the market is kind, so we do not have to locate the key precisely.

The novice private trader must find this middle ground quickly because his initial survival is threatened by inexperience. Many successful traders believe the worst introduction to trading for the novice is an early series of successful trades. The beginner believes he does not have to take a loss. "You have to be willing to make mistakes regularly: there is nothing wrong with it," Bruce Kovner, perhaps one of the world's largest interbank currency and futures traders, asserts in *Market Wizards*. A string of early wins does not teach the novice trader how to take losses.

Bear markets probe for weaknesses in our trading and in our beliefs about our relationship with risk. No trader is immune so if we intend to survive, and prosper, we need to revisit our options for handling risk. Good traders find little need for change. Traders who built success on the back of the bull market need to make significant changes. The novice has a more difficult task because he must learn all the skills at the same time as he grapples with the increased real risk of loss. All learn to trade again in new market conditions.

On the trading floor, in front of the screen or in the comfort of home, the trader has only one way to control risk once he has purchased a financial instrument. He must know when and how to take a loss.

This translates into a simple action – pick up the phone, ring your broker or key in the sell order and click 'send' on the Internet screen. Do whatever it takes to quickly exit the position. As suggested in Chapter 15 there are times in a bull market when delay is profitable. In the bear market the lessons of this random reinforcement come home to roost like a flock of vultures. Delay is fatal.

EXTREME RISK

Stock selection, diversification, technical analysis and trading techniques all help the trader shape risk to fit his personal profile. In re-shaping our risk profile it is useful to consider the extremes of risk control as reflected by attitudes to loss. Frank Partnoy wrote *F.I.A.S.C.O.* based on his experiences with the Morgan

Stanley derivatives trading division. He appears to have been a successful salesman rather than a trader, but the actions of his colleagues capture one aspect of risk control. We use this to define one extreme edge.

Richard McCall is author of *The Way of The Warrior Trader*. His approach defines the other extreme edge of risk control, drawing upon military and martial arts lessons. In many ways it reflects controlled aggression. Our objective is to use these extremes to find the middle ground because in the final analysis the way we handle loss is our only way of controlling risk.

Our purpose here is to look briefly at the extreme edges so we do misrepresent McCall. His trading approach is much more complex than we suggest. Although it is tinged with a level of aggression which I find uncomfortable and unsuitable for good trading, there are many successful aggressive traders. Those who are able to channel their aggression in the ways he describes will become better traders and we do recommend *The Way of The Warrior Trader* for this purpose.

Partnoy need not fear misrepresentation. His experiences, and the attitudes he reveals are unfortunately typical of many institutional trading houses and brokerages. In F.I.A.S.C.O. they seem extreme, but delve back just a little way into recent financial history and we discover they are not substantially different from the attitudes in the late 1980s. Michael Lewis reminiscences in *Liar's Poker* tell of same hot-house of financial dealings and unfortunate attitudes. Such popular books do give traders a bad name.

UNCONTROLLED AGGRESSION

Big losses go with big men – or so some institutional egos claim. They are taken as a sign of strength because only the really big men can afford to play the game with such high stakes. The book *Liar's Poker* takes its name from a game played in brokerage dealing rooms. A group of players form a circle. Each holds a dollar bill close to his chest. Each player attempts to fool the others about the serial numbers printed on the face of his dollar bill. The bidding escalates until all players agree to challenge a single player's bid. Only then do the others reveal their serial numbers and determine who is bluffing whom.

Lewis describes the time when Salomon Brothers chairman, John Gutfreund, challenged one of Salomon's finest bond traders, John Meriwether with "One hand, one million dollars, no tears." Meriwether raised the bid to ten million. That is, one game of Liar's Poker with ten million dollars at stake with 'no tears.' The loser was expected to suffer a great deal of pain but wasn't entitled to complain or moan about it. Even though Gutfreund declined to play for higher stakes, the message is clear: sharks win because they have more money so they can take risks others cannot. Size does not offer immunity, as John Meriwether discovered when his firm, Long Term Capital Management, had to be rescued from derivative trading difficulties in late 1998.

As private traders we swim with these sharks, but we are not them. We trade with limited capital, so there is a fine dividing line between the devil-may-care approach and serious pain. Fast deals, lots of cash and loads of attitude make *F.I.A.S.C.O.* exciting reading with a devil-may-care attitude to losing money as its theme. Partnoy blurs the line, suggesting 'real' traders treat money and trading risk as issues too inconsequential to worry about.

It is easy for them. They deal with institutional money, not their own. We should reject this extreme when we develop a plan to cope with the increased probability of loss in the new bear market. Books like these are good bedside reading[1], but our danger is that we too may come to believe the publicity generated about traders.

When we first become involved in the market we were often given the standard warning by all our friends and family. It is a message reinforced by some of the popular market magazines we read. The warning is always along the lines of, "Only use the money you can afford to lose."

This well-intentioned advice, if accepted at face value, has the potential of killing us. The advice implies it doesn't matter if we lose a lot of money. This is only a short step away from Partnoy. It is the most dangerous implication of all because it discourages the development of any risk control strategy and does nothing to develop the discipline necessary to manage risk.

NO FEAR

Fear paralyses, turning muscled traders into wimps unable to pick up the phone and close a losing position. Fear interferes with everyday motor functions, making if difficult to switch on the computer to see the latest price action. Fear changes visual perceptions so charts showing prices in freefall look ready for an immediate rally. These fears are all the fear of loss. Partnoy, and other well intentioned family advisers, suggest we ignore the loss. McCall takes the opposite view, suggesting we get to know fear so well that we are comfortable with it.

He finds this solution amongst the codes of the Japanese samurai, explaining it in *The Way of The Warrior Trader*. He argues a samurai transcended fear because he accepted the inevitability of death. Once the samurai put his fear of death to one side, he was able to fully concentrate on developing his killing swordmanship skills.

---

[1] A frequently updated list of other bedside and market reading trading books along with short reviews is available at www.guppytraders.com.

This is quite different from the hedonistic European approach encouraging us to drink and be merry because tomorrow we may die.

English political philosopher, Thomas Hobbes could have been writing about mediaeval Japan when he suggested life was, "nasty, brutish and short." For the samurai death was not only inevitable, it was a constant possibility. James Clavell's heroes in _Shogun_ spend much of their time wading through a sea of dismembered bodies. The Japanese classic _Musashi_ by Eiji Yoshikawa seems to pause only briefly between artful death blows to follow more cultural pursuits.

From this nasty, brutish battlefield McCall salvages trading salvation. The samurai comes to terms with death. Traders should come to terms with loss – a virtual death. McCall equates the fear of significant financial loss – the risk inherent in every trade – as the trader's equivalent of the samurai's natural fear of death. He suggests the trader should treat the risk of financial loss with as much acceptance as a seasoned samurai warrior treated death. He provides a range of exercises to develop a better focus and understanding of this virtual death. We do not intend to consider these here as they are part of a distinct and detailed trading approach.

Our concern here is to use McCall to define another extreme. The danger of the samurai approach is that it is too easy for acceptance of loss to turn into contempt. This is one of the themes of _Musashi_ and the hero's chief rival, Ganryu, has difficulty in separating contempt for death from contempt for life and the living. For the trader our danger is the slip from appropriate risk based on acceptance of loss to total disaster arising from contempt.

TOO MUCH TO LOSE

The idea that somehow we have a virtual life, or fortune, to waste is disturbing. At these extremes we lose touch with reality.

I once stood three hundred metres underground, the darkness illuminated only by a small light on my hard hat, as a 6.8 scale earthquake shook the stope. Rocks tumbled from the roof and the walls shook. The experience confirmed my mortality, not my immortality. More recently I watched the material accoutrements of a life, my own, and many, many others, being washed down-river to end up somewhere in the Indian Ocean.

The conclusions I reached were quite different from those of McCall and his samurai warrior or from Partnoy and his immature colleagues. My life, and my financial life, are important to me and I cannot disregard them. Nor can I squander them.

In the face of large loss, or potentially large loss, it is easier to take a smaller loss. This is a question of perspective, not as McCall suggests an aspect of virtual-reality suicide. Partnoy perpetuates a similar error in *F.I.A.S.C.O.* Because he and his fellow dealers are so well paid, they lose perspective, both in terms of what is reasonable expenditure and financial risk. For them a 10% loss of trading capital is just as acceptable as an 80% loss. For us the differences are life threatening and we cannot pretend otherwise.

We need to understand both these perspectives are a long way from the world of the private trader. We do ourselves a disservice if we take either approach at face value, so finding and establishing our middle ground is important. We trade more effectively when we define our risk and manage it carefully. There is no room for disdain and contempt in the market.

WINNERS ARE LOSERS

Although we admire success, we are wary of instant success. Success, or winning, is usually found at the end of a long hard road. Winners have far more experience of losing. A loser only loses once. That is why he is a loser – he never gets up for a second go. David Kyte, a successful futures trader interviewed in *The Mind of a Trader* declares himself an expert on losing. "You should lose, and I know I can lose and should lose, it's just a question of quantity. If you lose more than you should have done that's when you get into trouble."

When we trade we have no desire to 'rip someone's face off' as Partnoy's colleagues enjoy doing. Nor do we want to do a samurai Lazurus, brushing closely with financial death before returning to real life. Trading survival means we cannot pretend risk does not concern us, as Partnoy implies. Unlike McCall, we cannot blithely accept total loss as unimportant so we can somehow trade better.

As private traders we do have a lot to lose and we cannot afford to think, or act, as if it is otherwise. Trading survival demands we pay full attention to risk, monitoring it daily. Our trading survival relies on our ability to develop and exercise our skills with care. Handling loss is an inevitable part of trading. Handling an increased incidence of losses is an inevitable part of trading a bear market.

THE WAY OF THE WORRIER

The mechanical techniques for defining risk, calculating it and managing it with charts, trade planning and money management are relatively straightforward. They do stretch our skills with a spreadsheet and force us to dredge up old mathematics lessons in standard deviation. They are basics applicable to any market and to any market condition just as using the accelerator, clutch and brake are basic to any road travel.

Despite our mastery of these basic skills, as soon as it rains the vehicle accident rate increases because many people drive in their habitual way in new conditions. And it doesn't work as well. The trading skills we developed in the bull market are the basic skills required in the bear market, but unless we change the precise application of those skills our trading will not succeed as well.

Pinning a number on risk, as shown in _Trading Tactics_, is the first skill for recognising and defining loss. How we put the plan into action in a way appropriate to the current market conditions decides our survival. Constantly assessing the reasons for our trading success and failure inevitably involves the specific physical ways we handle losses, such as delays in picking up the phone. Constant evaluation of completed trades is the way of the worrier. We do not ignore loss, nor embrace it. We accept it as an inevitable minor pain on the road to trading success.

Our friends are welcome to confuse our attitudes with Partnoy's – money doesn't matter – or with McCall's – I am comfortable with the prospect of total loss. The real trading danger arises when our friends are right about us.

CHAPTER 17

RULES TO TRADE BY

Bear markets make us pay for our mistakes. We reach deep into our bank balance to pay for the losses, or abandon trading when we run out of money.

Either of these circumstances is cause for reflection, but more often they are an excuse for blaming someone or something else. For the trading survivors, for those who see the bear market as an opportunity rather than a disaster, it usually means time to refresh their understanding of basic trading rules.

These are the rules of trading survival, and they are different in some important ways from the rough and ready rules traders applied in the bull market.

The bull market is easy. The rules are loose, the fools are many, and money seems inexhaustible. Traders from Main Street can, and do, make money apparently as easily as the traders from Wall, Bond, or Collins Streets. Superficially they are the same, but delve deeper and we find financial street traders follow a set of well-established rules.

A list of trading rules can be quite simple. Top trader Ed Seykota, interviewed by Jack Schwager in *Market Wizards* has just five.

- Cut Losses
- Ride winners
- Keep all bets small
- Follow the rules without question.
- Know when to break the rules.

These are deceptively simple, and as Schwager observes, on the surface the last two rules are cute because they are contradictory. Seykota believes in both, but mostly follows the rules.

Other traders supply an extensive list of rules, of dos and don'ts, including a mixture of specific trading rules and more generic, unremarkable rules. Some take the question to be about the internal rules of their trading system. They write books about these rules, and how to develop them with explanations running into pages of mathematical proofs. Such complex and apparently definitive rules give the novice comfort, but do not turn him into a trader.

Construction rules help the unskilled survive, but not to prosper. While working in the Gulf country of the Northern Territory I was faced with a major machinery breakdown and no mechanic. All this on the side of the road in the middle of the bush. Following the Caterpillar repair book instructions I successfully replaced the primary drive chain gearing and grader bearings. I achieved this with some competence but never in my wildest imagination would I compare the process or the result with those achieved by good mechanics. They read from the same book, but do not rely on it word for word for their prosperity.

All traders read from the same book. The novice is at a disadvantage because the insights he has into the market are going to be those typical of all beginners. The expert is someone who sees beyond these typical responses to develop a deep understanding of the market.

What follows is not so much construction rules as observations. I do use these observations as trading rules and the combination is uniquely my own. They are developed from experience to suit my trading style, my personality and to compensate for my weaknesses. The specific rules you adopt will be different, although they may well be drawn from the same type of observations.

Novice traders tend to discover the first two rules last − if they survive long enough to discover their relevance.

Serious traders will already have developed a list of rules, although they may not yet have written them down. A bear market provides an opportunity to refresh the rules and tighten them up because our survival margin is too thin to trade successfully with approximations. Take what is appropriate from below, adding and modifying these observations to suit your trading style.

These rules offer protection, but they are not shark-proof.

RULE I

Understand trading discipline − trade development

This is most commonly understood to mean the discipline to follow our trading system and approach. Better traders understand it also includes meeting the challenge of cutting losses and taking profits cleanly.

Initially the novice concentrates on entry conditions and the challenge is developing the discipline to wait until all the entry conditions are satisfied.

Patience is a profitable virtue in this situation. If the target entry price is $1.47 and prices appear to hesitate around $1.55 then the novice must discipline himself to be patient. Price oscillation within a trend is normal, and getting too close to intra-day price action distorts the view.

It takes time, experience and observation to make the best use of real-time information. It is too easy to forget the minute-by-minute relationship between the bid and the ask may change quite quickly and quite dramatically. The novice is better equipped for position trading based on end-of-day data where decisions are made without the interference of the market froth and bubble. Ed Seykota refuses to have a live market feed. Instead he gets his price data after the close each day.

Before the more experienced trader dismisses this entry approach as baby steps inappropriate for his level of market expertise we ought to note this position trading technique is the basis of many trading strategies. "Patience is an important trait many people don't have," Tom Baldwin, at one time the single largest individual trader in the Chicago T-bond pit, says in *Market Wizards*. "They end up forcing the trade rather than waiting patiently. They forget that the reason they made money in their early trades was because they waited a long time."

The discipline the novice must master is the discipline to act on his entry signals even if it means being out of the market for a long time. Just because this is the first skill learned does not mean it is the least important. Without it, a trader cannot grow. With it, as position trader Sekoyta shows, a trader can grow very large indeed.

Trading discipline is the ability to exit a trade under either one of two conditions. The first is to realise a loss and the second is to take a profit.

Selling is more difficult because we can never be sure which way the market will perform in the future. We buy for one reason, but we sell for many reasons. This side of the trading process is much more complex and challenging. Unless traders develop a disciplined approach to the exit their trading suffers.

In understanding the way discipline applies in this trading rule we build on our understanding that a loss is not the same as losing. Until we accept this distinction it is difficult, in fact almost impossible, to exit a trade at a small loss. This lack of discipline rapidly destroys all our accumulated profits, assisted by the most discouraging market law of all – A 10% loss cannot be made up by a 10% gain.[1] This is the toughest market law. It applies at all times, but perhaps more loosely in

---

[1] Starting with $100 and taking a 10% loss leaves the trader with $90. To bring this up to $100 his next trade must make at least 11%. Over 12% is needed when brokerage is included.

a bull market. The bear uses it as a weapon to destroy those who have not developed the discipline to cut losses at pre-defined levels. Developing the discipline to take a profit sounds so simple that it is almost irrelevant. Yet failure in this aspect allows us to turn an unrealised profit into a substantial loss.

There are several ways to develop the discipline required to take profits. I find the most useful is to set defined financial targets before I enter the trade. You may feel more comfortable with defining a set of exit conditions based on a series of chart indicators. The exact method used is not as important as having a pre-defined exit plan formulated before the trade is entered. It is difficult to exercise discipline if we make up new exit conditions every day. The discipline of planning builds the discipline required to exit to take profits cleanly.

Lusting after the last few ticks in a price move leads to trades filled with regret. Legendary investor, J.P. Morgan is reputed to have said, "I always sold too early" but this did not appear to have a serious impact on his wealth creation. Nor will it destroy the trader.

Experienced traders understand trading discipline includes these three elements – the patience to follow a plan or method, acting on stop loss point and taking profits cleanly without regret.

RULE 2

Understand trading discipline – emotional development.

The very successful traders have another understanding of discipline separating them from the average. They do not let their emotions, their temper or their frustrations, get in the way of their trading.

A novice trader talks of losses as being caused by a mythical beast – the market. "I was taken by the market," they say. Then they go on: "I was so annoyed that I bought more as they fell." This is revenge trading, aiming to get even with the market. These traders let their emotions dictate their trading strategy.

Sometimes our broker encourages this emotional deception. "Remember those Pasminco shares you bought last week at $1.80? They are trading at $1.26 today. It's a good opportunity to get them at even better prices."

This subtle attack on emotional discipline is seductive and successful. Instead of exercising the discipline to get out, we go for emotional comfort, trading for revenge. With two parcels of Pasminco we calculate how to average down the trade.

More frightening, because it is less frequently acknowledged, is the impact of anger and frustration on our trading performance. Trading rage is even more deadly than road rage.

Take a moment of quiet reflection. How many times have your losing trades been driven by external emotions – by anger, frustration, revenge or the need to prove something to somebody else? How many of these trades have been used to satisfy emotional needs that have absolutely nothing to do with the market? Finding the answer takes some hard searching through your soul rather than your trading records and contract notes. All of us have been guilty. It is part of the process of moving from novice to journeyman to craftsman. The essential separating the skilled journeyman from the craftsman is this emotional discipline. With it eventually comes trading intuition where the exercise of the skill is achieved so effortlessly it seems almost casual.

The relationship between skill and intuition is explored in *The Intuitive Trader* by Robert Koppel. It is a complex subject beyond the scope of this collection of trading rules. We do note absolute trading discipline is a prerequisite for expert intuitive trading that marks some traders as market wizards.

RULE 3

Accept total responsibility for your actions

Trading is an activity where personal responsibility is unavoidable. Despite the efforts of the regulatory authorities to coddle and protect investors from the consequences of their decisions based on investment advice, the trader has no such protection, and ultimately, seeks no such protection.

The novice trader and the wannabe, look for trading programs to automatically provide buy or sell triggers and which claim to turn users into successful traders.

People who believe these claims and are prepared to buy products of this nature are also often enticed by the flush of tax-effective investment schemes appearing in the twilight weeks of the tax year. A mechanical trading system developed by someone else is a convenient crutch which allows the novice trader to avoid responsibility. It is easier to blame the system. When the bull market collapses they try to make money by sueing the system promoters.

Exploring and understanding different trading approaches is one of the first steps towards developing trading responsibility. Rarely is a single trading approach adopted wholesale. Each trader brings his own experience and interpretations to every approach, whether he uses count back lines, Gann swings, Elliott wave, trend lines or MACD triggers. Having assembled the pieces himself the trader accepts the responsibility for the outcome.

When your broker gives you trading advice that turns into a loser then accept responsibility. After all, you took the advice and acted upon it. It was you who chose not to initiate any stop loss procedures.

Very occasionally errors do happen, but not often enough to blame your broker more than once every few years.

Although you may use the proceeds of trading to improve your lifestyle and the lifestyle of your family, you are ultimately trading for yourself. You cannot trade to meet the expectations of others. If your partner tells you how to trade, then encourage them to trade their own account. Do not let them set your trading objectives.

Responsibility is nourished by trading discipline. It is difficult to develop true trading discipline without accepting responsibility for trading action and outcomes. Surprisingly, this is the major obstacle standing between many traders and success.

Why we succeed or fail in the market depends more on ourselves than on any other factor. Work towards understanding this every day, and when you can accept it, work on understanding why you are succeeding or failing.

RULE 4

Plan the trade: Trade the plan

The trading cliche above my computer reads "Plan the trade and trade the plan." If only trading were so simple.

Everybody plans to trade, but only the successful traders have a trading plan. This is often reduced to just a few notes, small enough to stick on the side of the computer. What goes into the reduction is important. We covered some of the mechanics of developing the trade plan in *Trading Tactics* but here are some other ingredients underpinning the planning process.

This single rule has many sub-clauses, including:

- ☞ Have a clear reason for being in the trade
- ☞ Know your exit conditions in advance
- ☞ Ride winners
- ☞ Cut losses quickly
- ☞ Money management
- ☞ Keep positions small.

RULE 5

Have a clear reason for being in the trade

Why am I in this trade? Put aside the glib answer: To make money. Concentrate on the myriad other potential reasons. These deflect us from our objective, or guide us to the exact outcome.

Traders are often reluctant to probe the reasons for each individual trade even though it is an essential part of the planning process.

Why am I in this trade? A selection of good answers includes the following:

- ☞ To exploit this short-term rally
- ☞ I am trading momentum
- ☞ I am trading the long-term trend and this is the best entry point
- ☞ A major news event, i.e. the budget, will probably cause a rally. I am trading that rally
- ☞ This is a recovery trade to rescue a position that is under water
- ☞ I am trading the triangle break-out
- ☞ This is a trading channel trade.

All of these answers, and others like them, are a useful part of the trade planning process. Answers like those below are less useful.

- ☞ I have spare cash so I feel I ought to be in the market
- ☞ Everyone else is making money
- ☞ This broker/magazine/newspaper recommendation sounds so good that I would be a fool not to trade it
- ☞ After the last loss I need to get some money back
- ☞ The stock is now worth half what it was when I bought it. I will average down.
- ☞ I need some money for a holiday/boat/car/tax bills
- ☞ At this price it is a bargain or it has to be a bottom
- ☞ If I wait much longer I am going to miss out
- ☞ The margin loan facility has been cleared. What can I buy?

These do sound far-fetched in cold hard print, but if there is a tiny twinge of recognition, then take the time to put in writing the answer to the question that begins every real planning process.

"I am in this trade because ...."

RULE 6

Know your exit conditions in advance

The first exit condition is designed to cut losses quickly. This rule is up there with the hardest trading rules of all. Ignore it, and it becomes the mass murderer of market nightmares. Our protection is in the trading plan.

The summary impact of this plan is to ride winners and cut losses quickly. It is the public core of trade planning and usually the starting point for the progression from novice to better trader. We have examined this in detail in previous chapters, so here we just note its importance in summary.

    ☞ The first exit condition is designed to cut losses quickly.

    ☞ The second exit condition is to protect and lock in profits.

RULE 7

Money management

Money management is the key to trading survival. Get almost everything else in the planning process wrong, but if the money management aspect is right, we will survive.

Conversely, if every other aspect of the trading plan is perfect, we fail if money management is incorrect. Without money management all the wins, big and small, may be destroyed in just a few losing trades.

Money management is a complex topic. In *Share Trading* we look at the impact of several different money management approaches under the same trading conditions. One money management model does not suit all, but without some form of money management we are extremely vulnerable in the market.

RULE 8

Keep positions small

Traders with limited capital often think this trade planning rule does not apply to them. Although they readily agree it is foolish to take a million dollars of trading capital and put it into a single stock or position, they are less agreeable to applying it to their own trading. All $6,000 of their trading capital sits with Southcorp.

The small private trader is locked into greater risk because he has limited capacity to diversify the risk profile across the market. It can be done, and in the chapter, Six to Twenty One, in *Share Trading* we explored the steps.

No matter how large our trading capital, the objective is to match position size with risk. Each position puts at risk only 2% of total trading capital, and our exit is based on this figure.

This is one trading survival strategy. There are many others and they all concentrate on ways to keep position size small, relative to the overall portfolio, so the risk of failure has diminished impact. Amateur traders, and amateur gamblers, bet big. Survivors take many small positions and many small losses in pursuit of the winner they ride for major wins.

RULE 9

Trade the market, not your opinion of it.

There is only one right answer and the market has it. If we catch ourselves thinking, "The market should not have done that", or "I didn't expect the market to drop today" – then immediately examine all of our open positions. We are paid for trading the market, not our opinion of what the market should be.

This rule is mostly ignored by experienced traders. Quite suddenly they lose touch with the market, and losing trades begin to accumulate. If trading discipline is strong, the losses don't amount to much in dollar terms, but the losing trades still hurt in emotional terms. The temptation is to add to the losing position until the market finally comes to its senses and understands their view is the correct one.

This rule is rarely broken by the novice because he has a clear understanding of his position in the market. Unlike Alexander Elder, author of *Trading for a Living*, the novice does not have to remind himself every day, "I have it in me to do serious financial damage to my account today." He understands this already.

Ego grows only when we gather some success and with it a dangerous certainty that we can pick the market direction. The private trader is generally food for larger market sharks, and those who forget these limitations become shark food.

My computer screen saver scrolls the reminder: "I manage risk. Trade the plan." The standard Windows 95 start-up and shut down procedures include mindless muzak. My start-up sound file replaces the music with another reminder of my trading limitations; "This Guppy is shark food unless I am careful."

The shut down sound file has a more upbeat note; "All stop losses executed. Excellent." Both are a useful reminder of my trading limitations and make a change from notices pinned to the wall – and Microsoft muzak.

RULE 10

Trade with the crowd, not where it has been

I tell my blue heeler cattle dog, "Don't chase moving truck wheels." There is just no way she can catch a fast-moving road-train even though she has a choice of over 50 wheels spread between three trailers. As traders we cannot profitably catch fast-moving prices, no matter how many there are. If we run after a market too far we soon run out of puff and cash.

The objective of every trade is to move with the crowd, taking a bite out of a trend trade or a fast-moving rally. Sometimes we move in anticipation of the crowd movement, trading trend breaks and rallies from support levels. Later we trade with the crowd.

When we trade where the crowd has been we buy stock from better traders busy selling into the market strength. We pile onto silver stocks when renowned investor, Warren Buffett, announces he has been buying silver. There may be a few ticks left in the move as even bigger fools bid higher to get on board, but just as with the 1997 Buffett-inspired silver rally, it is usually a better time to sell.

On every price spike at the very top of a rally a single buyer has tried to trade where the crowd has been. We avoid this by trading in the direction the crowd is travelling.

RULE 11

Take what the market will give you rather than what you would like it to give you

Many times the market does not behave as anticipated. Carefully calculated profit targets are nearly reached, but the momentum slides away. By monitoring open positions we make a better judgement about the probability of our sell, or buy, order being filled.

Here we ride in dangerous territory. There is a fine balance between micro managing the trade and paying too much, or accepting too little. For the position trader, this micro-management can be unproductive. Generally it is more useful to set our parameters and wait for the market to meet them particularly on the buying side of the equation. If we do miss out it means we have the cash to commit to the market elsewhere.

In selling, the advice is less useful. If we do not sell, our open profits are eaten away by falling prices. If there are clear reasons for exiting the trade below our initial profit targets, then we should act on them.

RULE 12

Manage every trade, every day

Every single open position must be monitored and managed. Many times management is no more difficult than peeking into a room at the end of the day to check the baby is sleeping well. At other times more serious action is required. If we lock the trade away in a bottom drawer we cannot tell when emergency action is needed.

Management comes from planning. At the end of each day bring up a new chart of each open position and ask these six questions.

- ☞ What is my trading plan?
- ☞ Is it still valid?
- ☞ If no, then what is my amended plan?
- ☞ What are my exit plans?
- ☞ Have these been triggered?
- ☞ Are they close to being triggered?

A Yes answer to the last two questions means we spend more time looking at this trade to decide if we need to take action on the next trading day. Most days this is a five-minute exercise. It's not much to ask, but it is a life-saver.

The active trader watches the market every day, even if they have no spare cash and even if it is only for a few extra minutes to check the All Ordinaries and potential trades. Some with less time read market newsletters that focus on trading techniques. The objective is to keep them in touch with the developing market and allow them to develop and test other trading approaches without risking any capital. When the time comes to trade they already know which techniques are working best in the current market.

RULE 13

Always analyse winners and losers, but never agonise

We need to learn from the mistakes of others because we cannot live long enough in the market to make them all ourselves. Additionally, we should also learn from our own mistakes because we have paid real money to make them. Learning cannot take place in an environment of self-flagellation.

Assemble the objective circumstances and conditions that made each trade successful, whether it turned a healthy profit, or incurred a small loss.

Study your trading errors so you can avoid repeating them. Reward your successes. I enjoy a good cigar. You might choose an expensive meal.

When we agonise over what could have been we lose sight of the very real success of the actual trade in locking in a profit. Each trade is an island in an archipelago of our own design, so we step from one to the next, but without regret.

RULE 14

Trading is about lifestyle, so we can do without stress

By circumstance you may have to work in a less than satisfactory day job. Private trading is an optional choice. No one forces you to trade, or be involved in the market. If trading is unpleasant work then you can probably get similar returns with less stress and less risk from other occupations.

For stress junkies the market is the ultimate place to be. Stress is self-imposed and ordered to measure. If it is not stressful enough then take an extra futures position against the trend. Need more stress, then trade it on the margin.

Stress and survival are a mixture of pain and masochism I cannot understand. Had Dante lived in modern times I am sure *The Divine Comedy* would have included an extra level in hell dedicated to these traders.

Bill Williams is a leading trader using fractals and the emerging science of chaos to day trade US markets. He notes in *The Day Trader's Advantage* that in his, "trading room we don't get real excited. We normally sit here with the cat and the dog in the room with classical music on." My cattle dog lies on the floor snoring and snuffling, chasing phantom cows in her dreams while the geckos scamper across the roof. I prefer mediaeval music and the hollow resonance of bamboo wind chimes. Apart from these minor differences both Williams and I sleep well of a night.

If you cannot sleep at night then the chances are you are trading in inappropriate ways. Trading is about lifestyle without stress.

RULE 15

Be humble

Never forget where you came from. The market can send you back there very quickly. Your trading approach should work for you. Beyond that is only uncertainty and the market.

THERE IS A RISK OF LOSS

These 15 rules come with no guarantees. There is not a lucky rabbit's foot hiding amongst them, nor is there the financial equivalent of a dollar-proof kevlar vest. Trading success is a constantly expanding mixture of knowledge and skill. We make an error if we confuse rule-based trading with market mastery. The IBM mainframe Big Blue may be a good chess player but there is little evidence of such mechanical rule based success in fast moving markets.

Treat these trading rules as guideposts on the side of the road. They show you where the road is, but they do not tell you where the road is going. These rules cannot define your destination or your fate because those are a decision between the market and yourself.

CHAPTER 18

PARADISE LOST?

S low bear or fast bear, any bear market looks tough. They are tough, but this doesn't mean there are no opportunities for profit. In a bull market we shoot for the stars but when we hunt with the bears we look into the pits of darkness and despair. How we react to the bear is a measure of ourselves as traders. The seventeenth century English poet, John Milton tells us "The mind is its own place and in itself, can make a heave'n of hell, a hell of heav'n." What we make of a bear market depends on the mind game we choose to play.

Do we want to be here? Our answer is a clear "Yes." If opportunity doesn't knock then we build a door. We dip into the technical analysis tool box and select the old tools and a few new ones. Building the door – a trading screen door – is not difficult. Opening it takes more courage because fear and anger are traditional emotional responses to danger and risk. Historically these emotions have served us well, but now danger is more likely to leap out of a trading screen than jump out from behind a tree. Old responses are inappropriate so when the crowd wakes in what they think is hell it is useful to understand how they might react.

The bull market brings a crowd of recent arrivals to the market place. To them, the bear market is financial hell. If they believed the market was mainly about fast money then they are most likely to discover just how rapidly trading and investment profits can disappear. Undoubtedly they will blame the market, their broker, their financial advisors – anybody but themselves – for their losses.

But amongst this crowd of recent arrivals are a few who discover that trading is more than just a respectable gamble. Slowly they discover trading is about the management of risk. This first step separates them from the newcomers and the novices. Later they understand trading success comes from accepting personal responsibility for every trading decision in every market condition.

It takes courage to accept this personal responsibility without blaming the market and even more so in a bear market. In the classic 1660 poem, PARADISE LOST, Milton writes of the mental struggle to recover from defeat. Lucifer, the fallen angel hurled to the 'bottomless perdition' of hell asks his followers to decide how they should survive in these 'regions of sorrow.' We ask how we may survive in the new bear market.

Traders grow accustomed to bull markets and many find the bear market means paradise lost. Not unlike Belial, a prince amongst the fallen angels, who "With words clothed in reason's garb, counselled ignoble ease and peaceful sloth," many commentators believe our only choice is submission. Taking this advice and licking their wounds, many investors and traders leave the market, taking what remains of their cash to safer havens, Adverse to risk they flee to property and bank fixed interest term deposits. Many of them have learnt little about trading, confusing the bull market with brains.

A smaller group is all for a "study of revenge, immortal hate." The desire to get even runs deep, but as observed by some "Revenge is a dish best served cold." Revenge trading taken in the heat of the moment is most often disastrous. It includes a new entry on every promising rally, but unlike the skilled traders, these people remain in the trade convinced it is a new uptrend and convinced this trade is going to return all of their losses – and more.

We should admire their courage and marvel at the results in the same way as exploding fireworks provide entertainment. This do or die revenge leaves a nasty taste and the survival rate is appallingly low.

The smallest group of all includes experienced traders and new traders who have taken the time to understand just how their new found wealth has been created by the bull market. This is our group. It includes warrant premium traders, equity spike and rally experts and those skilled with trading channel tactics. They do not trade for revenge , but nor have they given up the fight.

Our challenge is to emulate them and to decide how our task "is attempted best, by force or subtlety." Instead of subverting God's creation, mankind, as Milton's epic poem narrates, our struggle is with ourselves. Good trading tools and mental resilience give us the courage to trade more directly against the professional and institutional traders. Our real challenge is to pay more than just lip service to the idea of taking personal responsibility for our decisions. There is no place to hide in trading. You have to live with yourself and that is more difficult than many people first imagine.

The skillful combination of bear trading strategies with equity and derivative trading instruments show the way to survival, and beyond that, to profits. The path is impassable until we learn to master ourselves. The secrets of success do not lie with the tools of trading. They are freely available and easily understood. Many software programs carry full explanatory notes and copious help files. Anyone can build a door.

The secrets of success lie with the way these tools are selected and combined to develop the most appropriate trading strategy for the market conditions, and then to modify that strategy with the personality of the craftsman using the tools. Not everyone can open the door.

In this book we have shown you some of the opportunities available in this unaccustomed and difficult market. It is not a trading hell. Nor is it paradise lost, although you can make it so. Every market, bull or bear, calls on us to be architects of our future, not its victims. Risk and risk control is all a state of mind so we welcome the challenge to trade both the long and short side of the market with skill and confidence.

INDEX

INDEX

DISCOUNT COUPON — TRADING WORKSHOPS

10% off the regular seminar fee — single and group rates
(These workshops are held in all Australian capitals and also in Asia.)

Trading looks easy, but it takes skill. How best to approach your market and survive is a skill that can be learned, and improved. Trading success means knowing how to GET IN by identifying a trade. It means knowing how to manage the trade so you GET OUT with an overall profit.

You can become a better trader by attending a half-day workshop because Daryl Guppy will teach you how to understand the market from a private trader's perspective, how to use those advantages, and how to manage a trade to lock in capital profits.

All traders — those considering entering the market and those who want to improve their trading — will benefit from this workshop.

Nobody can give you the ultimate trading secret, but Daryl Guppy will show you, using local examples selected by the audience on the day, how a private trader identifies and manages a trade. You will enter the market better informed than your competitors.

Daryl Guppy holds regular Trading Workshops. Dates and details are posted on www.guppytraders.com eight weeks before each workshop.

How to claim your workshop discount

When you book your seminar mention that you own *Bear Trading* and get 10% off the advertised fee. Bring this book with you to confirm your discount. It can be autographed for you if you wish.

Some comments from workshop participants

"The workshop, like your book, was practical and informative. I enjoyed it, and more importantly, I learned from it. For me it brought a lot of the theory into perspective. Let me know when the next one is scheduled so I can mark it in my diary."

— Private equity trader

"If you get one good idea from a seminar, it is worthwhile. Your workshop gave me two very profitable ideas."
— Futures 'local' floor trader